Learn at Home
Grade 1

From the Editors of American Education Publishing

Table of Contents

Learn at Home, Grade 1

Welcome!

Congratulations on your decision to educate at home! Perhaps you are a bit nervous or overwhelmed by the task ahead of you. *Learn at Home* will give you the guidance you need to be sure that you are providing your child with the best first grade education possible. However, this book is only a guide. You are encouraged to supplement your child's curriculum with other books, activities and resources that suit your situation and your child's curiosity.

Create an inviting learning environment. It should be comfortable and attractive, yet a place where your child can work without distractions. Your child's work area should include a desk or table, a chalkboard or dry-erase board, an easel, appropriate writing and art materials, a cozy area for reading (perhaps with pillows or a bean bag chair), a bulletin board for displaying work and shelves for books and storage. You should also collect blocks or other building toys, old magazines and a variety of small manipulatives. Hang a clock and a calendar in the room also.

The Learn at Home Series

Learn at Home is an easy-to-use resource. It includes an introductory section called **Background Information and Supporting Activities** with general information and activity ideas, as well as 36 weeks of instruction in six curricular areas: Language Skills, Spelling, Reading, Math, Science and Social Studies. Each week is then further divided into three sections: **Lesson Plans, Teaching Suggestions and Activities** and **Activity Sheets**.

Each week's **Lesson Plans** include lesson and activity suggestions for all six curricular areas. The **Lesson Plans** are brief, but further explanation is provided in the **Teaching Suggestions and Activities** section.

The **Teaching Suggestions and Activities** section provides helpful background information in each curricular area and lists the materials, supplies and books needed for the week's lessons and activities. This section also provides more detailed directions for activities listed in the **Lesson Plans**, as well as a variety of related activities.

Activity Sheets immediately follow each week's lesson plan. The sheets are grouped by subject and in the order in which they appear in the **Lesson Plans. Activity Sheets** are highlighted by **bold** print in the **Lesson Plans** and **Teaching Suggestions and Activities** sections.

Background Information and Supporting Activities

 **LANGUAGE SKILLS**

It is difficult to separate reading from grammar, writing and spelling. Therefore, the Language Skills, Spelling and Reading sections of this book are interrelated. In some weeks, lessons in one section parallel those in another. Language skills should not be isolated but rather taught in real contexts and in all relevant subject areas. Language is used, modeled and explored in one's daily life more than any other subject.

Topics covered in the Language Skills section include handwriting skills, parts of speech, vocabulary development, punctuation, recognizing and understanding sentences and questions, sequencing, poetry and letter-writing skills.

Learning to write is a process developed much like learning to speak. Provide your child with modeling and reasons to write, then applaud his/her attempts. Although the lesson plans teach a variety of writing skills in the first half of the year, you should also incorporate relevant writing activities. First, emphasize fluency in your child's writing, then move toward accuracy. Emphasize one writing skill per writing piece so that your child will not be discouraged by negative feedback. Once your child has mastered a skill or a spelling, hold him/her accountable for that skill. Use a reminder such as *How should you begin a sentence*? Then, have your child correct that mistake throughout the piece of writing. Keep a folder of your child's writing. From time to time, encourage your child to improve an old story or look over the year's work to check for improvement.

▶WRITING IDEAS

1. Beginning on the first day of instruction, your child should write in a daily journal. Provide a writing tablet with wide-spaced lines. Journal entries are usually anecdotal and personal. Encourage your child to ask questions, describe dreams or write accounts of his/her day in the journal.

2. Give your child a sentence starter, such as *When I was little. . . .* Start sentences related to the topic of study, such as *The numbers two and four . . .* , *Pumpkin seeds . . .* , or *Martin Luther King, Jr. was. . . .* Use the starters to prompt your child to write on a topic.

3. Provide the beginning of a poem. Have your child copy it and complete it with rhyming words. Then, have him/her draw a picture to go with the poem.

4. Teach your child to write rebus sentences, in which pictures stand for some of the words or parts of words.

5. Encourage your child to spell words the way they sound, unless he/she has already learned the correct spelling. Once he/she is comfortable doing this, focus on content.

6. Begin a dialogue journal between you and your child. Each of you takes a turn writing and responding to the content written by the other.

Learn at Home, Grade 1

SPELLING

Your child's spelling ability is just beginning to develop. As your child's reading skills improve, so will his/her spelling. The spelling lessons in this book will help your child learn to spell familiar words, as well as work with the sounds that make up the English language. When writing, encourage your child to spell unknown words the way they sound to him/her. To help your child with spelling, expose him/her to print in as many forms as possible. Read books, keep charts containing familiar words and play word games such as "Hangman" and "Boggle."

READING

Teach reading with books that fit your child's ability and interests, using a variety of books obtained through bookstores and the public library. Before asking your child to read a book independently, activate your child's prior knowledge of the book's subject. Then, read the book aloud and discuss the story elements. For example, discuss the stages of a butterfly's life cycle and what caterpillars eat before reading Eric Carle's *The Very Hungry Caterpillar*. Provide books that your child can read independently the first time, while also reading books aloud that are at a higher level than your child's independent reading level.

▶BUILDING WORD RECOGNITION

1. Fill your child's learning environment with print.

2. Label objects around the room. Ask your child to name objects as you write their names on index cards. Use masking tape or poster putty to attach the labels. Label objects, such as window, door, chalkboard, desk, file, table, globe, books and shelf.

3. Label containers and locations for frequently used materials, such as blocks, pencils, paper, scissors, stapler and glue. These labels can be taken down and used as flash cards from time to time.

4. Write brief, predictable notes to your child, such as *Have a nice day* and *You did a nice job* or write reminders of routine assignments.

5. Write poems and songs in large print on construction paper and hang them on the walls of your classroom.

6. Hang your child's written work on the walls. Make a practice of reading environmental print on the classroom walls and on familiar products and signs.

As you read with your child, teach the reading skills emphasized by the author. If you notice something in a book, such as rhyming words or a frequent use of blends, take the opportunity to teach that skill in context. Use the following list of suggested reading skills as a guide. Teach one skill at a time, but if possible, use the same book to teach more than one skill. For example, in the book *Sheep in a Jeep* by Nancy Shaw, the author uses many rhyming words with the *ee* and *ea* spelling. The book also contains several blends. You could also discuss story elements, such as characters, setting, problem, events and solution. Tailor your lessons to your child's readiness level and interest.

▶SUGGESTED READING SKILLS

Phonics

Look for opportunities to teach the following skills in context: beginning, middle and ending sounds; blends and digraphs; rhyming words; vowel sound families; contractions; compound words; possessives; and common prefixes and word endings. Make charts to hang around the room for each vowel sound, and add words as your child encounters them in the books he/she reads.

Decoding/Building Vocabulary

When encountering a new word, encourage your child to use three different cues: think about the context (meaning), analyze the sense of the sentence (syntax) and/or sound the word out phonetically. Use some of the following suggestions to help your child learn and remember words:

1. Once a book is read, present words that your child did not know or had difficulty with. When you present the unknown word, underline it and use it in a sentence. Ask your child to define the word.

2. Make flash cards of words that your child needs to practice. Maintain a word bank of words that your child is learning. Keep a separate bank of learned words to be reviewed periodically.

3. Have your child write words he/she has difficulty with in his/her dictionary (see Reading, Week 2, Tuesday).

▶LANGUAGE EXPERIENCE

Have your child write stories, in his/her own words, to be used as his/her reading text. This low-risk writing experience builds proficiency with language, and it helps him/her make the connection between the spoken and written word. Because this writing is in your child's own words, he/she will feel successful in reading at a very early stage. That confidence will help him/her be a successful reader of other printed materials. Use some of the following ideas to build your child's experience with print:

1. Provide a topic such as an event, a pet, a family member or a favorite toy. Write down your child's words as he/she says them, adding punctuation as needed. Read the story together several times. Then, encourage your child to read it on his/her own, using a pointer to point to the words as he/she reads them. Have your child add illustrations and save each story for repeated readings.

2. Have your child keep a daily journal of day-to-day events, feelings and plans.

3. Have your child tell a story for a wordless picture book. Write down your child's words and cut them into sentence strips. Attach each sentence strip to the corresponding page with a paper clip. Then, have your child read the story aloud.

4. Write each sentence from a familiar poem or song on individual pages. Have your child read and illustrate each page. Staple the pages together to form a book he/she can read aloud.

Learn at Home, Grade 1

▶LISTENING

Provide ample opportunities for your child to listen to songs, poetry and stories. Use some of the following listening activities to help develop his/her listening skills.

1. With your child's back to you, tap a pencil on a table top. Have him/her tell how many times you tapped. Repeat this activity several times.

2. Have your child turn his/her back to you while you make noises with a variety of familiar things for your child to identify. **Examples:** tear paper, cut paper, turn pages of a book, open a drawer, sharpen a pencil, etc.

3. Record a short story on a cassette tape. Ask your child to recall details from the story.

4. **Game:** Play "Simon Says."

5. With your child blindfolded in the center of the room, walk to various places in the room and whistle or make another small sound. Have your child point in the direction of the sound.

6. **Music:** Have your child march to marching band music, counting and keeping the beat. Play other kinds of music with a strong beat and have your child clap along.

7. Whisper something in your child's ear. Have him/her repeat what you said.

8. Record various household noises and have your child identify each one.
    Examples: can opener, hair dryer, telephone, vacuum cleaner

▶FOLLOWING DIRECTIONS

Build your child's comprehension skills and attention to detail by teaching him/her to follow directions carefully. Give oral or written directions for your child to interpret and carry out. Whenever possible, let your child work independently and learn from his/her mistakes.

1. Give directional clues that lead your child to a hidden object. **Example:** *Take three steps forward. Turn left and hop forward twice. Then, take two giant side steps to the right.*

2. **Music:** Sing and do the "Hokey Pokey." Once your child is familiar with the song, change the order of the commands.

3. Write step-by-step directions for your child to read and complete.

4. Give a series of oral directions to create a picture. **Example:** *Fold a sheet of paper in fourths. Number the boxes left to right, starting at the top left. Draw a blue butterfly in box number three, an orange sun with a red face in box one,* and so on.

5. **Physical Activity:** Give commands using position words, such as right, left, up, down, next to, under and over. **Examples:** *Put the book on the left side of the table; sit on the chair next to the door;* and *write a three over the picture of the kittens.*

6. Have your child work at the chalkboard while you give step-by-step directions to create a drawing.
    Sample directions for drawing a house:
    a. Draw a square.
    b. Draw a triangle on top of the square.
    c. Inside the square, draw a rectangle touching the bottom line.

7. Have your child write directions to solve a problem and then give them to someone else to follow.

▶READING APPRECIATION

Read to and with your child every day. Build a love of reading through positive experiences with books. A child who loves reading will be a more successful reader. Read a variety of books aloud, and let your child choose books that interest him/her to read independently. Help your child find books in his/her interest areas. Ask librarians or booksellers for good book suggestions.

1. Set aside an uninterrupted 10-minute period every day when your child reads a book of his/her choice.

2. Make frequent trips to the library with your child. Meet the librarian. Ask the librarian to explain library rules, show your child how books are arranged and teach him/her about other library services. Obtain a library card for your child and allow plenty of time to browse and make selections. Attend story times at the library.

3. Once your child has mastered a book, have him/her read the book to a friend.

▶COMPREHENSION

The goal of reading is to acquire meaning from text. Use the following comprehension-based activities to assess whether your child understands what he/she reads.

1. Summarize the story.

2. Find a sentence or paragraph that describes. . . .

3. Tell the problem in the story.

4. Discuss issues raised in the story.

5. Restate the main idea of a paragraph.

6. Describe or explain what the character meant by. . . .

7. Make a time line of events in the story.

8. Make a diorama representing the central theme of the story.

9. Tell what the author meant by. . . .

▶RECOGNIZING THE MAIN IDEA

1. Show your child a magazine photo from an advertisement or article. Ask him/her to describe in one sentence the main message of the picture or ad.

2. Read a paragraph to your child and have him/her paraphrase the message.

3. Write short paragraphs on index cards. Write the main idea of each on another set of index cards and have your child match each story with its main idea.

4. Write a short story and read it to your child. Give your child a choice of three titles and have him/her choose the best title for the story.

Learn at Home, Grade 1

▶RECALLING DETAILS

1. Arrange two objects on a tray. Let your child look at the objects for a minute. Then, remove the objects from the tray and ask your child to put them back on the tray in exactly the same positions. Repeat the activity, increasing the number of objects. Ask your child to close his/her eyes. Take one object away and have your child identify which one is missing.

2. Have your child read a descriptive paragraph. Ask him/her to find and underline sentences that answer specific questions.

3. Say or write two sentences; one should include more information. Ask your child to identify the sentence that gives more information.

   Example: a. Tammy got dressed for the party.

   b. Tammy wore her blue dress to the birthday party.

4. After reading a story, have your child answer who, what, where, when and why questions.

▶STORY ELEMENTS

1. After reading a book, identify and find a creative way to represent the story elements. The story elements are characters, setting, problem, events and solution.

2. Before reading a book, look over the pictures with your child and have him/her predict what the story elements might be. After reading, compare the actual story elements to the predictions.

3. Before reading a book, choose ten vocabulary words from the story. Have your child read the words and sort them under headings of the story elements. These will obviously not match their placement in the actual story, so encourage your child to imagine how the words might fit. When all the words are placed, have him/her complete a story frame (below), using the vocabulary words as they were organized under the story elements. **Hint:** A bird could be a character or a problem (the bird is getting into someone's garden). Then, read the story and make any necessary changes.

   Story Frame: The story takes place _____. The main character is _____ who _____. The problem is _____ _____. First, _____ _____. Then, _____. _____. Finally, _____. The problem is solved when _____. The story ends when _____.

4. Have your child use the story elements (or a story frame) as a guide for planning a story, so that he/she can be sure that his/her creative story contains all the necessary elements.

▶SEQUENCE

1. Have your child describe a familiar routine in sequential steps. Routines include getting ready for bed, getting ready for school, brushing teeth, mealtime and cleaning a bedroom. Write the steps he/she describes in order. Have your child reread the steps independently.

2. Create an original four-sentence story.
   Example: Dad picked up his shopping list and said good-bye. He walked to the store. Dad bought chicken, beans, potatoes, apples and cookies. When he got home, he started to make dinner.

   Scramble the sentences. With your child, read the sentences and discuss whether they are in sequential order. Then, have your child arrange them in the correct order.

3. **Spelling:** Scramble each spelling word. Ask your child to unscramble them and write them correctly.

4. Cut apart a comic strip. Have your child put the frames back in order and read the captions.

5. Write events from a story on sentence strips. Scramble them and have your child arrange the sentences in the correct sequence.

▶CHARACTER ANALYSIS

1. Discuss the different emotions that characters can feel. Have your child draw faces that show these different emotions.

2. Brainstorm a list of words that describe one's character, such as friendly, thoughtful, rough and curious. Have your child choose words that describe him/herself and/or family members. Save these words to use to describe characters.

3. Help your child analyze a character in a book. What kind of a person is the character and how does he/she feel in the story? Your child should support his/her ideas with examples from the book.

4. Have your child think about a character's actions in a story. Does your child agree with what the character did? Would he/she have done something differently?

▶CAUSE AND EFFECT

1. Discuss specific events/situations that have a cause-and-effect relationship. Make sure your child understands the connection between the two events—that one event happens because of another. **Example:** Heavy rains may cause flooding; a crying baby may cause Mom to come; and finishing a book may cause you to pick up another.

2. After reading a book, ask questions such as *What caused the children to forget their promise?* or *What happened as a result of the man showing everyone the gold?*

Learn at Home, Grade 1

▶FANTASY AND REALITY

1. A story or event is considered fantasy if it cannot happen. If a story or event has happened or could plausibly happen, then it is realistic. Write a variety of sentences, some realistic and some fantastic. Read and discuss each one with your child and have him/her sort the sentences into categories of fantasy and reality.

   Examples: a. A little pig flew a kite.
   b. A little girl saved money in a piggy bank.
   c. A dog chewed on bones.
   d. The bear talked to a little girl.

2. Read a make-believe story to your child. Draw a line down the middle of a chart-sized sheet of paper. Write *Fantasy/Not True* at the top of the left side and *Realistic/True* at the top of the right. Ask your child what things in the story could never happen; list these under *Fantasy*. Then, ask what things in the story could actually happen; list these under *Realistic*.

3. Teach your child about fiction and nonfiction stories. Go to the library and find books in each section. Allow your child to make comparisons and choose books from each category to take home and read.

4. Teach your child about fantasy through fairy tales. Read and discuss several fairy tale books.

   a. **Art:** Have your child create a magic wand by wrapping crepe paper around a dowel, drizzling glue on it and sprinkling glitter on the wet glue. Let him/her use it to act out parts of a story that are fantasy.

▶COMPARE AND CONTRAST

1. Have your child compare him/herself to a friend by listing interests and attributes that are alike and different.

2. Make a Venn diagram:

   a. Write the name of a character above each circle. List attributes in each circle. List the attributes the two have in common where the circles overlap.

   b. Use the Venn diagram to compare two books with a similar theme.

   c. Compare two books written by the same author.

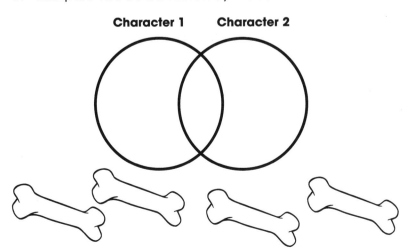

Character 1   **Character 2**

▶PREDICTING OUTCOMES

1. Make up short stories without endings. Have your child predict what will happen next.

   Example: Maria's cat, Toby, climbed the tree to get away from Mr. Sweetly's dog. Maria called to Toby but he wouldn't come down. Maria was worried because it was getting dark.

2. Cut out a comic strip. Cut off the last frame. Glue the comic to a sheet of paper, leaving space for your child to draw what he/she thinks the outcome will be.

3. While reading aloud a chapter book, stop after each chapter to let your child review what has happened and predict what might happen next.

4. While reading a book the first time, stop at logical stopping points and ask your child what will happen next. After reading on, discuss your child's prediction.

5. Using the front cover of a book, have your child predict what it will be about.

▶CLASSIFICATION

1. Your child frequently uses classification skills in math. Be sure to provide many opportunities to classify ideas, such as food, names, animals and books. Let your child choose category titles and sort the words accordingly.

2. Make a book of lists. On each page, have your child brainstorm a different list. Encourage your child to add to the lists as opportunities arise. Ideas for lists include things that are red, friendly animals, words that begin with z, friends, relatives, books about cars, toys and words that are fun to say.

3. Give your child words on index cards and have him/her sort them into groups.

▶INFERENCES

1. Explain to your child that information is sometimes implied rather than overtly stated in poems and stories, and the reader must infer the meaning. Look for opportunities to ask your child *How did you know that?* or *What gave you that idea?*

   Examples:
   a. Cassie and Jackie went to the beach. They swam in the water and ran on the sand all day long. At the end of the day the girls looked very red. If anyone touched them, they said, "OUCH!"

   Ask your child: *What happened to the girls? How did you know?*

   b. Mother bundled Maria in two thick sweaters and three pairs of socks. Mother also made her wear two pairs of mittens and a scarf. Maria could hardly walk when she went out to play.

   Ask your child: *What season is it? How did you know?*

Learn at Home, Grade 1

▶DRAWING CONCLUSIONS

1. Tell brief stories from which your child can draw conclusions. **Example:** *Shandra wrapped the box in brightly colored paper. She placed the box under the tree in her living room. She told her brother he would have to wait five more days until he could open it. What conclusions can you draw?* (It is Christmas and she has wrapped a present for her brother.)

2. Read books, such as *Nate the Great* by Marjorie Weinman Sharmat, in which a detective must draw conclusions from evidence. Have your child try to solve the mystery before reading the solution.

▶CRITICAL THINKING

1. Change one aspect of a familiar story and ask your child to write how the story might have changed as a result. **Examples:** Cinderella never went to the ball, Red Riding Hood walked on city streets or the Gingerbread Boy walked.

2. Have your child read a book until he/she knows the problem. Then, stop reading and ask your child to describe how he/she would solve the problem.

▶EVALUATION

1. Ask your child to evaluate a character's actions: whether the character was right or wrong, should have done something different, etc.

2. Make up realistic situations. Have your child propose how he/she should handle each one.

    a. Jack took the ball away from Larry at the playground and would not give it back. Larry tried to kick it out of Jack's arms.

    b. Marti was shorter than anyone else she knew. Her brother teased her and made her cry.

    c. Carole pushed ahead of others at a friend's party, took the largest cookie and drank the last of the grape juice.

MATH

To teach math to your first grader, use hands-on activities and concrete objects to explain new concepts. Once your child has practiced a new skill with manipulatives, he/she can solve problems without them. It is important that your child understand the concept underlying a problem and not just how to solve it. During his/her first-grade year, your child's focus should be on addition and subtraction. Your child should learn the basic facts through eighteen and work to memorize them. He/she should also learn to solve 2-digit problems, without regrouping or carrying, and column addition, which involves adding three or more numbers together in one problem. Also covered this year will be measurement, including using a ruler and scale, telling time, identifying and counting money and graphing information.

▶MATH IDEAS

1. Relate math skills to daily living activities by creating problem-solving situations. For example, when preparing for a meal, tell your child five people will be eating, but you only have three plates out. Ask your child how many more plates you need and how he/she will solve the problem.

2. When you are at the store, have your child count out the needed change or the change you receive back. Have him/her count your change at the end of the day.

3. Have your child keep a math journal in a notebook or writing tablet. He/she can use this to write the steps involved in solving a problem, illustrating a concept such as adding, predicting how long an object is and noting the actual measurement, creating his/her own story problems or recording anything else related to the concept or skill he/she is working on.

SCIENCE

Science, like math, should involve hands-on activities, allowing your child to explore and make discoveries. Allow your child to explore the materials he/she will use before beginning a science activity. Then, guide your child through the scientific process, helping him/her to discover on his/her own the goal of the lesson.

▶SCIENTIFIC PROCESS

1. Have your child make a hypothesis.

2. Plan the experiment with your child.

3. Help your child carry out the experiment.

4. Have your child make observations and record his/her results.

5. Encourage your child to make a conclusion.

During this school year, your child's science learning should focus on living things, plants and animals, the human body, the five senses, seasons and weather, the solar system and simple machines. To find more information on the topics covered or ideas for experiments, consult the following resources, if available in your area: the local library for videos, informational books and books containing experiments; a science center or museum of natural history; a garden center or botanical garden; the park system or forest service; nature stores; magazines such as *Ranger Rick*, *National Geographic World* and *Scienceland*.

Learn at Home, Grade 1

SOCIAL STUDIES

The concepts taught in the social studies lessons will give your child a basic understanding of him/herself, social skills, the community, famous Americans, maps and places of the world. As you are teaching the lessons, provide your child with experiences which will help make the concepts as real to him/her as possible. When studying early America, for example, try going to an antique store or museum. Find the different locations you study on a map and help your child figure out how far they are from your hometown. Seek out people from your community who have visited or lived in other parts of the world and are willing to share their experiences, pictures, etc. with your child. In addition, make use of videos from the library or video store showing places you are unable to visit.

Language Skills	Spelling	Reading
Monday — **Handwriting** Teach the correct formation of the letters of the alphabet on lined paper. Enlarge a copy of the **Handwriting Chart and Paper** on page 20 for your child to refer to. Have your child trace each letter with his/her finger. *See* Language Skills Week 1, numbers 1 and 2.	**Beginning Consonants** Have your child say the alphabet aloud. *See* Spelling, Week 1, number 1.	**Letter Recognition** Make a set of lower-case and upper-case alphabet cards. Assess your child's recognition of the letters of the alphabet. Read *Chicka Chicka Boom Boom* by Bill Martin, Jr. Teach your child the names of the letters of the alphabet. *See* Reading, Week 1, number 1. Have your child complete **ABC...Follow Me!** (p. 25).
Tuesday — Copy the **Handwriting Chart and Paper** on page 20. Have your child practice writing the lower-case letters of the alphabet on lined paper. Have your child identify the lower-case letters before writing.	Introduce the beginning consonant sounds *b, t, s* and *c. See* Spelling, Week 1. Use the letters *b, t, s* and *c* in activity number 1. *See also* Spelling, Week 1, numbers 2 and 3. Have your child complete **Beginning Sounds I** (p. 21).	Have your child lay out the alphabet cards used in yesterday's lesson and match the upper-case to the lower-case letters. Then, scramble both sets and ask your child to identify a given letter, such as upper-case *B*. Play a memory game in which your child finds and matches upper- and lower-case letters from cards turned facedown. Have your child complete **Sea Search** (p. 26).
Wednesday — Go through the formation of each lower-case letter. Call attention to the letters that go below the bottom line *(g, j, p, q, y)*. Notice how each letter touches the middle line. Have your child practice writing the lower-case letters on lined paper.	Introduce the beginning consonant sounds *d, m, r* and *f. See* Spelling, Week 1. Use the letters *d, m, r* and *f* in activity number 1. *See also* Spelling, Week 1, numbers 2 and 3. Have your child complete **Beginning Sounds II** (p. 22).	Copy **Alphabet Letters** (p. 27). On one copy, smooth glue over each letter and let your child sprinkle sand, glitter or crushed cereal over the glue. Have your child trace the dry, textured letters with the index finger of his/her writing hand while saying each letter to reinforce tactile memory. Copy **Alphabet Letters** on construction paper, cut out the letters and have your child arrange them in alphabetical order. *See* Reading, Week 1, number 2.
Thursday — Have your child write the lower-case alphabet on lined paper without looking at the alphabet chart. After he/she finishes, let your child compare his/her own work to the alphabet chart. Have your child rewrite any missed or sloppy letters on lined paper.	Introduce beginning consonant sounds *g, p, n* and *h. See* Spelling, Week 1. Use the letters *g, p, n* and *h* in activity number 1. *See also* Spelling, Week 1, numbers 2 and 3. Have your child complete **Beginning Sounds III** (p. 23).	Teach your child the consonants and the vowels. Using lower-case alphabet cards, isolate and teach the vowels. Teach him/her that vowels are special and are needed to make words. Each vowel makes at least two sounds—long and short. Tell your child that the remaining letters of the alphabet are called consonants and make only one sound, unless combined with other consonants. Have your child complete **Letter Lift** (p. 28).
Friday — Have your child write a description of your home classroom. Encourage him/her to paint a picture with words so that someone who lives far away could read his/her words and know what the room is like. Have him/her use sound spelling—he/she spells the words as he/she hears them. Let your child read his/her description to you. Below your child's words, write the conventional spelling of each word.	Introduce beginning consonant sounds *w, j, k* and *v. See* Spelling, Week 1. Use the letters *w, j, k* and *v* in activity number 1. *See also* Spelling, Week 1, numbers 2 and 3. Have your child complete **Beginning Sounds IV** (p. 24).	Mix up the alphabet cards. Choose a letter. Have your child identify the letter before and after it in the alphabet. Also, ask your child to find the letter that falls between two given letters. Read *Chicka Chicka Boom Boom* again. Let your child act out the story using the letter cards.

Learn at Home, Grade 1

Math	Science	Social Studies

Counting
Start the **Math Assessment Record Sheet** (p. 29). Have your child count by 1's. Record the date and the number to which your child counts confidently. Write the numerals 1–10 on index cards, one per card. Using small familiar objects, have your child place the number of objects called for on each card.
Have your child complete **Sheepish Shepherd** (p. 30).
	Human Body
	Ask your child to list the five senses. Explain the five senses and give examples. Brainstorm words related to the senses. Have your child copy and complete the following:
	    I see with my _____.
	    I hear with my _____.
	    I smell with my _____.
	    I taste with my _____.
	    I feel with my _____.
		All About Me
		Have your child look in the mirror and answer questions about him/herself. What do you see? What color is your hair? Is it curly or straight? What color are your eyes? *See* Social Studies, Week 1, number 1. Have your child draw a picture of him/herself and write a description.

Have your child count again. Record the date and number reached. **Note:** Continue to assess counting ability daily or weekly until your child is counting comfortably to 100. Let your child choose a favorite number from 1 to 10, draw it on construction paper and decorate it with the given number of buttons or other small manipulatives. Then, encourage him/her to write a story about the number.	Ask your child to list descriptive words that tell about what his/her eyes notice (color, shape, brightness, etc.). Make a chart of your child's words and post it for future reference. *See* Science, Week 1, numbers 1 and 2.	Help your child explore his/her emotions/feelings. List a variety of emotions on the chalkboard. Using a mirror, have your child show faces that express each emotion. Have your child explain what might make him/her happy, excited, annoyed, etc. Have your child complete **When I Feel...** (p. 33).
Have your child count numbers on a copy of the **Hundred Chart** (p. 31). Have your child underline and read every other number, starting with 2. Have your child practice counting by 2's with and without looking at the chalkboard. On drawing paper, have your child draw several people holding their hands up. Have your child write the total number of hands by 2's under each person.	Make a series of noises with familiar objects. Ask your child to list words that describe the sounds he/she hears (loud, soft, bang, rip, etc.). Make a chart of your child's words and post it for future reference. *See* Science, Week 1, numbers 3, 4 and 5.	**Art:** Help your child make a life-size figure of him/herself out of paper and paints, stuffed with newspaper. *See* Social Studies, Week 1, numbers 2 and 3.
Begin assessing your child's ability to count by 2's. Have your child practice identifying and counting numbers on the **Hundred Chart**. Have your child circle and read every fifth number, starting with 5. Have your child practice counting by 5's. On drawing paper, have your child trace his/her hand with fingers outstretched ten times. Then, have your child count by 5's and write the number of fingers on the hands.	Collect several objects with different textures. Put each one in a separate paper bag. Ask your child to touch each object without looking at it and to describe what he/she feels (rough, cold, hard, prickly, etc.). Make a chart of your child's words and post it for future reference.	Help your child make a personal fact sheet to be filed in the *All About Me* folder. Have your child complete information on his/her name, birthdate, age, height, weight, eye and hair color, address and telephone number.
Review and assess counting by 1's, 2's and 5's using the **Hundred Chart**. On a copy of the **Hundred Chart**, have your child color and read every tenth number, starting with 10. Then, have your child practice counting by 10's with and without the chart. On paper, have your child write the numbers used when counting by 2's, 5's and 10's to 100. Have your child complete **Caterpillar Count** (p. 32).	Prepare a variety of objects for your child to smell safely (orange, onion, flower, toothpaste, vinegar, soap, leather, etc.). Ask your child to smell each object and describe its smell without naming it (strong, light, fruity, flowery, pungent, etc.). Make a list of your child's words on a chart. Post it with the other sensory charts for future reference.	**Poetry:** Write your child's name vertically on a large sheet of writing paper. Ask your child to think of a word or phrase beginning with each letter that tells or describes something about him/herself. Write the words across, forming an acrostic poem.

17

TEACHING SUGGESTIONS AND ACTIVITIES

Language Skills (Handwriting)

▶ 1. Copy the **Handwriting Chart and Paper** (p. 20) as a practice sheet for your child. The lower half of the sheet contains lined paper for your child to practice writing the letters neatly. Use lined paper like this, which may be purchased in bulk at a teacher supply store, for your child's writing and handwriting.

▶ 2. Show your child the correct way to hold his/her pencil.

Spelling (Alphabet)

Spend as much time as is necessary teaching the alphabet and letter sounds. Do not start teaching spelling until your child is able to recognize the letters of the alphabet and their sounds. (*See* Reading and Language Skills lesson plans.) Spelling skills are developed and improved through reading and writing, so begin these activities right away.

▶ 1. Write each letter of the alphabet on a large index card. Choose four to eight of the alphabet cards and lay them out on a table. Say a word that begins with one of the letters and have your child identify the beginning sound. (Avoid naming words that begin with blends and digraphs such as *frog* or *shop*.) Repeat with other alphabet letters.

▶ 2. Give your child appropriate letter cards. Say a word that begins with one of these letters. Use the word in a sentence. Then, say the word again. Have your child listen for the beginning sound and identify the appropriate letter.

▶ 3. Using four consonant letter cards, point to a letter and have your child name a word that begins with that letter.

Reading (Letter Recognition)

A reader must recognize the lower- and upper-case letters of the alphabet before making an association between letters, their sounds and reading. Coordinate the teaching of the letters of the alphabet and letter sounds with the first three weeks of Spelling.

▶ 1. Have your child touch each letter of the alphabet while singing the alphabet song.

▶ 2. Read *Grover's Own Alphabet*, a Little Golden Book by Sal Murdocca. After reading the book, have your child attempt to form each of the letters as Grover did.

Math (Counting)

There is a difference between rote counting and understanding the meaning of counting. Help your child develop an understanding of numbers through a variety of concrete counting experiences. Have your child practice counting sets of actual objects, rearranging them and counting again. Activities such as these will help develop your child's understanding of one-to-one correspondence.

Learn at Home, Grade 1

Science (Human Body)

▶ 1. Put ten objects on a tray. Let your child look at it for a minute. Tell your child to close his/her eyes. Remove one object. Have your child open his/her eyes and tell what is missing. Repeat, taking away one or two objects.

▶ 2. Remove the tray from your child's sight. Give your child a piece of drawing paper and have him/her draw the objects that were on the tray. Compare the drawing to the tray.

▶ 3. Here is a list of sound words to get you started: *soft, loud, low, high, booming, clanging, whisper, murmur.*

▶ 4. Ask your child to be absolutely quiet for 1 minute and to pay attention to any sounds that are present. List all sounds your child can hear and identify.

▶ 5. Explain that sound is made by vibrations. Ask your child to put a hand on his/her voice box and talk. Ask what your child feels. Take your child's hand. Put it on your voice box. Say something, and then say it again without voice. Ask your child to tell you the difference.

Social Studies (All About Me)

Help your child build a positive sense of self through an awareness of what makes him/her unique. As your child's teacher and parent, you have a great responsibility in building your child's positive self-image. Deliberately share with your child the specific strengths and qualities which make him/her unique. Provide positive experiences and participate in activities that your child enjoys. Guide your child to analyze his/her likes and dislikes so he/she may continue to gain self-awareness.

▶ 1. Make an *All About Me* folder. Give your child a file folder in which to keep all papers completed in this unit. Your child may decorate the folder with his/her name and a self-portrait.

▶ 2. **Preparation:** Have your child lie on a large sheet of butcher paper. Trace around your child to make an outline of his/her body. Place another sheet of large paper under the body outline and cut out both so you will have two identical body cutouts. Staple them together, leaving the head and shoulders open.

▶ 3. **Art:** Instruct your child to paint the front of the life-size figure to look as much like him/her as possible and to put features on the face that will show how he/she is feeling. Instruct your child to crush newspaper into small balls and to stuff his/her figure with it. Staple the shoulders and head shut when the figure is completely stuffed.

Learn at Home, Grade 1

Handwriting Chart and Paper

Learn at Home, Grade 1

Beginning Sounds I

Say each picture name. **Circle** the beginning sound for each picture. **Color** the pictures.

b t c s   b t c s   b t c s

b t c s   b t c s   b t c s

b t c s   b t c s

Beginning Sounds II

Say each picture name. **Write** the beginning sound for each picture. **Color** the pictures.

Learn at Home, Grade 1

Beginning Sounds III

Draw a line from each letter to the pictures which begin with that sound. **Color** the pictures.

Learn at Home, Grade 1

Beginning Sounds IV

Say each picture name. **Write** the beginning sound for each picture. **Color** the pictures.

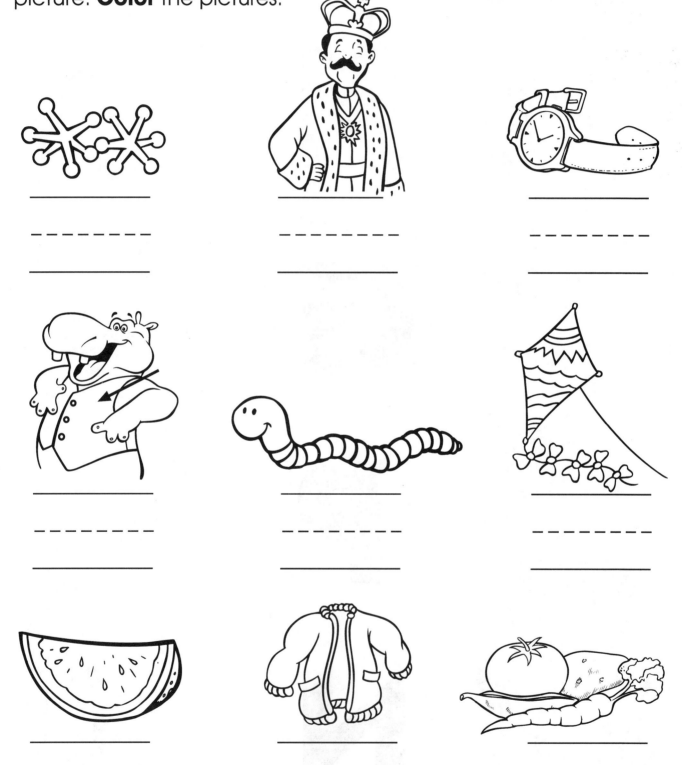

Learn at Home, Grade 1

ABC...Follow Me!

Draw a line to follow the alphabet from **A** to **Z** in the correct order.

Sea Search

Week 1

Help the boat sail to the island! **Color** the fish:

upper-case letters – *orange*
lower-case letters – **blue**

Learn at Home, Grade 1

Alphabet Letters

a b c d e
f g h i j k
l m n o p
q r s t u v
w x y z

Learn at Home, Grade 1

Letter Lift

Cut out the letters below.
Glue each letter on the correct balloon.

Consonants

Vowels

w	s	m	a	q	h	d	o	r	j	x	p	y
f	g	t	i	l	b	e	n	v	u	c	k	z

Learn at Home, Grade 1

Math Assessment Record Sheet

Start assessment when each skill is introduced. Continue assessment until your child has mastered the skill. When no improvement is being made, reteach with a new approach.

Skill → Date ↓	Counting to 100	Counting by 2's to 100	Counting by 5's to 100	Counting by 10's to 100	Number Combinations Through 10	Identifying Shapes (name the shapes)	Addition Facts	Subtraction Facts	Counting Coin Values Through 99¢

Sheepish Shepherd

Count the sheep on each hill. Then, **write** that number on each tree.

30

Hundred Chart

1	2	3	4	5	6	7	8	9	10
11	12	13	14	15	16	17	18	19	20
21	22	23	24	25	26	27	28	29	30
31	32	33	34	35	36	37	38	39	40
41	42	43	44	45	46	47	48	49	50
51	52	53	54	55	56	57	58	59	60
61	62	63	64	65	66	67	68	69	70
71	72	73	74	75	76	77	78	79	80
81	82	83	84	85	86	87	88	89	90
91	92	93	94	95	96	97	98	99	100

Caterpillar Count

Count by 5's.
Draw triangles around each number in the box.

1	2	3	4	5	6	7	8	9	10
11	12	13	14	15	16	17	18	19	20
21	22	23	24	25	26	27	28	29	30
31	32	33	34	35	36	37	38	39	40
41	42	43	44	45	46	47	48	49	50

Count by 5's

5 **10** ____ ____ ____ ____ ____ ____

____ ____

Count by 10's.
Draw boxes around each number in the box.

1	2	3	4	5	6	7	8	9	10
11	12	13	14	15	16	17	18	19	20
21	22	23	24	25	26	27	28	29	30
31	32	33	34	35	36	37	38	39	40
41	42	43	44	45	46	47	48	49	50

Count by 10's

10 ____ ____ ____ ____

Learn at Home, Grade 1

When I Feel...

Complete each sentence.

When I feel happy, I ...

_____

- -

_____

When I feel sad, I ...

_____

- -

_____

When I feel angry, I ...

_____

- -

_____

When I feel scared, I ...

_____

- -

_____

When I feel excited, I ...

_____

- -

_____

	Language Skills	**Spelling**	**Reading**
Monday	Go through the formation of each upper-case letter. The letters must touch the top and bottom lines and not stray outside the lines. Point out each letter's relationship to the middle line. Have your child practice writing upper-case letters on lined paper.	**Alphabet** Introduce beginning consonant sounds *l, q, y,* and *z. See* Spelling, Week 1. Use the letters *l, q, y* and *z* in activity number 1. *See* Spelling, Week 2, number 1. Have your child complete **Beginning Sounds V** (p. 38).	**Letter Sounds** Over the course of the week, provide samples of foods that start with each letter of the alphabet. Then, have your child write the beginning sound for each food and draw a picture of him/herself eating that food. Post your child's drawings around the room or help him/her make a *Food Alphabet Book*. Repeat this activity with other categories such as furniture, animals or colors.
Tuesday	Have your child practice writing the upper- and lower-case letters from *A* to *L* on lined paper.	Have your child write the alphabet first in upper- and then in lower-case letters. *See* Spelling, Week 2, numbers 2 and 3.	Help your child make his/her own alphabet book. Staple 26 pages inside a construction paper cover. Your child should label each page with a letter of the alphabet and decorate the cover. Your child may add words to this book at anytime throughout the year. Your child may add words from books, the environment or lessons. Your child can refer to the book to practice reading sight words and for help with spelling during writing activities.
Wednesday	Have your child practice writing the upper- and lower-case letters from *M* to *Z* on lined paper.	Teach your child to listen for the ending consonant sounds. *See* Spelling, Week 2, number 4.	Go for a "word walk." Have your child identify things seen on your walk and tell the beginning letter. **Example:** *I see a cat. Cat begins with c.* If your child is confused by the beginning sound of *tree*, explain that *tree* begins with the *tr* blend. Upon your return, have your child write the words in his/her alphabet book. Your child may illustrate each word.
Thursday	Have your child write his/her first and last name. Teach your child to use upper-case letters for the first letter of each name. Have your child practice writing his/her name neatly on lined paper. Then, have him/her circle his/her neatest handwriting.	Provide your child with practice identifying the ending consonants *b, k, l, m, n, r, s* and *t. See* Spelling, Week 2, number 5. Have your child complete **Final Sound I** (p. 39).	Have your child dictate a story describing your "word walk." Then, your child can copy the story and draw an illustration.
Friday	Write sentences about the day for your child to copy. Draw a line under the capital letters to call attention to them. Point out the period at the end of each sentence. **Examples:** <u>T</u>oday is <u>F</u>riday. 　　　　　<u>I</u>t is <u>S</u>eptember (twentieth). 　　　　　<u>I</u>t is sunny and cool.	Provide your child with practice identifying the ending consonants *d, f, g, p, x* and *z. See* Spelling, Week 2, numbers 6 and 7. Have your child complete **Final Sound II** (p. 40).	Copy a poem onto chart paper. Read the poem to your child while pointing to each word. Discuss the meaning and images of the poem. Then, read the poem again. Ask your child to read the poem with you a few times. Have your child identify the sounds, letters and words in the poem. Read the poem and identify phonics skills for several days. Repeat this procedure with other poems all year. Then, have your child read his/her own story from yesterday. *See* Reading, Week 2, number 1.

Learn at Home, Grade 1

Math	**Science**	**Social Studies**
Patterning Introduce the number words *one* through *ten*. Make number word cards and numeral cards with the corresponding number of stickers on each. Give your child a number word card. Have him/her match it with a numeral card and count out the correct number of manipulatives. Give your child a number word card and ask him/her to hop a given number of times.	**Sense** Prepare small amounts of salt, sugar, cinnamon, pepper, lemon, curry, garlic, chive, strawberry, raw turnip, cheese and capers for your child to taste. Have your child describe how each tastes. Make a list of tasting words on a chart. Hang it on the wall with the other sense charts. Have your child complete **It Makes Sense to Me** (p. 44).	Spend the week discussing and exploring the uniqueness of your child. Make a time line depicting significant events in your child's life. Include pictures. Have your child use his/her time line as a guide to writing an "autobiography."
Introduce patterns. Have your child listen to and copy several auditory patterns (snap, clap, snap, clap, etc.). Have your child continue the visual patterns you start. Do other patterns such as varying the volume of claps (soft, loud, soft). Use three different shapes in a pattern repeated two times (triangle, square, star, triangle, square, star). Have your child continue the pattern.	Read *My Five Senses* by Aliki with your child. Help your child make a book of the senses following a similar pattern. *See* Science, Week 2, number 1.	Have your child brainstorm favorite foods, sports, stories, etc. Draw an outline of a shield on paper. Have your child design a coat of arms by drawing pictures that represent his/her interests. Cut out and display.
Use foods such as small cereal pieces, crackers or dry pasta to create a pattern. Repeat the pattern twice before your child continues it. Have your child glue the patterns onto paper. Have your child complete **Plenty of Patterns** (p. 42).	Ask your child to name and identify the parts of his/her body. Write the words as your child names them (head, shoulders, chest, stomach, arm, etc.). Read the words from the list together. Have your child draw a picture of his/her body and label each part, referring to the written list. **Game:** Play "Simon Says," giving commands such as *Touch your knees*.	Teach your child how to make fingerprints using an ink pad. Make your own fingerprints and let your child compare them with his/her own to conclude that they are different. Let your child make a "fingerprint picture." Have him/her make a fingerprint imprint and then add details—head, legs, tail, etc.— to the fingerprint to create an animal picture.
Look for and create size patterns. Go for a "pattern walk" outside or around the house. Discuss patterns your child sees in familiar objects such as fabrics, furniture, wallpaper, tiles and landscaping. Have your child write and draw the patterns he/she has seen. Have your child arrange five blocks from largest to smallest. Then, have your child arrange other objects according to size.	Give a series of directions to your child. Each time, ask your child to identify the primary body part that he/she uses to carry out the direction. *See* Science, Week 2, number 2.	Have your child draw an outline of him/herself and divide it into sections. Have your child write a word or phrase in each section that describes him/her. Have him/her cut out the outline, turn it over and decorate it as him/herself. Then, he/she can cut apart the pieces to make a puzzle.
Provide your child with pennies, nickels and dimes to explore. Observe how he/she "plays" with the coins. You might encourage sorting, patterning, counting or identifying the coins. Have your child complete **My Very Special Name** (p. 43).	Make a copy of **Silly Skeleton** (p. 45). Provide books with pictures of the human skeleton for reference. Have your child cut out the bones and piece them together on black paper.	Read aloud the poems "Me I Am" and "Everybody Says" from the *Random House Book of Poetry*. Discuss what makes your child unique. Have your child complete these sentences in writing: *I feel happy when…* *I feel sad when…* *I feel special when…* *I am me because…* *I like me because…*

Learn at Home, Grade 1

TEACHING SUGGESTIONS AND ACTIVITIES

Spelling (Alphabet)

▶ 1. Give your child letter cards for *l, y, q* and *z*. Say a word that begins with one of these letters. Use the word in a sentence. Then, say the word again. Have your child listen for the beginning sound and identify the appropriate letter. Here are some words to get you started:

   lotion, lace, little, lizard   question, quack, quail, quote
   yard, yummy, yam, year   zipper, zero, zany, zoology

   Explain that the sound *q* makes is a combined sound of the letters *k* (as in king) and *w* (as in wing).

▶ 2. Give your child a sheet of drawing paper for each letter of the alphabet that he/she is practicing. Label each page with a letter. Have your child search through magazines and newspapers for pictures of objects that begin with the letter on the page, then cut them out and glue the pictures on the appropriate pages. Help him/her write the word beside each picture. Staple the pages together to make an alphabet book. It may take several days or weeks for your child to complete the entire alphabet.

▶ 3. **Game:** Make up letter riddles. **Example:** *I'm thinking of an animal that hops and whose name begins with r.* Have your child guess the answer.

▶ 4. Write a list of easy three-letter words and read the list to your child as you point to each word. On the second reading, have your child listen for the ending sound. As you read, emphasize the last letter with your voice and by pointing to it. Have your child name the ending sound.

▶ 5. Give your child the following consonant cards: *b, m, l, r, t, k, n* and *s*. Say some words that end with these sounds. Use each word in a sentence and repeat the word. Have your child identify the ending sound. Here is a list to get you started:

   bib, crab, tub, rib, web   vat, light, cut, bat, rat
   ham, ram, chum, sum, from   kick, pack, cluck, cook
   tell, bull, roll, pail, sill   won, pen, sun, tan, fin
   four, bear, war, burr, car   pass, guess, less, hiss, us

▶ 6. Give your child the following consonant cards: *f, p, x, g, d* and *z*. Say some words that end with these sounds. Use each word in a sentence and repeat the word. Have your child identify the ending sound. Here is a list to get you started:

   half, off, puff, calf   big, rag, leg, hug, hog
   tip, rap, cup, sip, mop   hid, said, lead, pod, pad
   six, fox, fax, mix, box   buzz, fizz, whiz, jazz, fuzz

   Note: The sound *x* makes at the end of a word is a combination of two letters: **k** and **s**. The letter *x* will not be used at the beginning of a word at this time.

▶ 7. Hold up a consonant letter card. Say a word. Have your child tell you whether he/she hears the letter at the beginning or end of the word.

Learn at Home, Grade 1

Reading (Letter Sounds)

Learning the letter sounds can be great fun. Use a variety of multi-sensory strategies to teach the letters and sounds so that learning is reinforced through all of the senses. Multi-sensory strategies involve visual, auditory, physical and musical activities as well as activities that involve words, pictures, group dynamics and quiet time.

▶   1.   An excellent resource for poetry is *Read-Aloud Rhymes for the Very Young* compiled by Jack Prelutsky. Choose poems weekly for their seasonal or topical relevance and copy them for your child on either a poster or a page on which your child can write and draw. Poems are excellent for teaching many phonics skills in context. Provide opportunities for your child to frequently reread and memorize poems.

▶   2.   Hang a clothesline across the room and provide clothespins. Have your child cut out the **Shirt, Pants and Sock Pattern** outlines on page 41 and trace them onto different colors of construction paper. Have your child look through magazines for a picture of an object whose name begins with *a*. Have your child cut out and glue the picture to one of the shapes and print the letter *A* on the shape. Repeat for each letter of the alphabet. Have your child hang the clothes on the line in alphabetical order.

Math (Patterning)

Patterns form the basis of mathematics and enhance problem-solving skills. Teach your child to recognize a pattern by modeling rhythmic and visual patterns. Have your child look for the core that is repeated in the sequence, then join in the rhythm or have your child complete the visual pattern. As your child gains experience in pattern recognition, he/she will point out patterns in clothing, on walls and elsewhere.

Have your child touch and name objects in a pattern to gain visual, auditory and kinesthetic reinforcement of the pattern. Vary the manipulatives with which patterns are presented, to focus on the relationships in patterns. Create the same pattern with different materials, such as buttons, two or three colors of blocks, pattern blocks, toothpicks, keys, acorns, printed symbols, musical notes and shapes.

Science (Senses)

▶   1.   Make a book of the senses modeled after *My Five Senses* by Aliki. Take a photo of your child pointing to each sense organ—five photos in all. Glue each photo to a page. Have your child copy the following sentence-starters on the photo pages: *With my eyes I see . . . , With my ears I hear . . . , With my mouth I taste . . . , With my nose I smell . . . ,* and *With my hands I feel . . . .* Following the photo page for each sense are four pages listing things that your child sees, hears, tastes, smells or feels. The final page of the book should make a closing statement such as *My senses help me understand my world.* Your child should illustrate each page and make a cover for the book. Your child may practice reading the book and keep it in his/her personal library.

▶   2.   Give the following directions to your child for Thursday's lesson:

Read a book.   *Give me a pencil.*
Talk to a friend on the telephone.   *Kick the soccer ball.*
Put on your coat and button it.   *Move this chair to the door.*
Blow out the candles on a cake.   *Jump as high as you can.*
Eat an ice-cream cone.   *Do five push-ups.*
Reach as high as you can.   *Lie on your back and pretend to ride a bike.*

Beginning Sounds V

Say each picture name. **Circle** the beginning sound for each picture. **Color** the pictures.

l q y z

l q y z

l q y z

l q y z

l q y z

l q y z

l q y z

l q y z

l q y z

38

Learn at Home, Grade 1

Final Sound I

Write the sound you hear at the end of each word. **Color** the pictures.

Final Sound II

Draw a line from each letter to the pictures which end with that sound. **Color** the pictures.

Learn at Home, Grade 1

Shirt, Pants and Socks Pattern

41

Plenty of Patterns

Continue each pattern below.

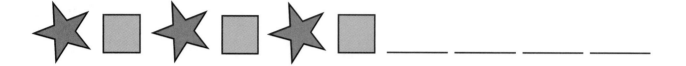 _____

 _____

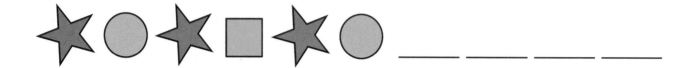 _____

 _____

1 5 2 5 1 5 2 _____

5 4 6 5 4 6 5 _____

9 9 8 9 9 8 9 _____

1 3 5 7 9 1 3 _____

Learn at Home, Grade 1

My Very Special Name!

Write the first letter of your name in the first box, the second letter in the second box, and so on. When you finish your name, **write** your name again without skipping any boxes. Continue until you run out of boxes. Next, choose one crayon to color all the first letters in your name, a different-colored crayon to color all of the second letters, and so on until your chart is full of color and creates a pattern.

Learn at Home, Grade 1

It Makes Sense to Me

Our five senses help us understand our world. Look at each group of pictures. Decide which sense is used for most of the things in each group. **Write** that sense on the line for each group. Then, **draw** an **X** on the picture that **does not** belong.

Learn at Home, Grade 1

Silly Skeleton

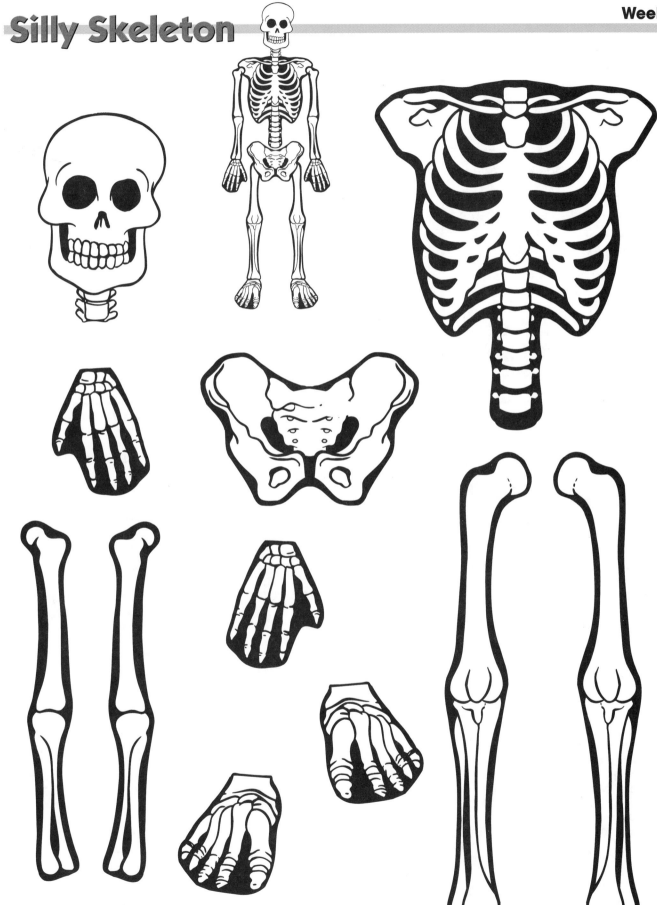

Learn at Home, Grade 1

Language Skills	Spelling	Reading
Monday Using a **Topic Web** (p. 50), brainstorm with your child some of the things that make him/her unique. Include interests, achievements, appearance, likes and dislikes and activities. Throughout this week, have your child write and illustrate sentences about him/herself to be included in his/her *All About Me* book.	**Short Vowels** Teach the short *a* sound as in *bat*. *See* Spelling, Week 3, numbers 1, 2 and 3. Have your child complete **Short a** (p. 51).	Have your child look through magazines for pictures beginning with each letter of the alphabet. He/she should cut out and glue each picture onto a sheet of paper with the letter written on it. Hang your child's alphabet letters on a clothesline in alphabetical order. Read *Brown Bear, Brown Bear* written by Bill Martin, Jr. Have your child complete **How Do I Begin? I** (p. 56)
Tuesday Have your child write a sentence that tells what he/she likes to do. Have him/her draw and color a picture to go with the sentence. Note your child's use of consonants. Is your child using vowels in his/her sound spelling? Is there any punctuation? Choose one skill to focus on in your child's writing as he/she reads the sentence to you. Then, help your child rewrite his/her sentence using the correct spelling. Be sure to praise your child's effort.	Teach the short *e* sound as in *bed*. *See* Spelling, Week 3, numbers 2 and 3. Adapt the activities to short *e:* **Words:** egg, east, end, add Have your child fill in the blanks: b__d, h__n, j__t, w__b and s__t. Have your child complete **Short e** (p. 52).	Reread *Brown Bear, Brown Bear* together several times. Discuss the beginning sounds of words found in the book. Have your child complete **How Do I Begin? II** (p. 57).
Wednesday Repeat yesterday's lesson but have your child write about his/her appearance. Your child may write more than one sentence per day, if time permits. Have your child rewrite his/her sentences neatly, using correct spelling. Have him/her glue each sentence on the matching picture.	Teach the short *i* sound as in *rip*. See Spelling, Week 3, numbers 2 and 3. Adapt the activities to short *i:* **Words:** is, itch, ill, ink, end Have your child fill in the blanks: m__x, b__g, h__p, w__n and l__p. Have your child complete **Short i** (p. 53).	Help your child use the pattern of *Brown Bear, Brown Bear* to write his/her own book. Encourage your child to use familiar objects in the story. **Example:** *Orange cat, orange cat, what do you see? I see a yellow mouse looking at me.* Have your child write a rough draft, spelling words by sound. Help your child edit the draft and write and illustrate a neat copy with standard spelling. *See* Reading, Week 3, number 1.
Thursday Have your child continue Tuesday's lesson to complete all the pages for the book *All About Me*. Have your child add sentences about his/her likes and dislikes and what makes him/her unique.	Teach the short *o* sound as in *top*. *See* Spelling, Week 3, numbers 2 and 3. Adapt the activities to short *o:* **Words:** odd, mom, cot, apple, bug Have your child fill in the blanks: d__t, m__p, g__t, p__d and l__t. Have your child complete **Short o** (p. 54).	Write your child's name in upper-case letters vertically down the left side of a page. Have your child write a word or draw a simple picture of an object that begins with each of the letters in his/her name. Repeat using the names of family members. **Example:** Ant Nest Duck Yo-yo
Friday Have your child make a front and back cover for the book out of construction paper. He/she should copy the words *All About Me* across the front cover. Have him/her write his/her name in large letters below the title. Help your child run a bead of glue over each letter in his/her name and sprinkle glitter over the glue. Staple the covers and sentence pages together, and let your child read his/her *All About Me* book aloud.	Teach the short *u* sound as in *sun*. *See* Spelling, Week 3, numbers 2 and 3. Adapt the activities to short *u:* **Words:** up, sun, under, cat, it Fill in blanks: c__t, d__g, h__t, n__t, r__n. Have your child complete **Short u** (p. 55).	**Cooking:** Make bread dough letters. *See* Reading, Week 3, number 2. Use the letters to form simple three-letter words (consonant-vowel-consonant). Have your child complete **Hidden Picture** (p. 58).

Learn at Home, Grade 1

Math	Science	Social Studies
Shapes Out of construction paper, cut several triangles, circles, ovals, squares, rectangles and diamonds of varying sizes and colors. Label each shape. Help your child identify shapes and their attributes through sorting and comparing. *See* Math, Week 3, numbers 1–3. Read *The Shapes Game* by Paul Rogers. Have your child complete **Find the Shapes** (p. 59).	**Body Systems** Begin an experiment with bones and calcium that will continue over the course of 2 weeks. *See* Science, Week 3, number 1. Have your child observe the bone and write down his/her observations before putting it into vinegar.	**Friends and Family** Read and discuss the book *Do You Want To Be My Friend?* by Eric Carle. Then, ask your child why some people make better friends than others and what your child looks for in a friend. Have your child name some friends and tell why they are friends. Make a chart of his/her responses.
Out of construction paper, cut hearts, stars, trapezoids and rhombuses. Add them to the previously explored shapes. Help your child identify the shapes and their attributes through sorting and comparing. Teach your child the shape word names. Write the names on index cards and have your child match the names to the cut-out shapes. Have your child use the cut-out shapes to create a picture and count how many of each shape is used.	The body has over 600 muscles, each with its own special job of helping a part of the body move. The muscles attached to your skeleton help you move. Have your child observe the muscles in his/her arm as he/she bends the arm at the elbow. Other muscles keep your food, blood and breath moving. A different kind of muscle makes your heart pump blood all over your body. *See* Science, Week 3, numbers 2–4.	Have your child write to a friend and then act out a conversation he/she might have with a good friend. Discuss telephone manners. Let your child practice making and receiving telephone calls.
Sorting and Classifying: Have your child brainstorm a list of attributes (red, four corners, etc.). *See* Math, Week 3, number 4. **Critical Thinking:** Place two attributes in a Venn diagram. Then, have your child sort all the shapes into the appropriate sets. Where the two circles intersect, have your child place objects that have attributes from both circles.	Observe and record your child's pulse and breaths per minute. Have your child do some jumping jacks for 1 to 5 minutes. Discuss how your child's body reacts (heartbeat, breathing, sweating, etc.). Record your child's pulse and breaths per minute again. Compare these to the readings taken before the activity. Have your child try other activities while you record his/her pulse and breathing: walking around the room, jumping, etc.	Have your child write or dictate a story about a special time he/she shared with a friend. Have your child draw a picture of him/herself with a friend.
Further discuss attributes and have your child classify other available objects such as toys, clothes and food. Have him/her sort into categories with two or more attributes (**Example:** summer clothes and red). Read *The Button Box* by Margarette S. Reid. Have your child complete **What Belongs?** (p. 60). Discuss your child's responses and brainstorm other possible answers. *See* Math, Week 3, number 5.	Discuss the location and function of the lungs (take in clean air and expel used air). *See* Science, Week 3, number 5.	Have your child make an invitation for his/her next birthday. Discuss the guest list, food, presents and games with your child. Have your child complete **Birthday Bonus Poster** (p. 61).
Using a small bag of snack mix such as cereal, peanuts and raisins, have your child sort and identify categories. Align the objects on graph paper. This is called a real graph. Label the graph. Encourage your child to use appropriate mathematics language to discuss the graph (fewer, two more raisins than peanuts, etc.). Then, have your child create a picture or bar (symbolic) graph from the information on the real graph.	Read the book *What Happens to a Hamburger* by Paul Showers. Discuss the process of eating, digesting and using food. Have your child draw a picture showing food going from his/her mouth into the stomach. Then, have him/her label the parts of his/her body.	Have your child draw a picture of someone in his/her family. Ask your child to tell you why this person is special. Write the family member's name and the sentence your child dictates with a marker. Repeat for other family members. Help your child assemble the pictures, make a cover and put it all together to make a family album.

TEACHING SUGGESTIONS AND ACTIVITIES

Spelling (Short Vowels)

BACKGROUND

There are only five vowels in the alphabet, but they are very powerful. A word cannot be made without a vowel present. However, because vowels can make more than one sound, at this time introduce only words which fit the following phonics rules:

- Short vowels in one-syllable words which are followed by one or two consonants with no other vowels in the word. **Examples:** *fat, hit, fond, that, run, lend, hug.*

- Long vowels (*see* Week 10) in one-syllable words will be the first of two vowels. In that case, the second vowel is silent. **Examples:** *clean, mate, cane, lone, cute, mine.* Long vowels can also be found when no letter follows the vowel as in *go* and *be.*

The above rules also apply to syllables. The word *secret* is made up of two syllables: *se* (no letter follows the vowel so it is long) and *cret* (the vowel is followed by one consonant so it is short).

▶ 1. Teach your child the vowels *a, e, i, o* and *u.*

▶ 2. Write the letter *a.* Draw and write the word *apple.* Have your child make the short *a* sound as in *apple.* Slowly say several words that begin with vowels. Tell your child to clap his/her hands when you say a word that begins with a short *a.* Here are some words to get you started: *ant, elephant, axe, animal, energy, ask, octopus, igloo, after, under.*

▶ 3. Teach your child to listen for the short *a* in the middle of a word as in *bat, tan* and *wag.* Write b_t, t_n and w_g. Ask your child to fill in the blank with the letter *a* and read the word. Repeat with other words such as c_b, d_d, f_t and m_p.

Reading (Letter Sounds)

▶ 1. To copy the pattern of the book *Brown Bear, Brown Bear,* ask your child to think of things he/she sees that he/she can write about. Place a new subject in each sentence but keep the rhythm. After your child has finished the rough draft, have him/her read the story to you once through. On a second reading, help your child write the standard spelling below his/her original words. Explain that standard spelling is necessary if he/she wants others to read what he/she writes. Then, have your child read the story again. The final step is for your child to publish the book. Your child should neatly write one sentence per page and draw and color an appropriate picture. Include a cover and title page. Save the book to be read again and again.

▶ 2. **Cooking:** Bread Dough Letters
Mix the ingredients listed below together and divide into 26 pieces.

3 ¾ cups whole wheat flour	2 cups buttermilk
¼ cup wheat germ	2 teaspoons baking soda
1 cup molasses	

On waxed paper, have your child roll out each piece of dough like a snake, then form each piece into a letter of the alphabet. Place the letters on greased cookie sheets and bake at 375° for 20 minutes or until they are golden brown.

Learn at Home, Grade 1

Math (Shapes/Sorting and Classifying)

First-grade children learn to identify simple shapes by name and attributes. Geometric solids, which will be studied later, are made up of these simple shapes.

▶ 1. Discuss differences and similarities between the shapes. **Example:** A square and a rectangle both have four straight sides.

▶ 2. Play a game in which you describe a shape and have your child identify the shape.

▶ 3. Draw one shape on a 9" x 12" sheet of paper. Have your child list or draw things in the room that contain or have that shape. Repeat with other shapes.

Sorting and classifying activities sharpen your child's observation, critical thinking and organization skills. Your child must observe the attributes of various objects, then analyze how objects are alike and different, and finally arrange the objects in groups. Your child will also exercise language skills while describing attributes and while explaining the reasoning behind each grouping.

▶ 4. Have your child sort manipulatives that have an obvious attribute, such as buttons that are red and blue. After your child sorts them, ask him/her to verbalize how he/she sorted them. Explain that color is one attribute. Repeat with other attributes such as shape and size.

▶ 5. Cut out several shapes in different sizes and colors. Ask your child to think of different ways they could be sorted—for example, shape, color, size, straight lines or number of sides.

Science (Body Systems)

▶ 1. Tell your child the skeleton is a framework of 206 bones that gives the body shape and protects the organs inside. Therefore, bones must be kept healthy. The outer part of bones is made of compact bone tissue containing calcium which keeps bones strong. This 2 week experiment will show what happens to bones if the calcium supply is weak.

  Experiment:
  a. Have your child clean all the meat from a chicken bone and wash it thoroughly.
  b. Then, have your child place the bone in a jar and fill the jar with vinegar.
  c. Your child should cover the jar tightly with a lid and let the bone soak for 2 weeks. Mark each day on a calendar so your child will gain a sense of the length of time.

▶ 2. Raise your child's awareness of the function of the heart muscles. Using a pair of knee-high socks, stuff one sock into the toe of the other sock. Push the inside sock down and twist and wrap the outer sock with a rubber band. Explain that this is about the size of your child's heart. To represent the contracting of the heart muscles, have your child squeeze the sock ball with one hand in a rhythmic pattern. The pressure of the contracting muscles sends blood out to the arteries.

▶ 3. Skeletal muscles can either pull or relax—they cannot push. Help your child carefully observe this by feeling the muscles in the front and back of the arm as he/she bends the arm forward and back.

▶ 4. Have your child contract muscles near the knee, hip and shoulder. Ask your child to point to the muscle that gets shorter (contracts) in each movement.

▶ 5. Tell your child to sit up tall in his/her seat and take a deep breath in through the nose. Have your child observe his/her chest move. Have your child blow the breath out of his/her mouth and describe the movement of the chest as he/she inhaled and exhaled. To demonstrate the action of the lungs, have your child blow into a balloon and then let the air out. Explain that when your child inhales, he/she is filling the lungs like the balloon.

Topic Web

Write the topic of the web in the big oval. **Write** four ideas that are parts of the topic in the small ovals. **Write** more about your ideas on the lines.

Learn at Home, Grade 1

Short a

Write a on each line. **Draw** a line from each word to the correct picture. Then, **color** the pictures.

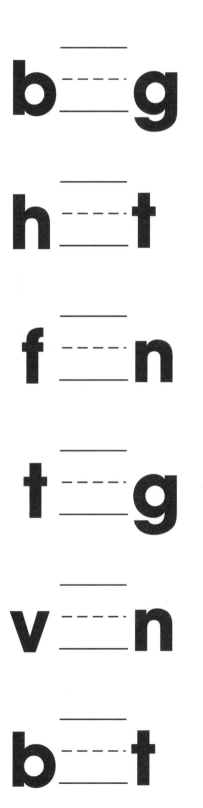

b __ g

h __ t

f __ n

t __ g

v __ n

b __ t

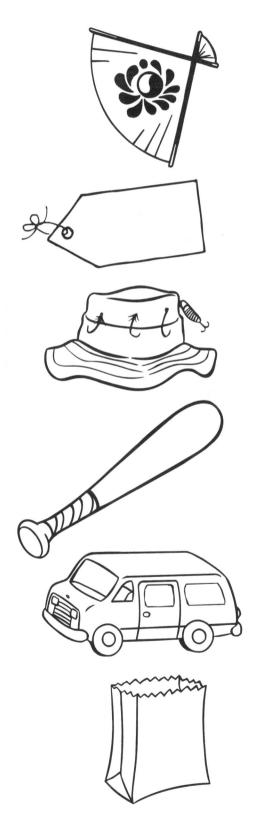

Short e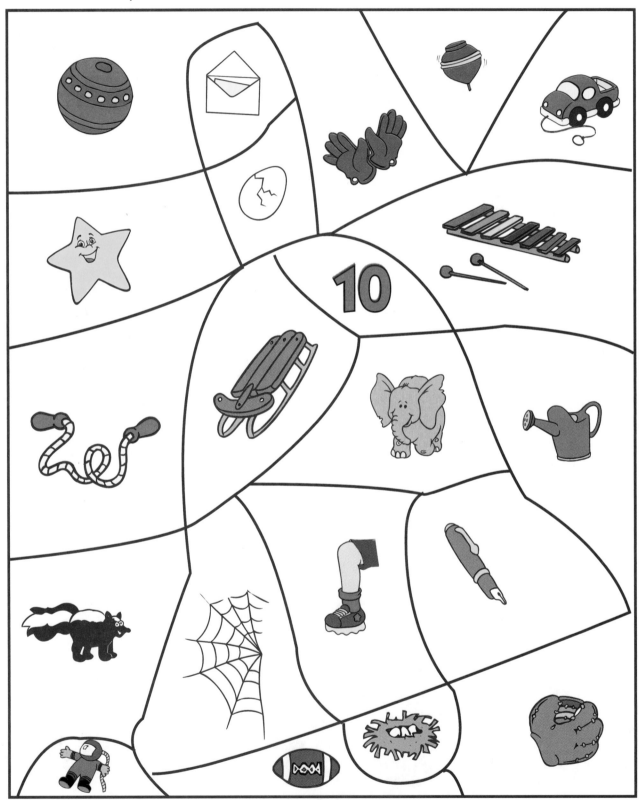

Say each picture name. If the picture has the sound of short **e**, **color** the shape blue.

Learn at Home, Grade 1

Short i

Write i on each line. **Color** the correct picture for each word.

p __ g

l __ d

s __ x

m __ lk

w __ g

g __ ft

Short o

Write o on each line. **Color** the sock the correct color.

d ___ g
red

m __ p
green

t __ p
orange

h __ t
yellow

b __ x
blue

d __ t
purple

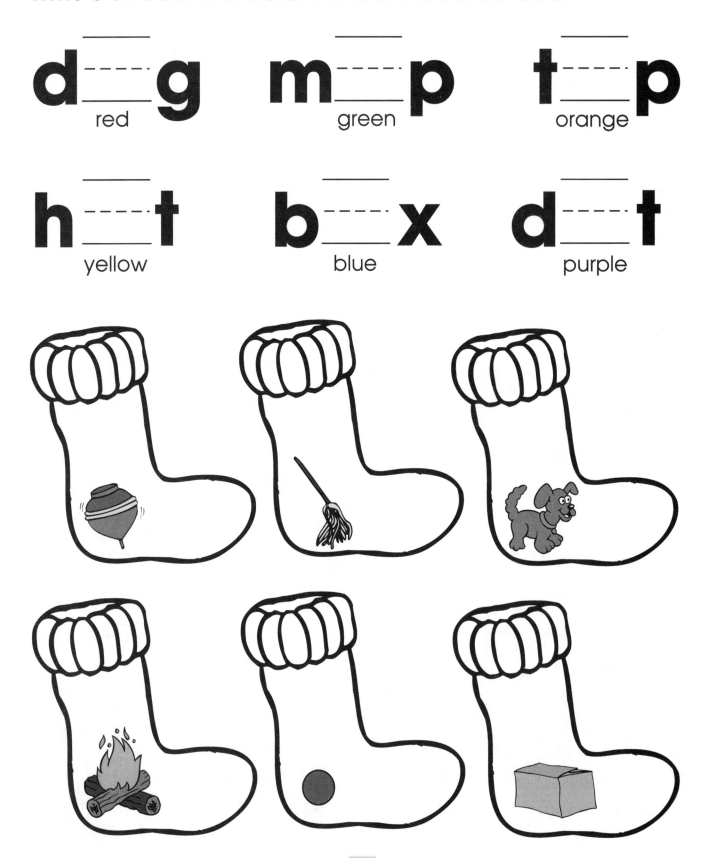

54

Learn at Home, Grade 1

Short u

Say each picture name. If the picture has the sound of short **u**, **color** it yellow.

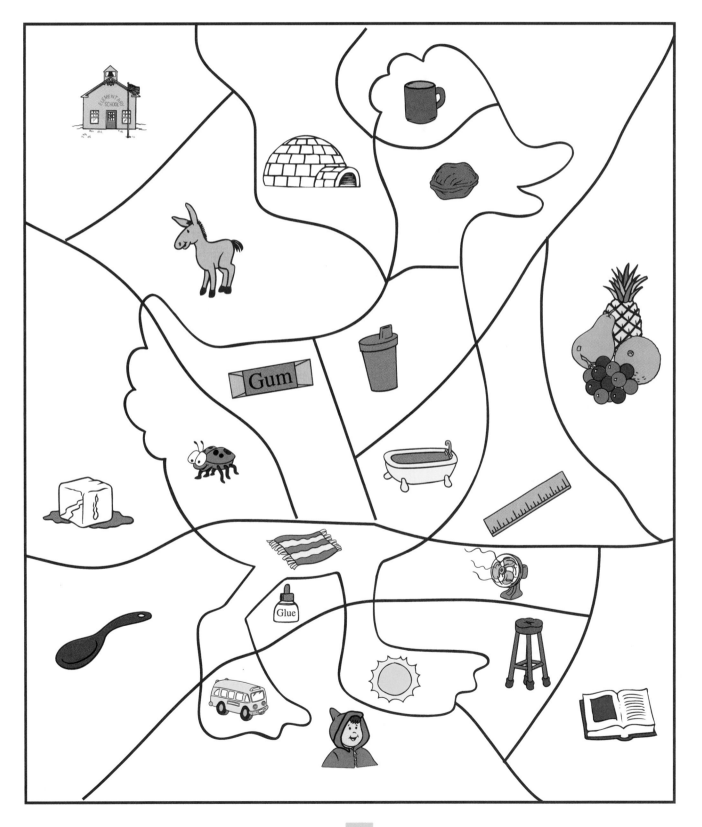

How Do I Begin? I

Say the name of each picture. **Write** the beginning sound for each picture.

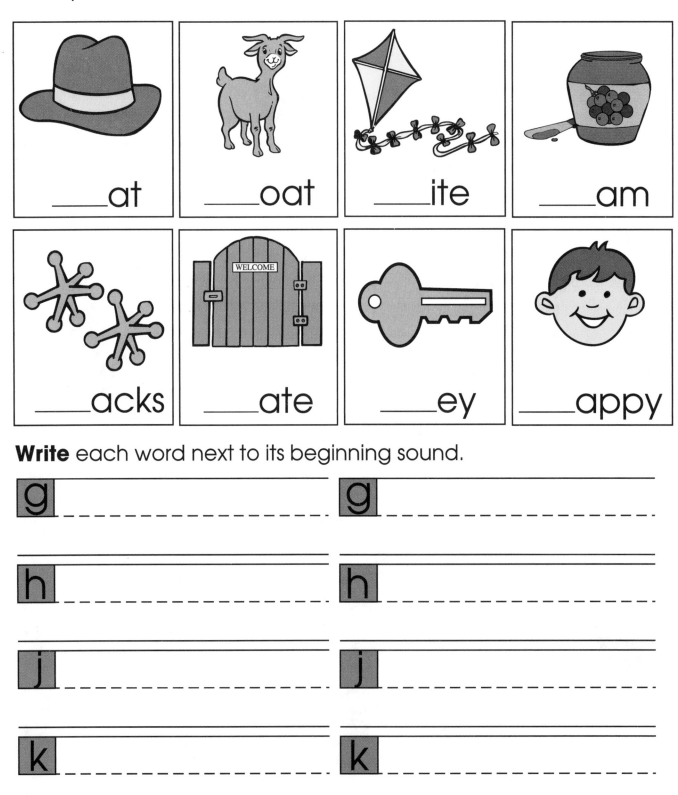

___at   ___oat   ___ite   ___am

___acks   ___ate   ___ey   ___appy

Write each word next to its beginning sound.

g _____   g _____

h _____   h _____

j _____   j _____

k _____   k _____

56

Learn at Home, Grade 1

How Do I Begin? II

Say each letter sound. **Color** the pictures in each row that begin with that sound.

Say the name of each picture. **Write** the beginning sound for each picture.

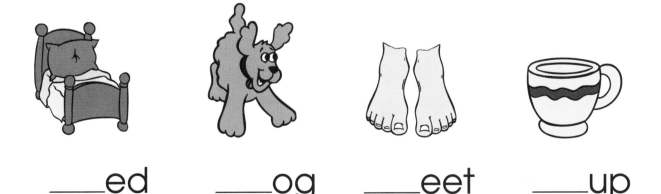

___ed   ___og   ___eet   ___up

Learn at Home, Grade 1

Hidden Picture

Say the name of each picture. **Write** the beginning sound for each picture. Then, **color** the picture.

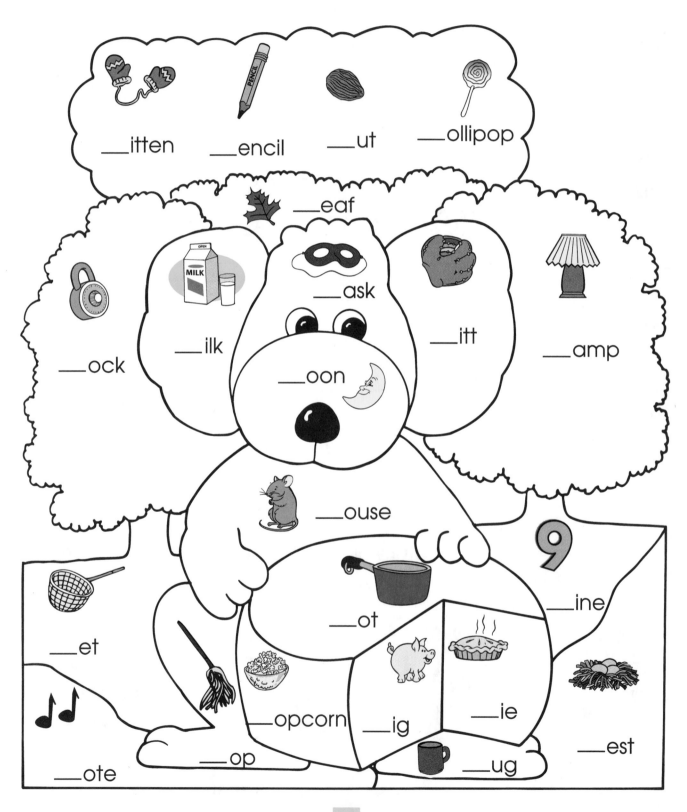

___itten   ___encil   ___ut   ___ollipop

___eaf

___ock   ___ilk   ___ask   ___itt   ___amp

___oon

___ouse

___ot   ___ine

___et   ___opcorn   ___ig   ___ie   ___est

___ote   ___op   ___ug

58

Learn at Home, Grade 1

Find the Shapes

Find each shape. Then, **color** the picture using the code.

red   green   blue   orange   yellow

59

What Belongs?

Look at the things in each circle. **Cross out** the thing that **does not** belong. **Write** a name for each group below the circle.

Learn at Home, Grade 1

Birthday Bonus Poster

My Cake

Name

_____

Date

_____

Where I'll Celebrate

How I'll Look

Age I'll Be (Make a big number and decorate it.)

Friends I'll Invite (Write their names and draw their pictures.)

My Gifts

My Birthday Dinner (Draw what you'd like.)

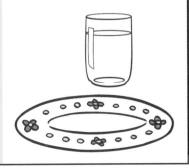

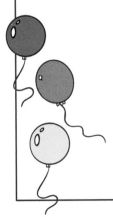

Learn at Home, Grade 1

	Language Skills	**Spelling**	**Reading**
Monday	**Nouns** Make three columns on a chart. Write *People* at the top of the first column, *Places* at the top of the second and *Things* at the top of the third. Have your child name people, places and things. Do not tell your child he/she is naming nouns until the lists are made. Have your child use nouns in spoken sentences.	Pretest your child on these spelling words: bat mat pan fat van sat cap jam Review the phonics skill of short *a* vowels.	Dictate the following list of three-letter words to your child. Have your child write each word and underline the ending consonant. Word list: pat, can, sit, pad, tin, top, fun, had, pin, sip, bed, run, tip, bag, peg, gab, not, sad, dim, fog, hop, jam, kit, led, mom, van, wet, yam, zip. Have your child complete **And Finally...** (p. 68).
Tuesday	Choose several sentences written by your child. Take the sentences from journal writings and stories. Have your child read each sentence and underline the nouns.	Have your child write the spelling words in sentences.	Read *The Three Bears* by Byron Barton. Discuss the word *bears* as a plural. Brainstorm other words that mean more than one (shoes, hands, bowls, books, etc.). Have your child make a poster showing all the objects in the bears' house that the bears had more than one of.
Wednesday	Introduce proper nouns. Explain to your child that a proper noun can be the name of a person and that proper nouns always begin with a capital letter. List the names of people your child knows. Have your child copy each name correctly, including the capital letter.	Have your child spell each word aloud while clapping the consonants and tapping the vowels. Have your child complete **Rocket Raccoon** (p. 67).	Have your child draw and/or cut out pictures of objects (nouns) and glue them on a large sheet of paper. On a chalkboard or chart, write the singular form of each object. Have your child label each picture, including the number of each (two balloons, etc.). *See* Reading, Week 4, number 1. Have your child complete **Middle Sounds** (p. 69).
Thursday	Teach your child that proper nouns are special names for places and things such as the name of a city, a monument or a specific location. Have your child name some special places he/she has visited (or would like to visit). Have your child copy each proper noun correctly, including the capital letter.	Scramble each word in this week's list. Have your child unscramble the words and write each word correctly.	Help your child write a story patterned after *The Three Bears*. After your child has written and edited his/her story, have him/her go back through the story and identify things that there are more than one of. Have him/her draw and label the objects on another sheet of paper. *See* Reading, Week 3, number 1.
Friday	Display a calendar. Ask your child to list the words on the calendar that are capitalized. Have your child complete **Proper Nouns** (p. 66).	Give your child the final spelling test.	Have your child choose one character from a book. Help your child make a character web that describes the identifiable characteristics of the chosen character. Include likes and dislikes, physical characteristics, decisions, personality, age and other traits. *See* Reading, Week 4, number 2. Have your child use the web to write a description of the character.

Learn at Home, Grade 1

Math	Science	Social Studies
Addition Facts to Ten *See* Math, Week 4, number 1. Repeat for as long as it is meaningful and it holds your child's interest. Have your child draw some of the sets he/she made.	Tell your child that the brain is the control center of the entire body. The brain controls thinking, speaking, feeling and moving. Play a game like "Simon Says" called Your Brain Says. Give commands such as *Your brain says smile.* If your command does not include the words *your brain says,* your child should not carry out the command. If he/she makes a mistake, remind your child that the body cannot do anything if the brain doesn't command it.	Look through and discuss the family album made in Week 3. Have your child write the names of family members on sheets of paper. Have him/her arrange them according to size (biggest to smallest) and/or age (oldest to youngest).
Number Combinations: Hold four small counters in one palm and let your child count them. Move some counters to your other hand and close your fists. Open one hand. Can your child tell you what is hidden in your closed fist? Repeat with different combinations of the four counters. Arrange four toothpicks in several different designs to spark creativity. Have your child use the toothpicks to create and describe designs in sets of four. Have your child practice writing the numbers 1–10.	Ask your child where the brain is located and why. Look at pictures in books. Discuss the spinal cord, an extension of the brain that is protected by the spine (or vertebral column), which is made of individual bones called vertebrae. Have your child act out how the brain would respond to given messages: *I'm hot, I'm tired, I hear the telephone, I can't hear the television, I'm thirsty.*	Have your child list qualities that describe each family member. Have him/her add the words to the pictures in the family album. Set up a corner for playing house. Observe your child's play. This is a good way to learn about your child's perception of family and each member's role.
Repeat Tuesday's assessment. If your child is confident with four, assess his/her ability with five counters. Have your child use a variety of materials (blocks, pasta, buttons) to build different arrangements in sets of five (or the number determined in your assessment). Talk about what makes up each design such as two black and three yellow. Have your child draw pictures of the combinations he/she made with the materials.	Guide your child through making a model of a human body—inside and out. Trace around your child's body and cut out two outlines. Help your child paint muscles, bones and organs on one or use paper towel tubes, popsicle sticks, etc. for bones. On the other outline, have your child paint the "outside" body parts. Then, staple it over the outline showing the "interior" parts.	**Setting Goals:** Discuss the meaning of goals with your child. Ask your child to think of an area in which he/she would like to improve. Discuss and lead your child to form a specific, realistic goal by a certain time period. The goal should be attainable in a few weeks so your child can see results. *See* Social Studies, Week 4, number 1.
Continue assessment to determine the number for your child to build. Introduce the **+** and **=** signs in horizontal equations. Have your child write and build addition sentences using number cards. Have your child complete **Addition Using Counters** (p. 70). **Note:** Continue assessing numbers weekly until your child is confident with combinations through ten.	Let your child continue working on his/her model of the human body.	Talk about long-term goals. Discuss how they are different from short-term goals. Is it likely that a long-term goal will remain the same over time? Why or why not? Help your child write some long-term goals such as career and personal achievement goals. Record the goals in a special place where your child can look at them in future years.
Use the **Addition Board** (p. 71) to introduce vertical equations. Place counters in the first two circles. Have your child count the counters in each circle, then pull all counters to the bottom circle and count. Let your child practice several times before using number cards in place of some or all of the counters. Write some simple vertical addition sentences for your child to build with blocks and record the answer.	**Cooking:** Use a sugar cookie recipe to bake cookies in the shape of gingerbread men. Have your child use frosting and candies to decorate the cookies showing parts inside and/or outside of the body.	Discuss the importance of carrying an identification card. What type of information should be included? Show your child different types of identification adults have, such as a driver's license or passport. Help your child design an ID card. Laminate the card and encourage your child to carry it with him/her. *See* Social Studies, Week 4, number 2.

TEACHING SUGGESTIONS AND ACTIVITIES

Spelling (Spelling Lessons)

GENERAL WEEKLY PLAN FOR SPELLING LESSONS

Name	Date
1	
2	
3	
4	
5	
6	
7	
8	
9	
10	
11	
12	

Monday

▶ 1. Give your child a pretest of the word list on lined paper. (See sample page at right.)

▶ 2. Read each word and spell it aloud as your child corrects his/her own test. Any words your child already knows need not be practiced that week.

▶ 3. To make the list complete, add words from science vocabulary, reading, personal writing or previously misspelled words.

▶ 4. Go through the list together in the following manner: Read the first word, spell the word and read the word again. Repeat with the entire list. Define any words if necessary, teaching your child how to use a dictionary.

▶ 5. Identify and teach the specific spelling or phonics skill of the lesson.

▶ 6. Have your child make an accurate copy of the spelling list from which he/she will study.

Tuesday

Have your child use each spelling word in a meaningful sentence. Your child may dictate the sentences and then copy them, or your child may first write the sentences using invented spelling (except the spelling word) and then copy them after you have edited the sentences.

Wednesday

▶ 1. Have your child complete the activity sheet provided for each week. Have your child write any additional words on the back.

▶ 2. Practice spelling each word aloud while singing, marching, clapping or doing any other physical activity.

Thursday

Have your child complete an activity that involves repeatedly writing, forming, tracing or reading the words. Use letter cards to spell the words.

Friday

▶ 1. Administer a test of your child's spelling list. Any missed words should be added to the list of vocabulary for the following week.

▶ 2. Add a "challenge" to the spelling test by having your child write simple sentences or write words that rhyme with those on his/her list. Remind your child to use correct punctuation and capitalization.

Learn at Home, Grade 1

Reading

▶ 1. Write a list of familiar objects. Have your child read each word aloud and use it in a sentence. Write each sentence for your child on lined paper. Skip two lines between each sentence.

Example: *boy*

The boy plays on the soccer team.

Ask your child to change the sentence so it tells about more than one boy. Write the second sentence under the first.

Sample Character Web:

Math (Addition Facts to Ten)

BACKGROUND
Addition is the combining of sets into a new whole. Provide opportunities for your child to discover that by creating and combining meaningful sets, a new set is created. While an eventual goal is memorization, it is essential that your child understand the concept of the part-part-whole relationships of addition and subtraction. A foundation with manipulatives is essential. It is valuable to be able to visualize that the number 5 is the same as 4 and 1, 3 and 2, 1 and 4, and 2 and 3. Addition as a mathematical process takes on more meaning for your child if there is a need for it. Therefore, present real-life situations where addition is required to solve a problem.

▶ 1. Use two different colors of counters. Fill several cups with combinations that add up to the same number. For example, in one cup place one blue and three yellow counters and in another cup place two blue and two yellow for the sum four. Do not have any sum go above ten at this time. Have your child dump the contents of one cup and count each group, saying the numbers aloud, *two and two*. Repeat the activity until each combination for that sum has been modeled at least once.

Social Studies (Setting Goals)

BACKGROUND
Everyone strives to improve at something. Setting realistic goals gives your child a focus and purpose. When the goal is reached, your child will feel a sense of pride and accomplishment.

▶ 1. Have your child complete a contract to help him/her attain a determined goal. A contract outline is given below.

Date _____

My goal is to_____.

To reach my goal, I must _____.

I will try to reach my goal by (date)_____.

Signed_____

▶ 2. On cardboard, reproduce a form similar to the sample at right. Glue a small photo of your child on the ID card. Have your child fill in the desired facts. Laminate the card and have your child carry it at all times.

Learn at Home, Grade 1

Proper Nouns

A **proper noun** is a special name for a person, place or thing. It always begins with a capital letter. **Write** a proper noun to name each person and pet. Use the word box.

| Rover | Sarah | Pedro | Jack & Jill | Piggy | Fluffy |

66

Rocket Raccoon

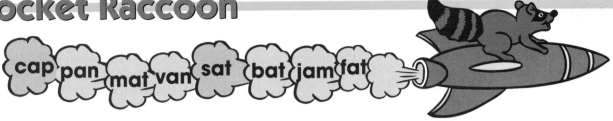

cap pan mat van sat bat jam fat

Write the spelling word that names each picture.

_____

- - - - - - - - - - -

_____

_____

- - - - - - - - - - -

_____

_____

- - - - - - - - - - -

_____

_____

- - - - - - - - - - -

_____

_____

- - - - - - - - - - -

_____

_____

- - - - - - - - - - -

_____

Write the spelling words that rhyme with the pictures.

_____ _____

- - - - - - - - -

_____ _____

_____ _____

- - - - - - - - -

_____ _____

_____

- - - - - -

_____

_____

- - - - - -

_____

Learn at Home, Grade 1

And Finally...

Say each picture name. **Write** the ending sound for each picture.

tu ___

pai ___

pa ___

lo ___

hoo ___

mu ___

boo ___

ha ___

shel ___

lea ___

cra ___

li ___

gir ___

bea ___

broo ___

Learn at Home, Grade 1

Middle Sounds

Say each picture name. **Write** the missing vowel **a**, **e**, **i**, **o** or **u** in the puzzle.

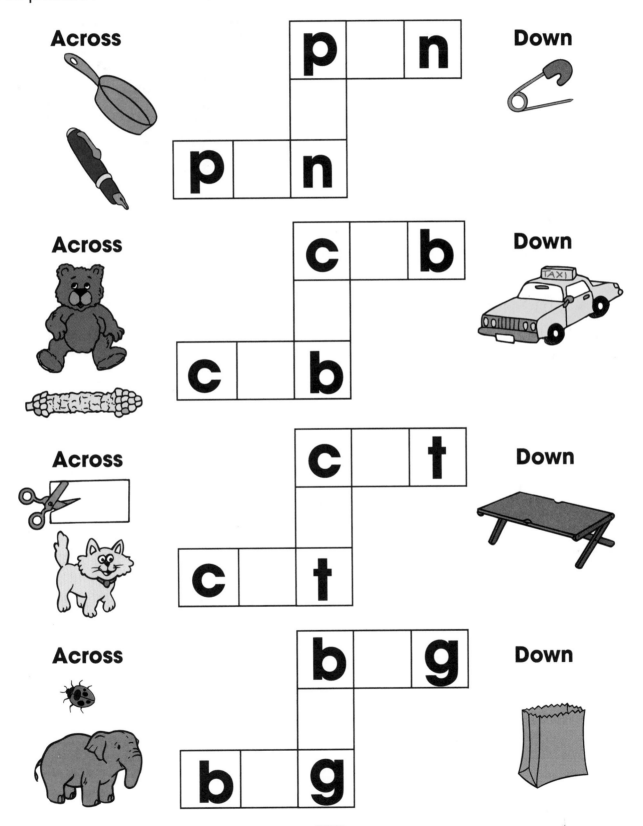

Across

Down

Across

Down

Across

Down

Across

Down

Addition Using Counters

Example: 2 + 1 = _?_

Use counters to add.

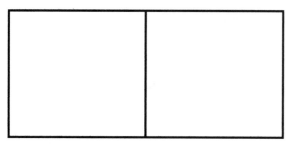

Put in 2.   Put in 1 more.

How many counters are there in all? _3_

2 + 1 = 3. The number that tells how many in all is called the **sum**. The sum of 2 + 1 is 3.

Use counters to find each sum.

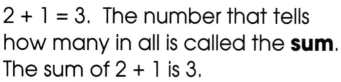

2 + 4 = _____

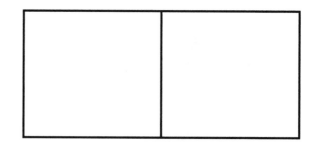

5 + 2 = _____

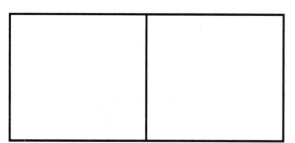

3 + 3 = _____

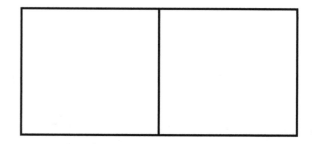

3 + 4 = _____

70

Learn at Home, Grade 1

Addition Board

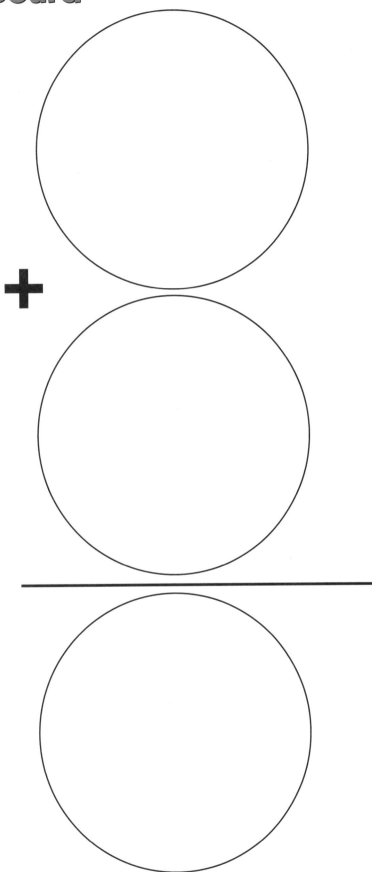

+

Language Skills	**Spelling**	**Reading**
Monday **Adjectives** Explain that adjectives describe nouns. Number words and color words are adjectives. Write nouns and adjectives on the chalkboard and have your child circle the adjectives. *See* Language Skills, Week 5, number 1.	Pretest your child on these spelling words: best nest pet jet set wet tent leg Review the phonics skill of short *e* vowels.	Read *Are You My Mother?* by P. D. Eastman and discuss the story. Brainstorm a list of baby animals, such as kitten and puppy, as well as the name of their parents. Have your child draw pictures of baby animals and their mothers, labeling each one.
Tuesday Tell your child adjectives can also describe the size and shape of nouns. Brainstorm with your child some adjectives that describe size and shape. Ask your child to point out round objects in the room, flat objects, small objects and other objects of different sizes and shapes.	Have your child write the spelling words in sentences.	Read *Are You My Mother?* again. Have your child finish this sentence: *If I were the baby bird, I would have....* Have your child complete **What's What?** (p. 77).
Wednesday Explain that adjectives can also tell how our senses perceive things. Have your child taste a lemon, listen to a loud noise or feel a prickly brush. Ask your child to describe how the lemon tasted, what the noise sounded like and how the brush felt. Write those words. Ask your child to list other adjectives that describe what we experience.	Have your child spell each word aloud while marching around the room. Have your child complete **Get on Track** (p. 76).	Teach the *es* plural ending that occurs after the letters *s, ss, sh, ch* and *x*. Write examples on the board. Have your child circle the endings and draw a line under the root words. **Examples**: fishes, foxes, hippopotamuses, porches, messes Have your child choose several of the words to write and illustrate.
Thursday Plan a tasting activity. Prepare foods of varying tastes and textures, including fruits, vegetables, peanut butter, dressings, meats and chips. Have your child describe how each food tastes. You may wish to blindfold your child so he/she can concentrate on the taste. Keep a record of your child's responses. Afterward, have your child write adjectives in sentences. (*The peanut butter was <u>sticky</u>.*) Have your child underline the adjectives.	Have your child write each spelling word in a unique design and decorate the letters. **pet** *tent* jet	**Game/Center:** Draw a bird on one card and write *bird* on another card. Draw two kittens on one card and write *two kittens* on another card. Make several pairs of cards with singular and plural objects. Your child may play a matching game or "Concentration" with the cards.
Friday Write several sentences on the chalkboard. Include a variety of adjectives that describe nouns. Have your child draw circles around the adjectives in each sentence. *See* Language Skills, Week 5, number 2.	Give your child the final spelling test.	Have your child create an advertisement for a book he/she has recently read and enjoyed. The advertisement should include information about the book's plot, descriptions of the characters and a quotation or passage from the story.

Learn at Home, Grade 1

Math	Science	Social Studies
Addition Use the **Addition Board** (p. 71) and counters for review. Review the + and = signs. Tell stories involving familiar events and people using addition vocabulary such as *plus, and, all together* and *in all*. Have him/her tell addition stories while demonstrating with counters. Then, have your child write his/her own story problems. Have your child complete **Cuddly Kitten** (p. 78).	**Health** Remove the bone from the jar filled with vinegar from two weeks ago. Have your child describe how the bone has changed. Ask how his/her findings compare to his/her observations in Week 3. Ask *What might happen to your body if you do not eat foods that keep your bones strong?* Use this as an introduction to nutrition. Explain that calcium is one thing the body needs.	**My Community** Ask your child to imagine how life would be different if you lived in a house hundreds of miles from any other people, stores or other community services. Discuss what aspects of the community you depend on. Brainstorm professional, production, trades, service and community workers that make up your community. Have your child complete **What's My Job?** (p. 81).
Draw two sets of circles on the chalkboard or put round stickers on paper. Count each set and write a total. Repeat, substituting a numeral for some sets. Have your child say the numeral and "count on" the circles. **Example**: 4 + • • • = ___ 5 6 7 Have your child complete **How Many in All?** (p. 79).	Ask your child to explain why he/she thinks we need to eat. Explain that the body is like a car—it needs fuel for energy. The more your body does, the more fuel it needs. Your body needs a variety of nutrients to keep it going. Teach about the different nutrients. *See* Science, Week 5, numbers 1 and 2.	Start each day with a riddle. *See* Social Studies, Week 5, number 1. Begin making a *Community Book*. Have your child make a page that describes and illustrates a person's job in the community or a location in the community. In order to have your child complete the book in 4 weeks, your child will need to complete one or two pages each day. *See* Social Studies, Week 5, number 2.

Draw sets of objects on the chalkboard. Have your child write the appropriate number sentence horizontally and vertically.
    000000 0000
    6 + 4 = 10
Write number sentences and have your child illustrate them. *See* Math, Week 5, numbers 1–5 for additional activities.
Have your child complete **Pet Picture Problems** (p. 80).
	Continue yesterday's lesson.	Discuss the qualifications and/or training required for different jobs. Which jobs involve working with people, numbers or words? Which jobs require college, apprenticeship or on-the-job training? Record the information you discuss on a chart.

Do another number assessment, writing the number for the assessment at the top of a large sheet of paper. Have your child build eight different designs, each one using that number of toothpicks or colored blocks. Help your child write a matching number sentence below each design. Remove the blocks and have your child draw a picture that illustrates each written math fact. Repeat with higher numbers as your child's ability increases.	Provide your child with a variety of food containers, boxes and cans with nutritional labels or take a field trip to a grocery store. Teach your child how to read the nutritional information and fill in the form provided. *See* Science, Week 5, number 3.	**Field Trip:** Take your child to visit city hall where he/she may visit with several community workers. Before the trip, help your child formulate several questions.
Cut out small pages (8" x 5") to make a number book. Cut small triangles out of two colors of construction paper. Choose one number (through assessment) to be the theme of the book. Have your child use two colors to make and glue a picture with the given number of triangles. Help your child write a sentence describing the picture and an appropriate number sentence. Repeat on several pages. Gather the pages and staple them with a cover.	Continue yesterday's lesson.	Discuss the field trip experience with your child. Encourage him/her to recall details of the experience and tape record a description of what he/she learned on yesterday's trip. Have your child write a thank you letter to the people he/she spoke to at city hall.

Learn at Home, Grade 1 © 1999 Tribune Education. All Rights Reserved.

TEACHING SUGGESTIONS AND ACTIVITIES

Language Skills (Adjectives)

▶ 1. On the chalkboard, write four directions for your child to follow. The directions should include number and color words. Your child should complete the directions on drawing paper folded into four boxes. Ask your child to identify the adjective(s) in each sentence.

   Examples:
   Draw six blue ▲.   Draw four green ♣.
   Draw three red ♥.   Draw ten purple ♦.

▶ 2. Have your child choose objects in your home and describe each noun using adjectives. Write each descriptive phrase as your child says it. Tell your child that his/her descriptive phrase is an adjective phrase.

Math (Addition)

▶ 1. Play "sum bingo." Make a 5 x 5 grid on drawing paper. Have your child write a digit (1–9) in each box, repeating numbers as necessary. On small cards, make at least 25 dominoes with values from 1–9 in different arrangements. To play, have your child choose a domino, add the two parts and state the total. Your child should then place a counter over that number on the bingo grid. Play continues until your child has five in a row—vertically, horizontally or diagonally.

▶ 2. Use Cuisenaire rods. Have your child lay out one rod and experiment with different ways that length rod may be matched using just two other rods. **Example**: a purple rod (4) matches two reds (2 + 2) or a white and a green (1 + 3). Have your child record his/her findings.

▶ 3. If Cuisenaire rods are not available, make homemade rods from construction paper or cardboard. Each rod should be 1 inch wide. Cut the longest rod (#10) 10 inches long. Cut the shortest rod (#1) 1 inch long. Make at least ten 1's, five 2's, three 3's, two 4's and two of every number through 10. Color each number a different color (1's = white, 2's = pink, 3's = blue). Have your child experiment with the rods as in activity 2 above. Have him/her record his/her findings. Use the rods to teach the commutative property (3 + 1 = 1 + 3) and also that a number is made up of two or more numbers.

▶ 4. **Language:** Write addition vocabulary on a chart. Discuss and add to it at appropriate times.

▶ 5. **Center:** Keep flash cards at a center for your child to practice number facts.

Learn at Home, Grade 1

Science (Health)

▶ 1. Write each of the following nutrients each at the top of a separate sheet of paper: carbohydrates, proteins, fats, water, vitamins, minerals and fiber. Explain to your child that: carbohydrates and fats give us energy; protein helps the body grow; water dissolves substances and moves them around inside the body and replaces fluids; vitamins and minerals keep a person healthy; and fiber helps move food through the body. Under each heading, write a subheading that tells what each substance does.

▶ 2. Work together to list foods on each page that contain the nutrient.

   Carbohydrates: rice, potatoes, pasta, breads, cereal, corn, crackers
   Proteins: meat, beans, eggs, tofu, split peas
   Fats: butter, margarine, oils, cream, cheese
   Vitamins and minerals: fruits and vegetables
   Fiber: whole wheat products, fruits and vegetables

   Have your child look through magazines for pictures of foods to glue on each page.

▶ 3. Duplicate the form below. Give your child one form and one food package to evaluate at a time. Repeat with other packages. When your child has completed the activity, ask your child to identify products that will provide certain health benefits such as energy.

```
Name of Product_____
Food Group_____
Nutritional Facts:
Carbohydrates _____        Fats _____
Vitamins _____             Proteins _____
Minerals _____             Fiber _____
```

Social Studies (My Community)

This 4-week unit teaches your child about the varied people who make up a community. They may be professionals, businessmen and women, service people or community helpers. Help your child build a sense of the interdependence of people in a community. Also, discuss the things that make a community a nicer place (parks, etc.). Four field trips are suggested, but also visit the locations unique to your community. Take a camera so your child may take pictures.

▶ 1. Start the Social Studies lesson each day with a riddle about a worker in the community. Give clues until your child can guess the occupation.

   Example: (the butcher)
      This worker cuts and packages food.
      This worker wears a white apron.
      This worker may work at a grocery store.
      This worker may often be found in a cool place.
      This person works with something that rhymes with feet.

▶ 2. **Community Book:** Help your child think of an occupation. Discuss this person's work in detail. Have your child dictate a sentence about the worker. Have your child draw and color a picture of that worker on drawing paper. Write your child's sentence on the bottom of the page. Include pictures from field trips. Ask your child to write captions.

Get On Track

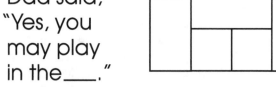
best wet set tent
jet leg nest pet

Write the spelling words in ABC order.

1. _____

2. _____

3. _____

4. _____

5. _____

6. _____

7. _____

8. _____

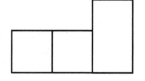

Read each sentence. **Write** the missing spelling word in the boxes.

1. Ned fell and cut his ___ .
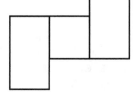

2. The hen is in the ___ .
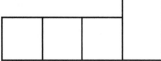

3. Please, help me ___ the table.
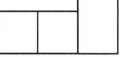

4. Do you have a ___ rabbit?
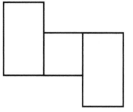

5. Ted did his ___ .
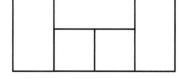

6. We will go on a trip in a ___ .
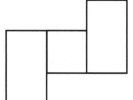

7. Dad said, "Yes, you may play in the ___ ."

8. The hat got ___ when it fell in the pond.

Learn at Home, Grade 1

What's What?

Write the words from the word box in the correct place.

Living	Non-Living
1. _____	1. _____
2. _____	2. _____
3. _____	3. _____
4. _____	4. _____
5. _____	5. _____
6. _____	6. _____

car

girl   hen
house

boat   plane
bird   dog   cow
          tree
window   rocks

Cuddly Kitten

Use counters. **Trace** or **draw** each group you make. Then, **write** how many in all.

How many?		How many more?		How many in all?
3	+	2	=	____
2	+	1	=	____
4	+	3	=	____
1	+	6	=	____

Think of a story for this picture. **Write** how many in all.

____ in all

78

Learn at Home, Grade 1

How Many in All?

Write two addition sentences for each picture story. Find how many in all.

Example:

___ 3 + 1 = 4

3
+1
―――
4

___ + ___ = ___

___
+___

___ + ___ = ___

___
+___

___ + ___ = ___

___
+___

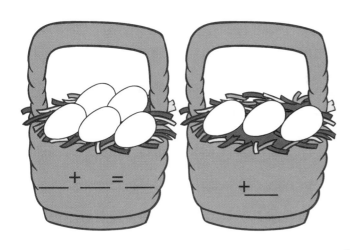

___ + ___ = ___

___
+___

___ + ___ = ___

___
+___

Pet Picture Problems

Circle the picture which matches the addition sentence.

1 + 2 = 3

3 + 2 = 5

2 + 4 = 6

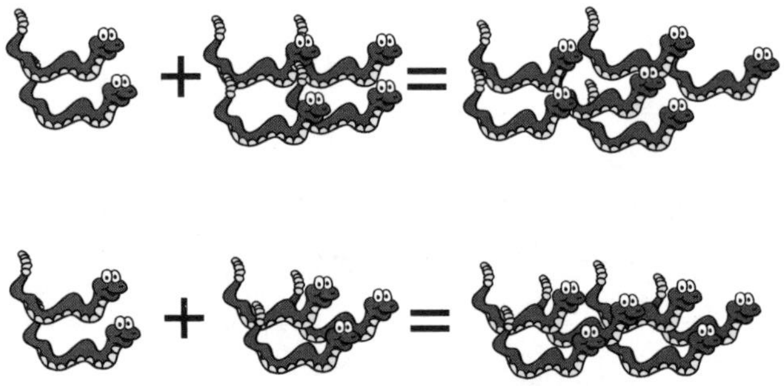

3 + 3 = 6

3 + 4 = 7

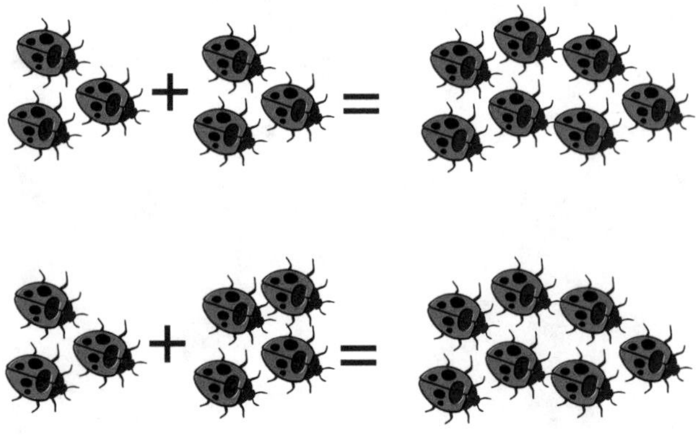

1 + 6 = 7

Learn at Home, Grade 1

What's My Job?

Write the correct word on each line. Then, color the pictures.

pilot farmer doctor builder plumber teacher

_____

A _____ helps us learn new things.

_____

A _____ helps people get well.

_____

A _____ flies planes many places.

_____

A _____ plants and grows crops.

_____

A _____ fixes many leaky pipes.

_____

A _____ builds new buildings.

	Language Skills	**Spelling**	**Reading**

Monday	**Verbs**
	Begin the lesson about verbs by throwing a ball to your child. Tell your child to catch it. Write on the chalkboard: *I throw the ball. You catch it.* Underline the verbs. Tell your child they are action words. Explain that a verb tells what a person, animal or thing does. Have your child name other action verbs. Make a list of them. *See* Language Skills, Week 6, number 1.
	Have your child complete **Verbs I** (p. 86).
		Pretest your child on these spelling words:
		    sit win
		    pin pig
		    fin hit
		    dig lid
		Review the phonics skill of short *i* vowels.
			Nouns
			Discuss nouns (persons, places or things). Have your child brainstorm a list of nouns from books and from looking around the room. Hang up the list of words on the classroom wall for your child's reference. Your child may choose some words to add to his/her alphabet book (Week 2, Tuesday). Read *How Many Snails? A Counting Book* by Paul Giganti, Jr.

Tuesday	Write several sentences on the chalkboard. Have your child circle all the verbs. Using the verbs and the list from Monday, have your child act out some of the situations. Have your child complete **Verbs II** (p. 87).	Have your child write the spelling words in sentences.	Reread *How Many Snails?* As you read, have your child count out the answer to each question. Challenge your child to think up other questions on each page. Write each of your child's questions on a separate page. Your child may illustrate each question with an appropriate picture.

Wednesday	Write two or three simple sentences. Omit the verb in each one. Have your child read each sentence fragment.
	Examples: The pig in the dirt. (rolls)
	               A man the house. (paints)
	               The wind loud noises. (makes)
	Discuss that the sentence makes no sense without a verb. Have your child rewrite each sentence including a verb.
		Have your child spell each word aloud while tapping his/her foot.
		Have your child complete **Picky Pigs** (p. 88).
			Teach your child the color words, and have him/her practice writing them neatly on lined paper. Have your child write the word once using the appropriate color crayon, and once using a pencil. *See* Reading, Week 6, number 1.

Thursday	Show your child pictures cut from a magazine. Have your child name an action in each picture, then write a sentence about each picture. Write the verbs in a list.	Make a word search puzzle using the week's spelling words. Have your child find and circle all the spelling words in the word search. Have him/her write the spelling words on the chalkboard. Then, let him/her trace over each letter with colored chalk.	Play "Ten Questions" (reduced from "Twenty Questions"). Have your child think of an object (noun) and tell you if it is a person, place or thing. Ask ten questions that will help you figure out what the object is. Your questions will model for your child how to ask questions that lead to the discovery of the object. Reverse roles and play again.
Friday	**Art:** Have your child make a mural of verbs. On a large sheet of butcher paper, write verbs that can be illustrated such as *run, hop, eat* and *throw*. Have your child paint or use crayons to draw a picture of each action.	Give your child the final spelling test.	In *How Many Snails?*, the author goes walking in places such as a meadow, a lake, a garden, the beach and the park. Ask your child to name other places to go walking (in your area). As an extension, list things you might see in those places. **Art:** Have your child design a new jacket for a book he/she has recently read. Make sure he/she includes all written information such as title, author and illustrator.

Learn at Home, Grade 1

Math	**Science**	**Social Studies**
Addition Introduce the concept of zero as an addend. *See* Math, Week 6, number 1. On each of two dice, cover the 6 face with a circular sticker. Write the numeral 0 on the sticker. Your child should roll the dice, add the dots and state the total. Play a game that uses dice or have your child write the dice rolls as math sentences. Have your child complete **Alien Problems** (p. 89).	Introduce the food pyramid. *See* Science, Week 6, number 1. Encourage your child to find copies of the pyramid on boxes of cereal and crackers and cut them out. Discuss foods that belong in each category.	Make a copy of **Time For Work!** (p. 95). Glue the cards on index cards. Discuss the picture on each card. Play a game similar to "Go Fish." Have your child match the workers with their work places. You may also use the cards to play "Memory."
Present and use the mathematics vocabulary *sum, total* and *addends*. Introduce the concept of missing addend. Write an addition sentence and cover one of the addends. Ask your child to create and verbalize a strategy for figuring out the missing addend. *See* Math, Week 6, number 2. Discuss your child's problem-solving strategy. Have your child complete **Bear Necessities** (p. 90).	Have your child keep a record of what he/she eats for the next 3 days. Have your child flip through magazines and cut out pictures of food and group them according to the food groups shown on the food pyramid.	Have your child act out hypothetical situations of a worker. *See* Social Studies, Week 6, number 1.
Make a flannel board and felt shapes. Display two sets joined by a + sign. **Example**: ♥♥♥♥♥ + ♥♥♥ Have your child count and find a flash card with the same equation. Repeat with several equations. *See* Math, Week 6, number 3. Give your child time to manipulate the flannel shapes into familiar patterned sets for quick recognition of numbers. Have your child complete **How Many Robots in All?** (p. 91).	Help your child plan a healthful breakfast, lunch and dinner menu following the recommendations of the food pyramid. Have your child draw pictures on paper plates of what he/she would eat.	Arrange to have your child interview different people about their work. This may be done by phone or in person. Help your child choose people from all types of work. After each interview, have your child write a job description. Also, have your child write a thank you note to each person. Arrange for several interviews over the course of 3 weeks. Have your child compile the job descriptions in a folder.
Present addition flash cards (with sums of 10 or less) to your child, without manipulatives, to encourage him/her to visualize the numbers. If he/she is unable to answer without using fingers, your child needs more time with manipulatives. *See* Math, Week 6, number 4. Have your child complete **Creature Count** (p. 92).	Watch a videotape of Slim Goodbody. In each 15-minute episode, Slim Goodbody teaches about one aspect of being healthy. Slim Goodbody episodes can be seen on Public Television. (Check the listings in your area.) You may be able to borrow a video of Slim Goodbody from the library or rent one from a video store.	**Field Trip:** Arrange to visit a professional, such as a medical worker, business owner, writer, teacher or accountant. Before the trip, have your child formulate questions about the occupation.
Make a game out of flash card practice, such as earning a sticker for every five correct responses. Encourage your child to use manipulatives, such as buttons, to solve flash card facts. Have your child write the equations on **Sum It Up** (p. 93). Have your child complete **Bee Addition** (p. 94). *See* Math, Week 6, number 5.	Review the foods your child has eaten over the past 3 days. Draw a large, empty pyramid on chart paper. Have your child draw a picture of each food eaten in one day on the appropriate place on the pyramid. Discuss what foods your child needs to eat more or less of in order to follow the pyramid guidelines.	Review the field trip experience. Interview your child to encourage him/her to recall details of the experience. Have your child tape record a description of what he/she learned on yesterday's trip. Have him/her write a thank you letter to the professional who spoke with him/her.

TEACHING SUGGESTIONS AND ACTIVITIES

Language Skills (Verbs)

▶ 1. Go on a walk through a playground. Discuss action words such as *swing, climb, run* and *jump*.

Reading (Nouns)

▶ 1. Draw a simple picture and write three to five directions using color words.

   Example: Draw a *yellow* flower under the tree.
   Color the leaves *green*.
   Color the apples *red*.
   Color the sky *blue*.
   Color the trunk *brown*.

Math (Addition)

▶ 1. Ask some silly questions to which the answer must be zero. *(How many elephants are in the room? How many purple trees do you see outside?)* Talk about what zero means. Name other words that mean almost the same as zero. Show there is just one way to write the numeral zero. Put three glasses filled with water on a table. Ask your child to write the number of glasses of water on the table. Place two empty glasses next to the glasses of water. Ask how many glasses of water were added to the original three. Ask your child to write that number (0). Ask how many glasses of water are on the table. Guide your child in writing or saying what the problem was (3 + 0 = 3). Continue in this manner using different objects, such as nuts in bowls, pencils with erasers and bags of counters.

▶ 2. Have your child hold up three fingers. Write 3 + ___ = 7 on the chalkboard. Ask your child to tell how many more fingers are needed to make 7. Record the answer on the line. Repeat several times with other numbers.

▶ 3. Make several sets of 2 to 9 small objects and place them in individual plastic bags. Choose two bags of objects whose sum does not exceed 10. Use a clothespin to clip each pair together. Write on a large sheet of paper, *How many are there in all?* Read the question aloud. Have your child read it. Explain that this question is often asked in addition problems that tell a story. Empty each paired bag and say, *3 pennies + 5 pennies*. Ask your child to answer the written question. Repeat this activity, then let your child work independently.

▶ 4. Have your child fold a 9" x 12" sheet of paper into fourths. Instruct your child to do one of the following activities.

   a. In each box, write an addition sentence. Draw a picture that illustrates each sentence.

   b. In each box, draw a picture of two sets. Write the addition sentence that matches the picture.

▶ 5. **Art:** Make an addition mural. It may have a theme, such as seasons, foods or animals. On a sheet of solid-colored shelf paper, have your child write at least six addition problems with a black marker. Then, have your child use different-colored markers to illustrate each problem.

Learn at Home, Grade 1

Science (Health)

▶ 1. Copy the food pyramid below. The pyramid illustrates the government's recommendations for daily food intake. The information is provided to Americans to help them make wise choices about eating. Notice that breads and cereals make up the largest section of the pyramid—you should eat the most foods from this group. Compare the size of a food group in the pyramid to the other groups to determine how much to eat from each group proportionately. Discuss which foods the pyramid suggests we should avoid. Also, discuss which foods contain high amounts of carbohydrates, vitamin and minerals, fiber and proteins.

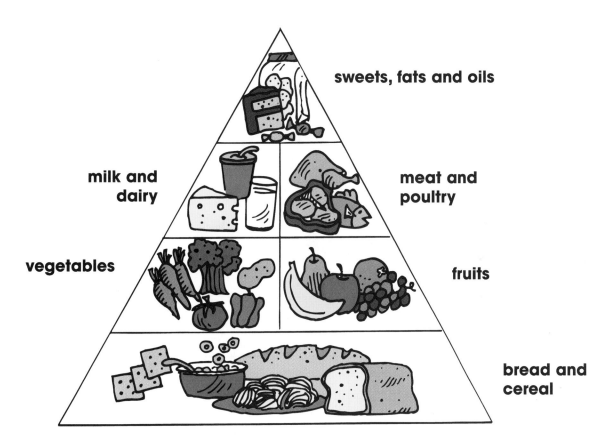

sweets, fats and oils

milk and dairy

meat and poultry

vegetables

fruits

bread and cereal

Social Studies

▶ 1. **Creative Dramatics:** Give your child a hypothetical situation to act out. Have your child take the part of the worker. You take the other part.

Situations: A policeman arrests someone for breaking a law.
A reporter interviews a rock star or other famous personality.
An automobile salesman tries to sell a car.
A doctor shows a patient a broken bone on an x-ray.
A nurse takes someone's temperature.
A firefighter rescues someone from a burning building.

Verbs I

A **verb** tells what a person, animal or thing does. **Example:** play, sing, stand. **Write** a verb under each picture. Use the word box.

| runs | cheers | chases | hits | catches | throws |

_____

- - - - - - - - - - - - - - - -

_____

- - - - - - - - - - - - - - - -

_____

- - - - - - - - - - - - - - - -

Learn at Home, Grade 1

How Many Robots in All?

Look at the pictures. Complete the addition sentences.

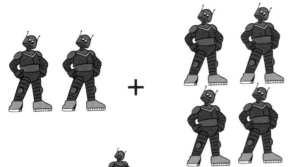 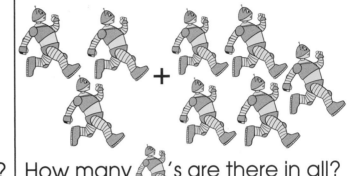

How many 's are there in all?   How many 's are there in all?

2 + 4 = **6**   3 + 5 = ___

 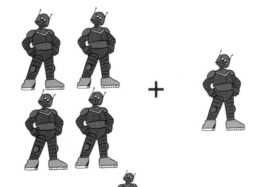

How many 's are there in all?   How many 's are there in all?

4 + 3 = ___   4 + 1 = ___

 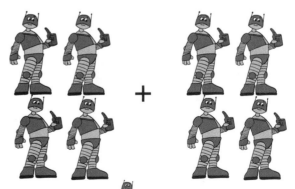

How many 's are there in all?   How many 's are there in all?

2 + 5 = ___   4 + 4 = ___

Learn at Home, Grade 1

Creature Count

Add to find the sum. **Write** each answer on a spaceship.

$4 + 6 = $ 10

$1 + 9 = $

$7 + 1 = $

$7 + 3 = $

$5 + 2 = $

$6 + 1 = $

$8 + 2 = $

$3 + 5 = $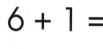

$6 + 3 = $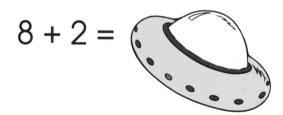

$6 + 2 = $

Learn at Home, Grade 1

Sum It Up!

_____ + _____ = _____

_____ + _____ = _____

_____ + _____ = _____

_____ + _____ = _____

_____ + _____ = _____

_____ + _____ = _____

_____ + _____ = _____

_____ + _____ = _____

_____ + _____ = _____

_____ + _____ = _____

Bee Addition

Add to find the sum. **Write** each answer on a beehive.

1 + 2 =  **3**

2 + 3 =

3 + 2 =

3 + 1 =

1 + 1 =

2 + 2 =

2 + 1 =

1 + 3 =

94

Learn at Home, Grade 1

Time For Work!

1. Shuffle and deal five cards to both players. Place the rest of the cards facedown.
2. Player One lays down any pairs he/she has. (Pairs must match workers with their workplaces.) Player One then asks Player Two for a card to match one of the cards that he/she has left.
3. If Player Two has the card, he/she must give it up. If not, Player One must "Go to Work" by drawing a card.
4. Players continue taking turns until someone runs out of cards. The person who runs out of cards first, wins the game.

Learn at Home, Grade 1

	Language Skills	**Spelling**	**Reading**
Monday	**Pronouns** Introduce the following pronouns: *I, you, he, she, it, we, they, me, him, her, us* and *them*. *See* Language Skills, Week 7, number 1.	Pretest your child on these spelling words: 　　hop　　not 　　hot　　got 　　mop　　lot 　　on　　mom Review the phonics skill of short *o* words.	**Adjectives** Give your child an object and ask him/her to describe it. Write all the words your child mentions such as *big, brown* and *cuddly*. Tell your child that these describing words are called *adjectives*. Have your child brainstorm a list of *adjectives*. Hang up the list of words on the classroom wall for your child's reference. Have your child complete **Animal Adjectives** (p. 102).
Tuesday	Look for pronouns in the books you and your child read together. Help your child identify to whom each pronoun refers. Explain that a pronoun always refers to a noun, usually a person or persons. **Hint:** If you are not sure to whom the pronoun refers, look in the previous sentence. Have your child complete **Pronouns** (p. 100).	Have your child write the spelling words in sentences.	Read *Quick as a Cricket* by Audrey Wood. Encourage your child to find all the adjectives in the book. Discuss how the author stretched the truth (using hyperbole) to emphasize the adjectives. You may wish to explore actual facts such as how quick a cricket is, the size of an ant or a whale and why a frog is cold.
Wednesday	Teach through modeling that using pronouns makes your writing more interesting. Read the following sentences: *Mrs. Brown went to the store. Mrs. Brown bought some apples. When Mrs. Brown got home, Mrs. Brown baked an apple pie.* Have your child replace "Mrs. Brown" twice with a pronoun and read again. Discuss with your child how the sentences are more varied and interesting with an occasional pronoun.	Have your child complete **Following the Flock** (p. 101).	**Art:** Review the definition and use of adjectives. *See* Reading, Week 7, number 1. Let your child create the "Adjective Flowers" described.
Thursday	Teach your child to use a pronoun rather than mention the same subject twice. Write a pair of sentences that share a subject. **Example**: *The elephant in the show danced.* *The elephant also stood on its head.* **Change to**: *The elephant in the show danced.* *It also stood on its head.* Provide several pairs of sentences as above for your child to practice replacing nouns with pronouns.	Let your child use dried beans, macaroni or cereal to form the letters of each spelling word.	Help your child think of adjectives that describe him/her. Have your child write a book about him/herself patterned after *Quick as a Cricket*. Help him/her edit the story. *See* Reading, Week 3, number 1. Have your child publish a "neat copy" of the book.
Friday	**Game/Center:** Give your child practice replacing the noun in a sentence with a pronoun that keeps the same meaning. Use the sentence strips and cards described in Language Skills, Week 7, number 2.	Give your child the final spelling test.	Discuss the meaning of setting. Have your child identify the setting in several familiar books. Have your child draw him/herself in a setting of his/her choice. Have him/her write two sentences describing the setting.

96

Learn at Home, Grade 1

Math	Science	Social Studies
Subtraction Facts to Ten Tell subtraction stories and encourage your child to act them out using the **Subtraction Board** (p. 103). *See* Math, Week 7, number 1. Many of the previous addition activities your child has done may be adapted to use with subtraction. Begin a subtraction vocabulary chart. Include the words *minus*, *take away*, *left over*, *more*, *less*, *hidden*, *difference* and *missing*.	Visit a nutritionist with your child. Discuss your child's eating habits and together set up a healthful diet for your child to follow.	Have your child continue to work on his/her *Community Book* and interviews.
To teach the concept of difference, have your child line up rows of counters and compare their lengths. **Example:** ◆◆◆◆◆◆◆ What is the difference? ◆◆◆◆◆ $7 - 5 = 2$ Demonstrate that comparing 7 and 5 produces the same answer as removing 5 from 7. Repeat with several subtraction facts.	Discuss other healthful habits. Ask your child to list healthful habits, such as brushing his/her teeth, taking a bath, drinking water and getting plenty of rest.	Read and discuss a book about a specific career. Discuss what is involved in that job and ask your child whether he/she would like it. *See* Social Studies, Week 7, number 1.
Start with five counters on the **Subtraction Board.** Write *5* on paper. Have your child take away one counter and write *−1* under 5 with a line beneath. Ask your child how many are left. Have your child record the answer under the line. Continue by having your child remove 2, 3, 4 and 5 counters at a time. Repeat with numbers other than 5. Have your child complete **Sea Creature Subtraction** (p. 104).	Introduce **My Body Homework** (p. 107). Tell your child to practice the healthful habits listed for a week. Make a copy for your child to use. At the end of the week, review the chart with your child and discuss the results.	Teach your child songs about different community workers. *See* Social Studies, Week 7, number 2.
Make subtraction flash cards and answer cards for the numbers 0–9. Have your child build the subtraction equations from the flash cards with counters and find the matching answer card. Have your child complete **Counting Kittens** (p. 105).	**Writing:** Have your child write a story about a real or imaginary trip to the doctor.	**Field Trip:** Arrange to visit a plumber, electrician or construction worker. Before the trip, have your child formulate questions to ask the worker.
While your child tells subtraction stories with a variety of manipulatives, write the equation for each of his/her stories. Help your child read the equation and relate it to the story he/she told. Have your child copy eight of the equations from this activity onto a large sheet of paper, drawing pictures to illustrate each. Have your child complete **Transportation Problems** (p. 106).	**Field Trip:** Arrange to visit a doctor or dentist's office. Have your child prepare a list of questions for the doctor, nurse and other health care workers. Arrange in advance that the tour include charts and models that illustrate healthful habits. After the visit, have your child read the story he/she wrote on Thursday. Have your child write a new story using the information he/she learned on your trip.	Review the field trip experience with your child. To encourage him/her to recall details of the experience, have him/her tape record a description of what he/she learned on yesterday's trip. Have your child write a thank you letter to the worker and to the health care professionals (from today's trip) who spoke to him/her.

<< **TEACHING SUGGESTIONS AND ACTIVITIES** <

Language Skills (Pronouns)

▶ 1. Write a sentence such as _My sister is three years old_, underlining the words _My sister_. Write the same sentence again, substituting a pronoun for the subject, such as _She is three years old_. Ask your child to identify the word that replaces _My sister_ but means the same thing. After repeating with other sentences, have your child circle each pronoun. Make a list of the pronouns and hang them up in the room.

▶ 2. **Center:** Prepare sentence strips by writing a sentence on each strip without a pronoun. On index cards, write pronouns that could replace the subjects of the sentences. Your child may work independently to match an appropriate pronoun card with each sentence.

Reading (Adjectives)

▶ 1. **Art:** Make a 6" diameter circle and a 6" long petal out of tagboard. Have your child trace the tagboard shapes onto construction paper (enough to make several flowers) and cut them all out. Using a marker, have your child write a different noun on each circle and six adjectives that describe it on the petals. Have him/her glue the petals around the center of each flower. Make a bulletin board to display the flowers. Hang a background of blue sky, add brown earth and green stems and put a flower on the top of each green stem.

Math (Subtraction Facts to Ten)

BACKGROUND

Use manipulatives to introduce subtraction in the context of stories that your child needs to solve. Working with manipulatives also helps your child grasp the relationship between addition and subtraction. Provide a variety of practice so your child will have a firm understanding of subtraction and its uses. Avoid using "take away" as the only synonym for subtract or minus. Comparisons such as _Juan has 3 candy bars; Sue has 2,_ do not involve "taking away" to find the difference. Subtraction also involves more, less and hidden sets.

▶ 1. Make two copies of the **Subtraction Board** (p. 103). Glue one copy onto poster board and laminate it if desired. Cut out the pelican from the other copy and laminate it. Give a number of counters (not to exceed ten) in a cup to your child. Have your child put the cut-out pelican on top of the laminated subtraction board. He/she should place some counters on the board, then "subtract" by sliding some of the counters "into" the pelican's beak. After your child has completed the above task, ask _How many counters did you begin with? How many were taken away? How many are left?_ Write the subtraction problem on a chalkboard or large chart for your child to see.

▶ 2. **Center:** Keep the **Subtraction Board** in the math center where your child may use it independently.

▶ 3. **Center:** Keep flash cards at the center for your child to use independently.

▶ 4. **Game:** Make a bingo board with five squares across and five squares down. Have your child fill in each space with a number from 0–9, repeating as necessary. Hold up one flash card at a time. Have your child place a counter on the correct answer on the bingo board.

Learn at Home, Grade 1

▶ 5. **Game/Center:** Cut two sections off an egg carton. Label the bottom of the remaining ten sections with the numerals 1–10. Put two small objects in the carton and close the lid. Write the directions for play on a card and tape it to the lid of the carton.

Directions: 1. Shake the carton. Lift the lid.
2. Write a subtraction sentence using the the two numbers landed on—the larger one should be first (the minuend). Then, write the difference between the two numbers.

Social Studies (Occupations)

▶ 1. **Reading:** There are many easy-to-read books about workers. Some are listed below for your convenience, but your local library may have others.

I Can Be a... series by Children's Press, Chicago.
Pilot by William Russell (Part of a career series that also includes broadcasters, farmers, fishermen, truckers and zoo keepers).
Fill It Up! by Gail Gibbons.
Going to the Dentist by Fred Rogers.
Flying Firefighters by Gary Hines.
My Mom's a Vet by Henry Horenstein.

▶ 2. **Music:** *Eye Winker Tom Tinker Chin Chopper*, a song book by Tom Glazer, has three finger-play songs about workers: "Down by the Station," "Shoemaker, Shoemaker" and "The Tailor and the Mouse." Another song, "The Farmer," may be found in *The American Songbag* by Carl Sandburg.

Pronouns

A **pronoun** is a word that can take the place of a noun in a sentence.

Example:

My dad is a pilot. **He** flies airplanes.
My dad loves to fly. **He** is a good pilot.

Circle the pronoun that can take the place of the bold words.

1. **My mother** is a pilot, too.   a. They   b. She

2. **Mom and Dad** own a small plane.   a. We   b. They

3. **My brother and I** have flown with   a. We   b. They
   them.

4. **My brother** wants to be a pilot.   a. It   b. He

5. **Mother** says flying is fun.   a. She   b. He

6. **Dad** loves to fly.   a. They   b. He

7. **My brother** is older than I am.   a. He   b. We

Learn at Home, Grade 1

Following the Flock

Write the missing spelling word in each sentence.

_____

----

1. Put it _____ top of the box.

_____

----

2. Will his _____ let us play?

_____

----

3. Bob _____ a rock in his sock.

_____

----

4. That pot is very _____.

_____

----

5. A rabbit will _____ on top of the log.

_____

----

6. We had a _____ of fun at the pond.

_____

----

7. Rob will _____ up the spilled milk.

_____

----

8. Ronda did _____ stop at the shop.

Animal Adjectives

Write a describing word in each sentence below. Use the word web to help you.

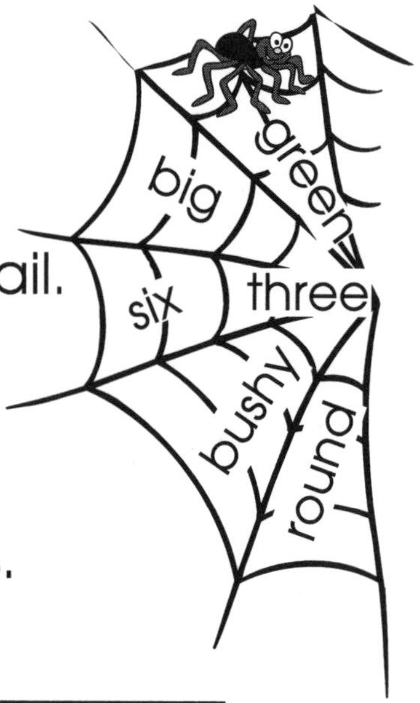

1. A  🐿 has a _____ tail.

2. A 🐞 has _____ legs.

3. The 🐟 will become a _____ frog.

4. A 🦫 has _____ teeth.

5. _____ hang by their tails.

6. An 🦉 has _____ eyes.

big   green   six   three   bushy   round

102

Learn at Home, Grade 1

Sea Creature Subtraction

Look at the pictures. Complete the subtraction sentences.

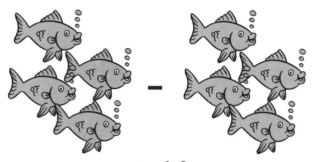

How many 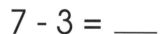's are left?

4 - 4 = __0__

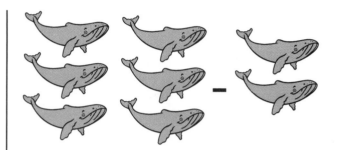

How many 🐋's are left?

6 - 2 = ___

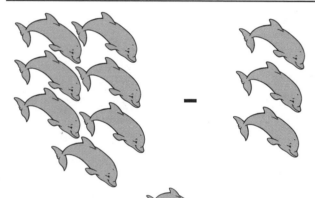

How many 🐬's are left?

7 - 3 = ___

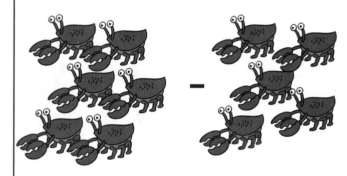

How many 🦀's are left?

6 - 5 = ___

How many 🐙's are left?

8 - 3 = ___

How many 🦭's are left?

5 - 2 = ___

Learn at Home, Grade 1

Counting Kittens

Use counters. Make a group, then take some away. **Write** how many are left.

_____
are left

Put in 4. Take away 1.

_____
are left

Put in 5. Take away 2.

_____
are left

Put in 7. Take away 3.

Think of a story for this picture. **Write** how many are left.

_____
are left

Transportation Problems

Circle the picture which matches the subtraction sentence. Then, complete the number sentence.

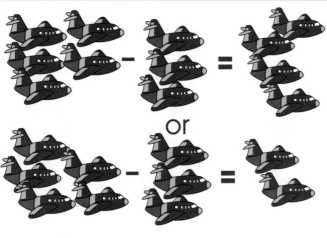

4 - 1 = __3__

6 - 2 = ___

5 - 3 = ___

7 - 3 = ___

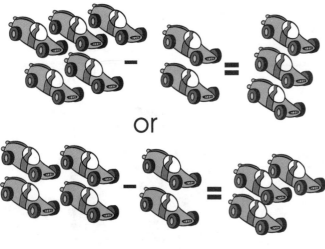

5 - 2 = ___

7 - 5 = ___

106

Learn at Home, Grade 1

My Body Homework

Use this check list to practice good health habits for the next week. Keep it on your bathroom mirror or next to your bed. It will remind you to do your "body homework"!

Name	Sun.	Mon.	Tues.	Wed.	Thurs.	Fri.	Sat.
I slept at least 8 hours.							
I ate a healthful breakfast.							
I brushed my teeth this morning.							
I ate a healthful lunch.							
I washed my hands after using the bathroom.							
I exercised at least 30 minutes today.							
I drank at least six glasses of water.							
I stood and sat up straight.							
I ate a healthful dinner.							
I bathed.							
I brushed my teeth this evening.							

Language Skills	Spelling	Reading
Monday — **Singular and Plural Nouns and Verbs** Write the following pair of sentences: *The owl flew after the mouse.* *The owls flew after the mouse.* Discuss with your child how the *s* added to owl in the second sentence changes the meaning. For guided practice, write several sentences with singular nouns and have your child rewrite each sentence with a plural noun. Have your child illustrate both sentences.	Pretest your child on these spelling words: bun rug / up tug / jug tub / us fun Review the phonics skill of short *u* vowels.	**Verbs** Review verbs with your child. Have your child act out verbs such as *stand, sit, roar, jump, sleep, eat* and *smell*. Remind your child that action words are called *verbs*. Read *Where the Wild Things Are* by Maurice Sendak. Have your child look through the book to find verbs and act them out. Add to the list of nouns begun in Week 6.
Tuesday — Draw or find pictures of single objects and sets of objects. Have your child say what each picture contains—for example, five eggs or six ducks. Fold a paper in fourths. In small letters, have your child write a singular noun in each box. He/she should draw more than one of the object named in each box. Then, have him/her write the number drawn and the plural form of each noun.	Have your child write the spelling words in sentences.	Have your child analyze Max's character, choosing where he falls on each of the following scales. Have your child write an explanation for each of his/her ratings above. **Example**: *Max is very powerful because he can command the wild things.* Obedient ⦿ ○ ○ ○ ○ Naughty / Loud ⦿ ○ ○ ○ ○ Quiet / Powerful ⦿ ○ ○ ○ ○ Weak
Wednesday — Write the following sentences and verbs: Sal ___ catch with my ball. (play) / They ___ catch with my ball. (play) / She ___ faster than Marty. (run) / Fran and I ___ faster than Chris. (run) / Jane ___ funny in that hat. (look) / The boys ___ funny in those hats. (look) Have your child fill in each blank with the appropriate verb form. Discuss why an *s* needed to be added to the verb in some sentences.	Have your child spell each word aloud while using American sign language. Have your child complete **Tub Fun** (p. 112).	Prove through examples that every sentence must have a verb. Show your child a picture from *Where the Wild Things Are*. Have your child make up a sentence describing the action in the picture. Write your child's sentences, and have him/her point out the verb in each. Repeat with other pictures from the book, as well as pictures cut out from magazines. Have your child complete **Circus Action** (p. 113).
Thursday — Teach your child when to use the *es* plural ending. It is added to words that end in *ch, s, ss, sh* and *x*. Have your child add the *es* ending to *itch, kiss* and *wish* for practice. Help your child look in the books you read together for verbs and nouns that end in *s* or *es*.	Have your child type each spelling word on the typewriter or computer.	**Game:** Ask a third person to write a different verb on each of several index cards. Have your child draw a card and act out the verb without speaking. You try to guess the verb. Alternate turns with your child.
Friday — Teach your child past-tense verbs. Provide examples of actions that happened in the past using what your child did the day before. Talk about the *ed* ending. **Examples:** You *walked* to the store yesterday. I *brushed* your hair. Casie *counted* the steps. Have your child complete **Past-Tense Verbs** (p. 111).	Give your child the final spelling test.	Discuss the beginning, middle and end of *Where the Wild Things Are*. Have your child draw the sequence of events from the story in a comic strip format. Have him/her write simple dialogue in balloons as in comic strips.

Learn at Home, Grade 1

Math	Science	Social Studies
Subtraction Lead your your child to discover that several subtraction problems can yield the same answer. $(8 - 3 = 5, 7 - 2 = 5, 10 - 5 = 5,$ etc.) *See* Math, Week 8, numbers 1 and 2. Have your child complete **Sweet Treats** (p. 114).	**Creative Dramatics** Write good health habits on index cards. Have your child pick one card at a time and act it out.	Have your child create a help-wanted ad for a community worker. Have him/her include the job description and necessary qualifications.
Read the book *Ten Sly Piranhas* by William Wise. Have your child act out the story with the crackers and count how many fish are still swimming. Repeat with different numbers and stories. Then, have your child invent and act out more "fish stories." *See* Math, Week 8, numbers 3 and 4. Use goldfish crackers as counters to solve the problems on **A Whale of a Job!** (p. 115).	Discuss the importance of breathing clean air and what can be done to keep it clean. With your child, brainstorm slogans to write on posters that encourage people and businesses to keep the air clean. Have your child choose one of the slogans and make a poster promoting clean air. After he/she completes the poster, ask a storeowner in your town to display it.	**Poetry:** Read "Cherry Stones" in *Now We Are Six* by A. A. Milne. *See* Social Studies, Week 8, numbers 1 and 2. Read some other poems about jobs. First, read a poem aloud to your child. Then, invite your child to read it along with you on a second and third reading.
Show your child how to use a number line to solve addition and subtraction problems. Have him/her practice counting forward and backward on the number line. *See* Math, Week 8, numbers 5 and 6. Have your child complete **Hop Along Numbers** (p. 116).	Discuss safety. With your child, brainstorm a list of safety rules. Have your child copy each safety rule on a page and draw a picture to go with it. Your child may publish the pages in a book called *Safety Do's and Don'ts.*	Have your child create a two-line poem as if he/she were talking to the worker. Your child should begin the poem by repeating the title such as "Doctor, doctor" or "Firefighter, fire-fighter."
Introduce "number families" using dominoes and Unifix cubes. Choose a domino with fewer than ten total dots. Have your child copy the dot pattern of the domino with the Unifix cubes. Lead your child to name the two addition facts and two subtraction facts using only the three numerals represented on the domino. Have your child repeat with other dominoes.	Continue yesterday's lesson.	**Field Trip:** Arrange to visit a store and talk to the manager, salesclerk and buyer. Before the trip, have your child formulate questions to ask each of the workers.
Help your child understand the inverse relationship of addition and subtraction. Addition and subtraction problems are made up of part-part-whole relationships. In addition, you add the parts to get the whole. In subtraction, you know the whole and one part and must find the other part. *See* Math, Week 8, number 7. Review color words. Have your child complete **Color Fruit** (p. 117).	**Field Trip:** Take your child to a bike shop to have a safety inspection conducted on his/her bicycle. Have your child accompany you when you get a car inspection. Discuss the need for such inspections.	Discuss the field trip experience. Encourage your child to recall details of the experience by having him/her tape record a description of what he/she learned on yesterday's trip. Have your child write a thank you letter to the people who spoke to him/her at the store.

TEACHING SUGGESTIONS AND ACTIVITIES

Math (Subtraction)

▶ 1. Have your child snap together Unifix cubes to form towers of numbers from 4 to 10. Have him/her "break" each tower, leaving the same number standing each time. Have your child write the subtraction problems as he/she builds each tower. Then, have your child read the problems aloud to review. **Example:** A tower of 9 loses 4 blocks and leaves 5 blocks standing $(9 - 4 = 5)$.

▶ 2. Write numbers that will serve as the minuends across a board or chart. Have your child subtract the same number from each one. Have him/her use towers of Unifix cubes as above to solve each problem.

Example:

6	7	8	9	10
-6	-6	-6	-6	-6
0	1	2	3	4

▶ 3. **Writing:** Cut out several interesting pictures from magazines and write a subtraction story problem about each one. When you have collected several story cards (picture and story mounted on construction paper), give them to your child to write a math sentence for each one. This may be done for addition problems, too.

▶ 4. Make up some simple addition and subtraction word problems. **Examples:** *Two boys were on the slide. Three girls joined them. How many children were on the slide?* or *Six monkeys lived in one cage. The zookeeper took three out. How many monkeys were left in the cage?* As you present each problem, have your child draw a picture and write the problem on paper.

▶ 5. To teach addition and subtraction using the number line, have your child imagine a rabbit that jumps forward and backward. Start the rabbit at 6 and have it make 2 jumps back to 4. Discuss the number sentence $(6 - 2 = 4)$. Repeat this activity using just subtraction (backward jumps). When your child seems confident, mix up addition (forward jumps) and subtraction problems.

▶ 6. **Physical Activity:** Draw a number line on the sidewalk with chalk. Space the numbers 0 to 10 1 foot apart. Call out addition and/or subtraction facts and have your child jump the calls.

▶ 7. Have your child write an addition problem and its answer on the chalkboard. Then, have your child reverse the problem and write a subtraction problem. **Example:** $4 + 5 = 9$ and $9 - 5 = 4$.

Social Studies (Occupations)

▶ 1. **Poetry:** Some poems are listed for your convenience, but your public library will have many more.

> "The Engineer" in *Now We Are Six* by A. A. Milne.
> "Waiters" in *Poem Stew,* poems selected by William Cole.
> "Archie B. McCall" in *The New Kid on the Block* by Jack Prelutsky.
> "Carpenters" in *A Child's Book of Poems,* Grosset and Dunlap, New York, 1969.

▶ 2. **Poetry/Physical Activity:** After reading "Cherry Stones" to your child, have him/her name several workers. Then, have your child make up poems similar to "Cherry Stones," putting four pairs of workers in each poem. Have your child jump rope to the rhythm of "Cherry Stones," and then jump to the poems he/she created.

Learn at Home, Grade 1

Past-Tense Verbs

A **past-tense verb** tells about something that has already happened. Add **ed** to most verbs to show the past tense. **Write** the past tense of each verb.

Example: pass**ed**   play**ed**   walk**ed**   crawl**ed**

1. push _____

2. want _____

3. help _____

4. heat _____

5. color _____

6. pull _____

Write the past tense of each verb on the blank.

1. I _____ Mom a gift.
   (hand)

2. She _____ it quickly.
   (open)

3. Mom _____ surprised.
   (look)

Learn at Home, Grade 1

Tub Fun

Write the words that rhyme with each picture.

bun   rug   up   tug
tub   jug   fun   us

1. _____   2. _____

1. _____   2. _____

3. _____

1. A kind of mat.

5. You and me.

2. You take a bath in it.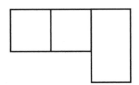

6. A good time.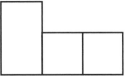

3. Not down.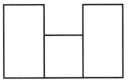

7. You can put milk in it.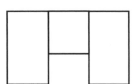

4. To pull on.

8. You eat a hot dog on this.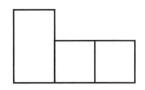

112

Learn at Home, Grade 1

Circus Action

Circle the verb in each sentence below.

1. The bear climbs a ladder.

2. Two tiny dogs dance.

3. A boy eats popcorn.

4. A woman swings on a trapeze.

5. The clown falls down.

6. A tiger jumps through a ring.

Sweet Treats

Solve the subtraction problems below. **Write** the number on the ice cream.

9
-1

10 - 1 = __

10 - 4 = __

8
-2

7 - 1 = __

9 - 2 = __

8
-1

10 - 3 = __

10 - 4 = __

8
-2

10 - 4 = __

7 - 2 = __

9
-4

10 - 1 = __

9 - 1 = __

Learn at Home, Grade 1

A Whale of a Job!

Put the number of counters needed on the page. Then, take them away by sliding them into the whale's mouth. **Count** how many counters are left.

$$\begin{array}{r} 7 \\ -3 \\ \hline \end{array} \qquad \begin{array}{r} 9 \\ -2 \\ \hline \end{array} \qquad \begin{array}{r} 6 \\ -4 \\ \hline \end{array} \qquad \begin{array}{r} 5 \\ -2 \\ \hline \end{array} \qquad \begin{array}{r} 8 \\ -3 \\ \hline \end{array}$$

$$\begin{array}{r} 9 \\ -3 \\ \hline \end{array} \qquad \begin{array}{r} 6 \\ -3 \\ \hline \end{array} \qquad \begin{array}{r} 7 \\ -5 \\ \hline \end{array} \qquad \begin{array}{r} 8 \\ -2 \\ \hline \end{array} \qquad \begin{array}{r} 5 \\ -1 \\ \hline \end{array}$$

8 - 4 = _____   6 - 2 = _____   7 - 4 = _____

Hop Along Numbers

Use the number line to **count back**.

Example: 8, _7_ , _6_

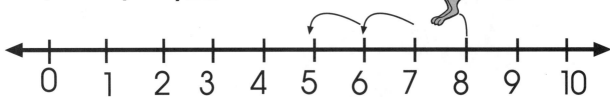

7 - 3 = ___

7, ___, ___, ___

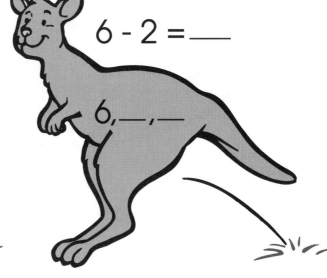

6 - 2 = ___

6, ___, ___

8 - 1 = ___

8, ___

7 - 2 = ___

7, ___, ___

116

Learn at Home, Grade 1

Color Fruit

Use an addition or subtraction board to solve the problems. Use the code to **color** the fruit.

3 = yellow   5 = orange   7 = yellow   9 = red
4 = red   6 = purple   8 = green   10 = brown

9
-4

3
+7

6
-3

1
+3

9
-2

7
+2

10
-4

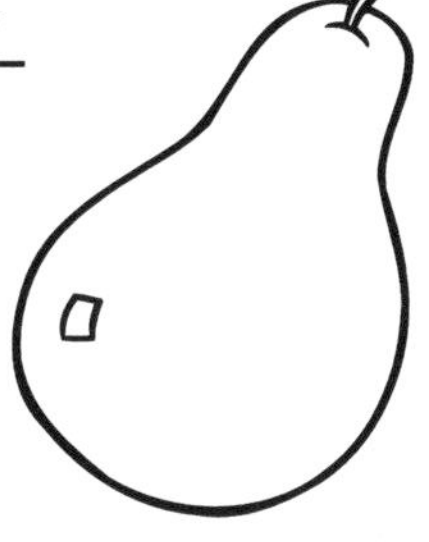

6
+3

8
-2

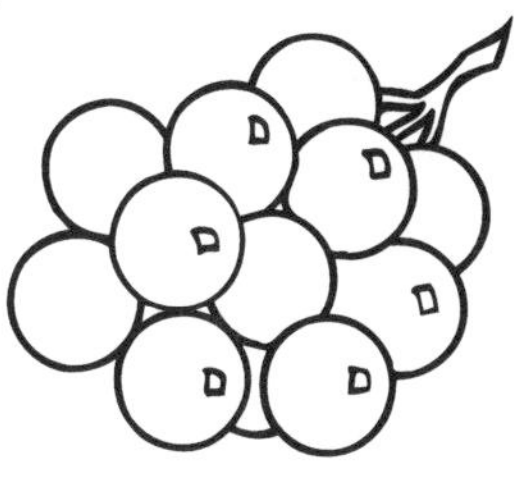

	Language Skills	**Spelling**	**Reading**
Monday	**Review Week** Review handwriting with your child. Give your child lined writing paper. Dictate the names of the letters at random and have your child write the upper-case and/or lower-case letters. Have your child neatly rewrite all the letters that were improperly formed or carelessly written.	**Review Week** Review beginning and ending sounds. Have your child complete **Start Your Engine!** (p. 122) and **Last Stop** (p. 123).	**Review Week** Review the alphabet with your child. Give your child a bowl of alphabet cereal. Have him/her find each letter of the alphabet, put them in order and name a word which begins with each letter. Have your child use **Balancing Act** (p. 124) to practice alphabetical order.
Tuesday	Review verbs with your child. Make a copy of the text from a story your child can read. Have your child underline all the verbs.	Using words from the past 8 weeks, have your child make a "dictionary" of spelling words. *See* Spelling, Week 9, number 1.	Have your child look at the headlines in a newspaper. Instruct your child to cut out a word that begins with each letter of the alphabet and arrange the words in alphabetical order. He/she can then glue the words on a sheet of paper.
Wednesday	Review nouns, proper nouns and pronouns with your child. Write ten sentences, including some proper nouns and pronouns. Have your child circle all the nouns in pencil, underline the proper nouns with a red pencil or crayon and draw a blue box around the pronouns.	Play "Bingo" with words from the past 8 weeks. *See* Spelling, Week 9, number 2.	Review nouns, adjectives and verbs with your child. Have your child look in books he/she has read for ten nouns, ten adjectives and ten verbs. Have your child sort and label the categories and then write three sentences using some of the found words.
Thursday	Have your child write (or dictate) an adjective and a noun that begins with the same letter for (nearly) every letter of the alphabet. **Examples:** angry ant, big bear, etc. *See* Language Skills, Week 9, number 1.	Write each letter of the alphabet on an index card. Play a spelling review game with the cards. *See* Spelling, Week 9, numbers 3 and 4.	Review plural nouns. Fold lined paper in half lengthwise. Write *Singular* and *Plural* above each column. Write a list of singular and plural nouns on the chalkboard. Have your child sort and write the nouns in their appropriate columns. Discuss with your child how he/she knows whether a noun is singular or plural.
Friday	Review singular and plural nouns and verbs with your child. Make an activity sheet of sentences, leaving blanks where words have been omitted. Leave out singular and plural nouns or verbs. Provide word choices for your child. Have your child write the correct word on the blank in each sentence.	Have your child make a word search using words from the past 8 weeks.	Review with your child the books he/she has read. Cut a 6" circle pattern from tagboard for your child to trace several times onto construction paper. Have your child write the titles of books he/she has read on the circles. On one circle, have your child draw a caterpillar face. Hang the circles on the wall, forming a caterpillar that can "grow" around the room as your child continues to read books throughout the year.

Learn at Home, Grade 1

Math	Science	Social Studies
Review Week Review counting by 1's, 2's, 5's and 10's. Make a copy of the **Hundred Chart** (p. 31). *See* Math, Week 9, numbers 1–3. Have your child go around the house, finding various numbers of objects. Have him/her count the objects by 1's, 2's, 5's or 10's. Using objects and numbers, have your child make a booklet entitled *How Many in My House?*	**Review Week** Review the **My Body Homework** (p. 107) activity sheet with your child (*see* Wednesday, Week 7). Discuss areas where improvement is needed. Tell your child the purpose of the activity is to build good habits. Copy page 107 again. Use the checklist as a reminder to build good habits. Work with your child to design a custom check list. Reward your child when weak areas improve.	**Review Week** Review your child's personal information with him/her.
Review patterns with your child. Have your child use pattern blocks to design a repeating pattern. Discuss what makes it a pattern. Have your child build or draw a variety of patterns using colors, numbers, letters, sizes and so on. *See* Math, Week 9, numbers 4–6, for further suggestions.	Review facts about the human body. Create a matching game of facts about the human body. *See* Science, Week 9, number 1.	Review your child's *All About Me* book with him/her. Look through the folder of pages collected. Ask your child what he/she has learned about him/herself. Allow your child to add pages to the folder if information is missing. Have your child make an *I Am the Best Me I Can Be* poster of him/herself. *See* Social Studies, Week 9, number 2.
Review the names of the shapes. Have your child match the shapes with their names. Play "I Spy," looking for shapes within objects in the room. Your child may say, *I spy a square in a gray rectangle.* Look around the room for the shape: the computer screen. Have your child use the shapes from **Shapely Figures** (p. 125) to make a picture or design with shapes.	Review the five senses. Read over the charts created for each sense from Weeks 1 and 2. Have your child write about a multi-sensory experience such as a hike through the woods. The descriptive story should use many of the words from the charts.	Review what your child has learned about his/her community. Sing songs and read poems learned during the unit about community workers. Discuss the visits to workers, comparing the jobs and workplaces. Encourage your child to read his/her *Community Book* and share it with someone else. Have your child complete **I Want to Be…** (p. 129) using the information learned.
Review classification and sorting. Have your child sort objects in the room or go for a nature walk, collecting small objects (pine cones, stones, leaves) to sort into categories. Have your child label the categories. *See* Math, Week 9, numbers 7 and 8.	Review parts of the human body. Have your child complete **Body Buddies** (p. 127).	Have your child make four posters—one for each worker he/she visited. Use photos taken at the site or have him/her paint a picture. Have your child dictate a sentence about each visit and give each poster a title.
Review addition and subtraction with your child. Use an empty margarine tub and a given number of small blocks. Have your child count all the blocks before you cover up part of the set. Have your child state the hidden number and write the addition or subtraction sentence. Repeat, hiding a different number of objects. Then, begin with a new total and hide various sets. Have your child play the **Counting-On Dice Game** (p. 126).	Review good nutrition. Draw an empty food pyramid. Have your child name examples of foods that belong in each section. Have your child complete **Food Fun** (p. 128).	Invite a worker to visit you. Your child may show the guest the *Community Book*. Ask the worker to sign the page that shows his/her kind of work. Have your child show his/her guest the posters and poems and sing songs for the guest. Have your child write a thank you letter to the worker who visited you.

A review week is like a "safety net." It is a chance for you to see if the concepts you have taught so far have been mastered or if any need to be reinforced. It is also a time for your child to "catch his/her breath" and work with familiar concepts.

Language Skills

1. **Art:** When your child has completed the adjective/noun alliterations, have him/her draw a picture of and label each one on a separate 9" x 12" sheet of paper. Staple the pages together to make a silly alphabet book.

Spelling

1. To make a dictionary, staple 26 sheets of writing paper inside a construction paper cover. Write one letter of the alphabet on the top of each page. Have your child look at the first letter of each spelling word and neatly and accurately write the word on the page with that letter at the top. Have him/her title the dictionary *Words I Can Spell*.

2. Make a bingo grid of five squares across and five squares down. Give your child a list of all the words studied in the past five lessons. Have your child write the words in random order on the grid until all the boxes are filled. To play, say a spelling word. If your child has written it on the bingo grid, he/she should spell the word aloud and place a penny on that space. When your child has covered five spaces in a row, column or diagonal, the game is over.

3. Lay alphabet cards faceup in front of your child. Choose a spelling word and tap the letters needed to spell that word. Have your child take those three cards and arrange them in order, spelling the word.

4. Say a spelling word. Have your child find the needed alphabet cards and spell that word.

Math

1. Have your child count by 1's, 2's, 5's and 10's. Copy the **Hundred Chart** (p. 31). Tell your child to circle the 10's in red, the 5's in blue and the 2's in yellow. Discuss the patterns he/she notices.

2. Have your child point to and name numbers on the **Hundred Chart**.

3. When you say a number (1–100), have your child write it.

4. **Poetry:** Read a short poem to your child in which the end rhymes have an ABAB pattern. Have your child dictate a four-line poem for you to write.

5. **Art:** Have your child make five paper chains, using patterns of three to five colors on each chain.

6. Collect several small objects, such as shells, buttons, coins and straws, in a shoe box. Have your child create patterns using the objects. Have your child repeat each pattern two or three times and say them aloud so he/she hears each pattern as well as sees it.

Learn at Home, Grade 1

7. On a large sheet of paper or poster board, draw vertical lines to make three or four columns. On separate small sheet of paper, write common attributes of objects, such as balls, toy cars, buttons, shells and cotton. You may list attributes such as hard, orange and round. Write an attribute at the top of each column. Then, have your child sort the objects and place them in the appropriate columns.

8. Draw a Venn diagram on a large sheet of paper. Cut out some figures with straight sides, some with rounded sides and some with a combination. Have your child place the objects in the appropriate part of the diagram.

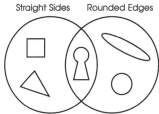

Straight Sides   Rounded Edges

Science

1. On index cards, write facts and other information you have taught your child about the human body during Weeks 1 through 4. Also on index cards, write a question to match each fact card. Mix up the cards and give them to your child. Have your child match the questions and answers.

Social Studies

1. Use a large sheet of drawing paper. With a black marker, write *I am the best me I can be* on it. Provide many colors of paint. Tell your child to paint him/herself at his/her best.

I am the best me I can be.

Start Your Engine!

Say the name of each picture. Then, **write** the beginning sound for each picture.

 _____ _____acket

 _____ _____oat

 _____ _____og

 _____ _____itt

 _____ _____ipper

 _____ _____ock

 _____ _____icket

 _____ _____an

 _____ _____opcorn

 _____ _____et

 _____ _____arn

 _____ _____uilt

 _____ _____ot dog

 _____ _____at

 _____ _____ug

 _____ _____ock

Learn at Home, Grade 1

Shapely Figures

Color and **cut out** the shapes below.
Glue them on another sheet of paper to
make a picture. Add details using crayons.

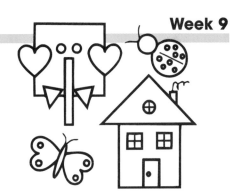

Learn at Home, Grade 1

Counting-On Dice Game

Roll a pair of dice. **Color** in the box that shows the sum. Which number got to the top first?

2	3	4	5	6	7	8	9	10	11	12

Learn at Home, Grade 1

Body Buddies

Write the letters in order to find a word that is part of your body.
Then, **color** each part.

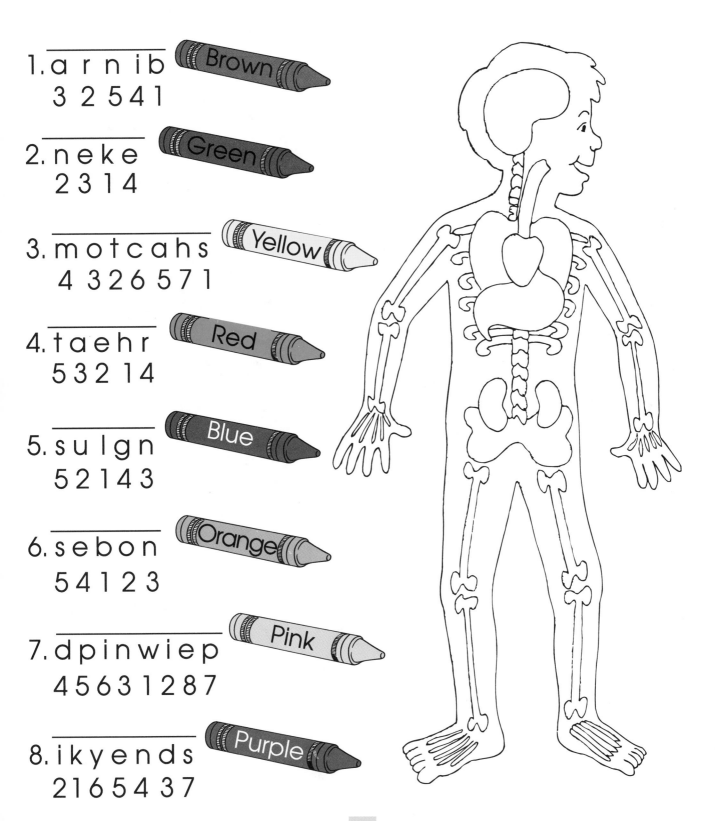

1. a r n i b   Brown
   3 2 5 4 1

2. n e k e   Green
   2 3 1 4

3. m o t c a h s   Yellow
   4 3 2 6 5 7 1

4. t a e h r   Red
   5 3 2 1 4

5. s u l g n   Blue
   5 2 1 4 3

6. s e b o n   Orange
   5 4 1 2 3

7. d p i n w i e p   Pink
   4 5 6 3 1 2 8 7

8. i k y e n d s   Purple
   2 1 6 5 4 3 7

127

Food Fun

Read the names of each food in the box. **Write** the words where they belong.

carrots   cherries   chicken   cheese   fish   ham
cake   lettuce   bagel   oranges   pears   rolls
beans   milk   toast   pie   yogurt   candy bar   cheese

VEGETABLE

GRAINS

FRUITS

DAIRY

MEATS

SWEETS

Learn at Home, Grade 1

I Want To Be . . .

Draw a picture of what you might look like when you grow up.
Then, **write** what you want to be when you grow up.

When I grow up I want to be a

_____

_____

because . . . _____

_____

_____

_____

_____

_____

	Language Skills	**Spelling**	**Reading**
Monday	**Complete Sentences** Teach your child how to identify a complete sentence. Write examples of sentences and phrases, such as *The house is old; the old house; The bird on the feeder is a wren;* and *the kid's ball.* Discuss what a complete idea (sentence) must contain. Have your child write the complete sentences from the examples on lined paper or change the phrases to complete sentences.	**Long Vowels** Pretest your child on these spelling words: day wait rain tail sail may say play Review the phonics skill of long *a* vowels. *See* Spelling, Week 10.	**Verb Agreement** Demonstrate that verbs can have a variety of endings, such as *s, es, ed* and *ing.* Write the following on the board: *I played pushed* *you play push* *they are playing pushing* *she plays pushes* Discuss root (base) words and word meanings. Have your child circle words in the newspaper with the given endings.
Tuesday	Look at yesterday's sentences with your child. Call his/her attention to the capital letter at the beginning of each sentence and the period at the end. Write several sentences without capitalizing the first letter or putting in a period. Have your child rewrite each sentence correctly.	Have your child write the spelling words in sentences.	Read *The Relatives Came* by Cynthia Rylant. Before reading the story, discuss a time when relatives visited from far away. Have your child describe his/her feelings about the visit—before, during and after the stay. After reading the story, ask some questions to assess your child's comprehension.
Wednesday	Draw a line down the middle of a sheet of chart paper. Write the beginning of five sentences on the left side of the line. Write the ending of each sentence on the right side of the line. Have your child draw a line connecting the beginning and ending of each sentence. Have your child read and write each. Have your child complete a copy of **Making Sentences** (p. 134).	Have your child spell each word aloud in a singing voice. Have your child complete **Lily Pad Leap** (p. 136).	With your child, look for verbs in *The Relatives Came.* Write a list of the verbs you find. Have your child sort the list into types of endings. Have your child write a story about your relatives, using some of the verbs from the list.
Thursday	Teach your child that a sentence should make sense. Provide the following sentence beginning and two choices for endings. Have your child circle the ending that makes sense. *The big dog...* a. for dinner. b. ran after the cat. Have your child complete **Completing Sentences** (p. 135).	Have your child use watercolors and a large sheet of butcher paper to write each of the spelling words several times.	Choose one picture in *The Relatives Came* with a lot of detail. Have your child verbally describe what is happening on the page. Encourage descriptive language and complete sentences. Extend the activity by having your child write a story about the picture.
Friday	**Center:** Have your child match sentence parts in a center activity. *See* Language Skills, Week10, number 1.	Give your child the final spelling test.	Have your child create an advertisement for a favorite book.

Learn at Home, Grade 1

Math	Science	Social Studies
Graphing Introduce a real floor graph by graphing shoes. Gather several shoes and sort them into categories like color, size, type of fastener or ownership. Choose two categories and label two columns of the graph. Have your child place the shoes in the appropriate columns of the graph. Talk about the graph using numbers and comparative language. *See* Math, Week 10, number 1.	**Living Things** Ask your child to name some things that are living. Have your child explain how he/she knows that each is living. Have your child complete **Living or Not Living** (p. 139).	**Mapping** Teach your child the difference between a picture of an area and a map of the same area. *See* Social Studies, Week 10, number 1.
Make several copies of **Picture This** (p. 137). Introduce picture graphs to your child. A picture graph is more abstract than a real graph but more concrete than a symbolic graph. A picture in each box of the graph represents the items on the real graph. Have your child convert yesterday's shoe graph to a picture graph using the two-column graph on **Picture This**. Have your child make a picture graph. *See* Math, Week 10, number 2.	Discuss the definition of living things. Write *Living* at the top of a sheet of green paper. Write *Not Living* at the top of black paper with white chalk. Have your child look through old magazines for pictures of living and non-living things. Have him/her neatly cut out and glue several living things on the green paper and several non-living things on the black paper.	Teach your child how actual objects are represented on a map. Teach your child how to use a key or legend. Draw a small box next to Map B labeled *Key*. Have your child draw the symbols from the map in the box and, next to each symbol, write what it represents.
With your child, graph real objects using more than two columns of the floor graph. Discuss each graph using quantity and comparative language. Ask questions to prompt your child: *How many more red books are there than brown and blue books? How many baseball cards do you have from the Tigers, Twins and Cardinals?* When you have completed the graph, have your child write two sentences that describe the information on the graph.	Help your child start a plant from a seed. Have him/her plant the seed in a pot of dirt. He/she should water the plant and place it in a sunny spot. Encourage your child to water the plant when needed and measure its growth. *See* Science, Week 10, numbers 1 and 2. **Preparation for tomorrow:** Soak three bean or corn seeds in a wet paper towel overnight.	Teach your child the direction names, where they are located in his/her environment and how they are shown on a map. Put up signs in the room showing each direction. Look at maps and show your child directions. On a map, have your child draw an arrow pointing north.
Help your child convert a real graph to a symbolic graph by filling in the boxes on **Picture This** to represent each object on the real graph. Compare and discuss the relationship between the real and symbolic graphs. Make extra copies of **Picture This** for your child to design his/her own symbolic graph. Your child can do a survey finding out people's favorite ice cream, color, etc.	Help your child plant the soaked corn or beans in a pot of dirt. Your child should measure the amount of water used to water the plant. Encourage him/her to keep a journal of plant care and observations. *See* Science, Week 10, numbers 3 and 4.	Teach your child to make a compass rose. Design a compass rose by drawing a plus sign with an arrow at each tip. Have your child label the four cardinal directions in appropriate positions. Have your child complete **A Venice Adventure** (p. 141).
Have your child use the **Candy Graph** (p. 138). Provide a small amount of colored candies and have your child place the candy on the graph. Then, have your child color the graph with crayons to match the candy. Have your child count and compare the columns and complete the bottom of the page.	Teach your child the parts of a plant and the job each part is responsible for in the plant's growth. Have your child complete **Plant Parts** (p. 140).	**Game:** Have your child play the direction game using grid or graph paper. *See* Social Studies, Week 10, number 2.

TEACHING SUGGESTIONS AND ACTIVITIES

Language Skills (Complete Sentences)

▶ 1. **Center:** Using books your child has read, write simple sentences on sentence strip paper. Cut each sentence into two parts so that neither part makes sense alone. Scramble the sentence parts. Have your child put the sentences together so they make sense.

Spelling (Long Vowels)

BACKGROUND
Long vowels say their names. The first vowel in a pair of vowels is long as in *pail, boat* and *pie*. The first vowel in a vowel-consonant-vowel pattern also makes the long sound as in *nice, tame* and *phone*. Finally, when there is one vowel at the end of a word as in *go* or *be*, the vowel is long.

Math (Graphing)

BACKGROUND
A graph is a tool for organizing and retrieving information. Interpreting a graph involves excellent practice in counting skills, addition and subtraction. The most important part of graphing is the experience gained in interpreting and discussing the data. Encourage your child to use comparative language (more/less) and write number sentences that add or compare columns.

When your child has had practice with real graphs, he/she can make pictorial graphs. In this type of graph, your child draws objects or uses precut pictures or stickers to place on the graph. This type of graph may be easily incorporated into daily routines by graphing the weather, the day's lunch selection, etc. Symbolic graphs may be used after much experience with concrete and pictorial graphs. In a symbolic graph, your child colors a space to correspond with each item he/she is counting.

▶ 1. Make a floor graph to use in the following and future graphing activities. A floor graph should be large enough to hold objects such as shoes, toys, books and other familiar items. Make a grid with 8"–12" squares on the sidewalk with chalk, a rug with masking tape or an old vinyl tablecloth with permanent marker. Inexpensive vinyl can be purchased at a fabric store.

▶ 2. Give your child several of four different designs of stickers. Copy the second blank graph on **Picture This** (p. 137). Have your child put like stickers in each row. When he/she is finished, have him/her compare the number of each kind of sticker.

Science (Living Things)

BACKGROUND
Certain characteristics are present in all living things. All living things obtain food and produce energy. All living things have the ability to grow and to repair tissue. Living things also reproduce and pass on specific characteristics to their offspring. Living things respond to stimuli. The response can range from a green plant growing toward sunlight to very complex behavior in higher vertebrates. All living things die at some time. **Plants:** Plants can be found all over the world. In order to survive, plants need air, water and sunlight. Plants grow taller and fuller as they receive nutrients. Since they cannot move around to find food, plants must make their own food through a process called photosynthesis. The parts of a plant include leaves, stem, roots and flowers. Most plants produce seeds for reproduction.

1. Have your child water the plant three times a week and observe how much the plant is growing. Have him/her record the measurements.

2. **To soak the beans or corn:** Have your child wet a paper towel and fold it in half. Have him/her put beans or corn kernels, that have been soaking for several hours, in the center of the damp towel. Fold the towel around the seeds one or two times. Put the damp towel and seeds inside a resealable plastic bag. Let them sit overnight.

3. Make an observation chart for the bean or corn seeds. On a sheet of lined paper, write *Day 1, Day 2, Day 3*, etc. down the left side of the chart, skipping four to six lines. Each day, have your child make observations. Your child may record how much water he/she added, the height of the plant and a description of any growth. Next to each day's record, have your child draw a picture of what he/she sees. As the plant grows, have your child draw what he/she observes and talk about and label each part.

4. To help your child measure how much water he/she is using, have him/her use a coffee scoop or other small scoop. Have your child count the number of scoops added rather than using standard measurements.

Social Studies (Mapping)

BACKGROUND
A map differs from a picture in several ways. A map is always shown from the perspective of someone looking down from above—i.e., a bird's-eye view—whereas a picture can be seen from the side or at various angles. A map also uses symbols to represent objects. An explanation of each symbol is given on a map key. A map may also include numbers and letters indicating the exact location of places on the map. Finally, a map includes a compass rose that points to the cardinal directions—north, south, east and west.
Preparation: Prior to this unit, take pictures of a familiar scene from different points of view.

1. Draw Picture A on the chalkboard. Discuss the picture with your child. Identify the building, trees and street. Draw Map B. Ask your child to point to the objects that were identified on the realistic picture. Explain that, on maps, objects are represented by symbols. The symbols are the design of the mapmaker.

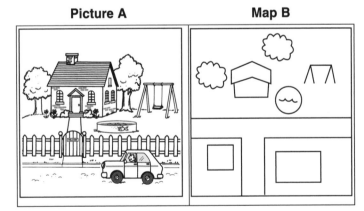

Picture A   **Map B**

2. **Game:** Give your child a sheet of grid or graph paper. Have him/her label the cardinal directions on each side of the paper. Then, have your child choose any square and color it in. Next, have your child place a penny on any other space. Give your child directions to lead him/her from the penny to the colored space. For example, *Move one space east; move three spaces north; move two spaces south.* When your child lands on the colored square, the game is over. Reverse roles and let your child direct you from your penny to your colored space.

Making Sentences

A **sentence** tells a whole idea. **Cut out** and **glue** each picture and group of words together to make a sentence.

Six candles

Glue

The rabbit

Glue

The apple

Glue

A little spider

Glue

has four carrots.

makes a web.

are on the cake.

is on a dish.

134

Learn at Home, Grade 1

Completing Sentences

A **sentence** must make sense. **Match** each sentence with an ending which makes sense.

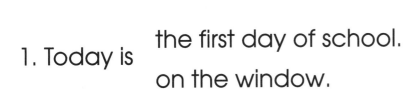

1. Today is   the first day of school.

on the window.

2. I like to   around the corner.

walk to school with my friend.

3. We eat lunch   at noon every day.

on the roof.

4. My class   under the old tree.

is learning to read.

5. I put my   pencil on my desk.

in the small box.

6. Our classroom   three more times.

has a map on the wall.

Lily Pad Leap

Complete each sentence with a spelling word. Then, **write** the words.

day play wait tail rain may sail say

1. My cat likes to chase its ___.

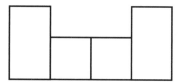

2. What did you ___ ?

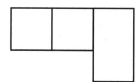

3. Do you like to ___ in a boat on a lake?

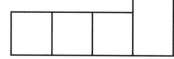

4. ___ I have a piece of cake?

5. We like to ___ in the ___.

6. Which ___ of the week do you like best?

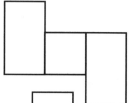

7. The train is late, so Pat must ___.

136

Learn at Home, Grade 1

Picture This

Graph Title

Graph Title

10		
9		
8		
7		
6		
5		
4		
3		
2		
1		

10				
9				
8				
7				
6				
5				
4				
3				
2				
1				

Candy Graph

purple	green	red	yellow	orange

Which Color?

Put your candy on the graph.

Which color do you have the most of? _____

Which color do you have the fewest of? _____

How many candies do you have altogether? _____

Learn at Home, Grade 1

Living or Not Living

tree

water

grass

turtle

flower

leaf

rock

Living things need air, food and water.
Living things grow.
Some living things move.
Some living things do not move.

What is not living in the picture? _____

Go outside. Find something living.

What is it? _____

Find something not living.

What is it? _____

Find other things.

Write them here.

Living	**Not Living**

Plant Parts

Label the parts of the plant. Read about the job of each plant part.

roots   stem
flower   leaf

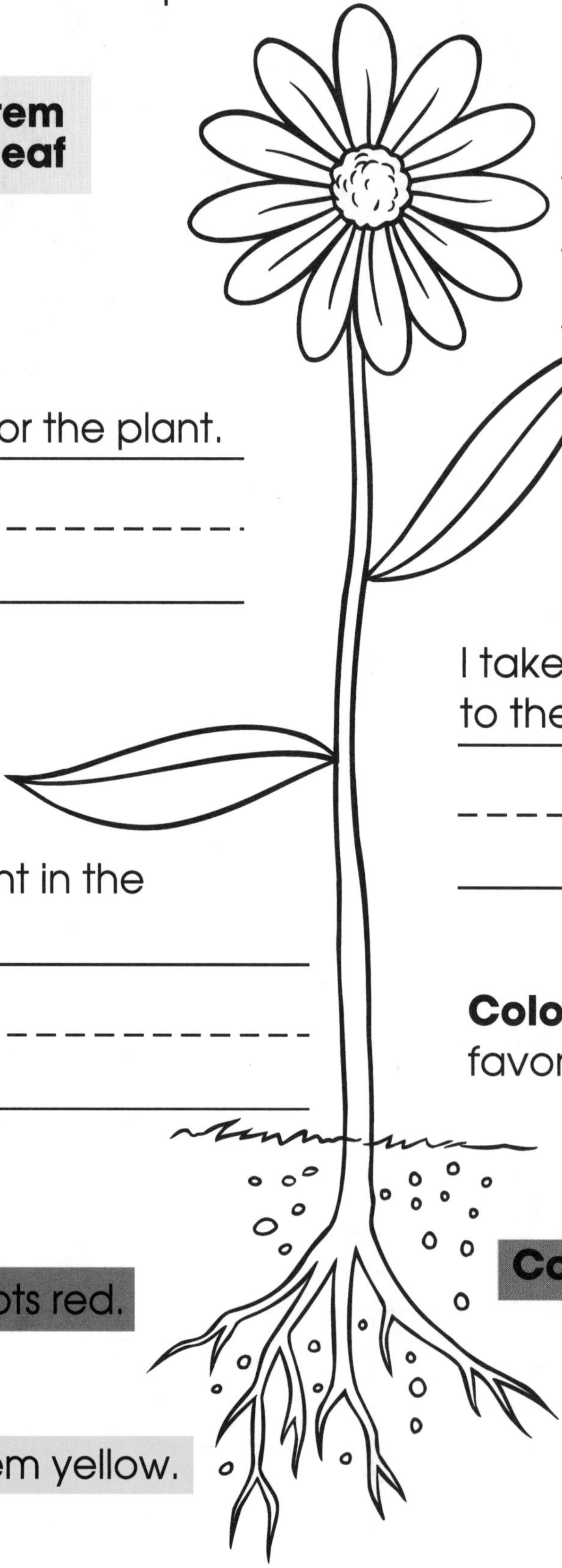

I make the seeds.

I make food for the plant.

I take water from the roots to the leaves.

I hold the plant in the ground.

Color the flower your favorite color.

Color the leaves green.

Color the roots red.

Color the stem yellow.

Learn at Home, Grade 1

A Venice Adventure

1. Start at the gondola. Move 2 spaces **south**. **Color** the box blue.
2. Go **east** 2 spaces. **Draw** a brown anchor.
3. Go **south** 2 spaces. **Draw** an **X** in that box.
4. Move one space to the **west**. **Draw** a red triangle in that box.
5. **Draw** an oar in the second box **south** of the triangle.
6. **Move** 2 spaces **east** to get to the dock at the finish.

	Language Skills	**Spelling**	**Reading**
Monday	**Subject and Predicate** Teach your child that the subject of a sentence tells who or what does something. It is usually near the beginning of a sentence. Write ten sentences. Have your child read each sentence and underline the subject. **Example:** The lady wore a funny hat today. Have your child complete **Subjects of Sentences** (p. 147).	Pretest your child on these spelling words: we me see feel keep bee peek he Review the phonics skill of long *e* vowels.	**Rhyming Words** Introduce rhyming words to your child. Read *Sheep in a Jeep, Sheep on a Ship, Sheep out To Eat* and/or *Sheep in a Shop*, all by Nancy Shaw. Have your child make a list of the rhyming words in each book.
Tuesday	Teach your child that the predicate of a sentence tells what the subject is or does. It usually follows the subject of the sentence. Write ten sentences. Have your child read each sentence and underline the predicate. **Example:** The children play soccer at the park. Have your child complete **Predicates of Sentences** (p. 148).	Have your child write the spelling words in sentences.	Teach your child about word families. *See* Reading, Week 11, numbers 1 and 2.
Wednesday	**Center:** Have your child match the sentence parts as described in the center activity. *See* Language Skills, Week 11, number 1. Have your child then invent silly sentences by mixing subjects and predicates. **Example:** *The gorilla ate ice cream at the park.* or *Charlie and Gabriel swung from the tree branches in the zoo.*	Have your child spell each word aloud and write it in the air. He/she should use his/her index finger like a pencil and write using large arm movements. Have your child complete **Sneak a Peek!** (p. 150).	Explain that rhyming words are not always spelled alike as in word families. Notice the spellings in *Sheep in a Jeep,* such as *cheap* and *jeep*. Have your child think of words that rhyme with *bear* while you write them. Have your child compare the spellings. *See* Reading, Week 11, numbers 3–5.
Thursday	Teach that using correct word order is important for expressing a clear thought in a sentence. Write an example of a mixed-up sentence, such as *the cat The tree is in*. Note that the sentence does not make sense. Help your child unscramble and write the words in the correct order. Repeat with other nonsense sentences. *See* Language Skills, Week 11, number 2. Have your child complete **Sentence Sequence** (p. 149).	Have your child form each of his/her spelling words using modeling clay. He/she should make "snakes" out of the clay, and then shape the snakes into the letters of each word.	Read nursery rhymes and other poems with your child. Have your child point out the words that rhyme. Have your child memorize a rhyming poem.
Friday	Teach your child how to edit his/her writing by changing sentence order. Just as using correct word order makes a sentence clear, arranging sentence order can make a story clear. After your child has written a story, work together to move sentences until the story flows fluently and clearly, adding sentences if necessary.	Give your child the final spelling test.	Introduce blends and digraphs to your child. From Tuesday's list of *Sheep in a Jeep* words, draw your child's attention to the varied beginning sounds such as *ch, sh, th, st* and *sw*. Have your child brainstorm other words that begin with each of the sounds. Write the words your child lists and maintain the list of words for each blend and digraph.

142

Learn at Home, Grade 1

Math	Science	Social Studies
Graphing Using coins, progress from a concrete (real) graph to a picture graph to a symbolic graph. *See* Math, Week 11, number 1. Make two copies of **Climbing Coins** (p. 151).	**Plants** Brainstorm with your child any words related to plants. Have your child use each word in a sentence. Add some of the new words to the spelling list. Have your child complete **Flower Fun** (p. 154) using the brainstormed words and other spelling words.	Show your child how to follow a route on a simple map. *See* Social Studies, Week 11, number 1. Have your child complete **Nick's Neighborhood** (p.156).
Ordinal Numbers Look for opportunities to use ordinal numbers in real situations. While in line at the store or waiting for a traffic light in the car, talk about your place in line. Discuss the position of others in line as well. *See* Math, Week 11, numbers 2 and 3. Have your child complete **Balls of All Kinds** (p. 152).	Teach your child where to find roots on a plant and discuss the purpose of the roots. *See* Science, Week 11, numbers 1 and 2. Have your child carefully observe the roots of a plant and draw a detailed picture.	Walk around the neighborhood. Discuss the direction you are walking and turning. Note street names. Help your child draw a rough neighborhood map, including his/her street and the neighbors' houses. He/she should not worry about the measurements at this time. Encourage your child to make a key that includes at least two symbols and a compass rose.
Go on an ordinal number field trip. Walk in the neighborhood or around the house and count items using ordinal numbers. For example, count (in order) fence posts, houses in a row, parked cars and street lights. Upon returning, have your child write a sentence describing something counted on the field trip. Have your child draw a picture of something you counted on your walk and label objects with ordinal numbers.	Discuss the purpose of leaves. Tell your child that the leaves make the food for a plant. Go on a leaf walk. Pick up leaves that have fallen on the ground. Compare the shapes and sizes of the leaves and then sort them. Have a leaf book available for your child's reference. Have your child complete **Leaves** (p. 155).	Teach your child to recognize map key symbols. Have your child follow the directions on **Time To Go Home** (p. 157).
Teach your child ordinal number words. Write the ordinal numbers to ten on cards. Hold them up like flash cards and have your child read them. Repeat with cardinal numbers. Randomly put all the cards out on a table and have your child match each ordinal number to the corresponding cardinal number.	**Art:** Have your child make leaf rubbings. Provide thin 6" x 9" paper. Have your child put a leaf under the paper and rub over the paper with the side of a crayon. On the bottom of the page, have him/her write *This leaf is* _____ and have your child complete the sentence. *See* Science, Week 11, number 3.	Help your child make a detailed map of a room in your house. The map should be drawn to scale and include doors, windows, furniture and permanent objects. Have your child design a key and a compass rose for the map.
Use ordinal numbers and a matrix. Teach columns and rows along with ordinal numbers. *See* Math, Week 11, number 4. Have your child complete **Let's Get Things in Order!** (p. 153).	Conduct an experiment with a green leaf and a dead leaf. *See* Science, Week 11, number 4.	Prepare a treasure hunt. Use a room in the house or a neighborhood park. Hide an object and draw a map. Give your child oral directions to follow, using the map to locate the treasure.

143

TEACHING SUGGESTIONS AND ACTIVITIES

Language Skills (Subject and Predicate)

▶ 1. **Center:** Write simple present-tense sentences on paper strips. Cut each sentence apart between the subject and predicate. Scramble the sentence parts. Have your child match a subject and predicate that make a complete sentence.

▶ 2. Copy individual words from a familiar book onto small cards. Scramble the words. Have your child arrange the words into a sentence that makes sense. Accept any sentence that makes sense even if it does not match the book's word order.

Reading (Rhyming Words)

▶ 1. Write *cat* on the chalkboard. Explain to your child that because he/she knows the word *cat*, he/she can also read other words in the same "family": *rat, mat, chat, fat, sat* and *bat*. Have your child read the words and underline the *at* in each word. Repeat this activity with the *an, in* and *et* families.

▶ 2. Challenge your child to think of and list other word families.

▶ 3. Create a folder of rhyming words for future reference. On a 9" x 12" sheet of drawing paper, write a word such as *me*. Have your child brainstorm and draw words on the page that rhyme with *me: tree, three, sea, bee, key, knee, pea* and *tea*. Help your child label (with correct spelling) each item drawn. Repeat with other word families. Encourage your child to add to or refer to the folder throughout the year and when writing poetry.

▶ 4. **Center:** Make up a list of ten sets of three rhyming words for a matching game. Copy and cut out the **Bird/Worm Pattern** on page 146. Trace and cut out the bird ten times on yellow construction paper. Trace and cut out the worm pattern on brown paper twenty times. For each set, write one word on a bird shape and two rhyming words on the worms. Repeat for the other nine sets.

   Game Directions: Have your child read the word on each bird and each worm. Have him/her match the bird and the two worms whose words rhyme.

▶ 5. Have your child write silly poems using the rhyming words developed in number 3 above.

Math (Ordinal Numbers)

BACKGROUND
Ordinal numbers are used to indicate order in a particular series, such as *fifth* in line or *second* place. Cardinal numbers are used in counting and for naming a quantity like *four* kittens. Teach the concept of ordinal numbers using concrete objects in a series. Use language as it arises, such as *We are fifth in line at the grocery store.*

▶ 1. Give your child a collection of pennies, nickels, dimes, quarters and half dollars. There should be no more than ten of each coin. Let your child sort them into similar groups and identify each coin by name. Give your child a copy of **Climbing Coins** (p. 151). Have your child arrange the coins in the columns, then carefully trace around each coin on its place on the graph. To make a symbolic graph, give your child another copy of **Climbing Coins**. Then, have your child color the spaces in each column to show the number of each coin.

▶ 2. Place four to six small objects in line. Ask your child to count them in order. Explain that there is another way to count things arranged in order. Count the objects for your child saying, *This one is first, This one is second, This one is third* and *This one is fourth.*

▶ 3. Practice ordinal numbers with your child in everyday contexts. For example, ask your child to point to the fifth day of the week on the calendar, the third button on his/her shirt, the eighth tile on the floor, etc.

▶ 4. Arrange small objects, such as shells, in ten rows. Put ten shells in each row. Ask your child to point to the first row, tenth row, etc. Then, ask your child to point to the fourth column, eighth column and so on. Next, have your child point to the shell in the third row, fifth column or ask for the sixth shell in the ninth row. Continue in this manner until your child is confident with ordinal numbers.

Science (Plants)

Have your child check the plant and bean or corn growth and record his/her observations. A tiny root and leaf should have emerged by now. Discuss where the leaf came from. Explain that the leaf came from inside the seed. The plant is getting nourishment from the seed until it can produce its own food.

▶ 1. The roots have two jobs: They anchor the plant firmly in the ground and absorb water and minerals from the soil. Have your child observe the roots from two or three plants under a microscope or magnifying glass.

▶ 2. Cut off a branch of a plant. A begonia, coleus or a philodendron work well. Put the cutting in a glass of water. Have your child watch for roots to form. Keep the cutting in water until roots are well established, then transplant it to a pot of dirt. As an alternative, have your child plant an avocado seed or potato (a root itself). Have him/her put three or four toothpicks into the side of the seed or potato. The toothpicks rest on the side of a glass of water. At least half of the avocado or potato should be submerged in the water.

▶ 3. **Art:** Have your child make a book of leaf rubbings. Have him/her staple the leaf rubbings between two construction paper covers. He/she should make two extra leaf rubbings, cut out around the leaf and glue them on the front cover for decoration. Encourage him/her to give the book a title.

▶ 4. Give your child at least one green leaf and one dead leaf. On a sheet of 6" x 9" drawing paper, have your child draw around the green leaf and color it to look like the real thing. Next to your child's drawing, have him/her rub the actual leaf on the paper, pressing hard. Ask your child to describe what he/she sees. Have your child repeat this using a dead leaf. Ask your child to describe what he/she sees. Have your child describe the characteristics of a green leaf and compare it to the characteristics of a dead leaf. Discuss what might cause the differences.

Social Studies (Mapping)

▶ 1. Draw an intersection like the one shown to the right. Draw a tree, house, seesaw and lake as shown. Have your child trace with a finger the route you describe. **Example:** *Leave the house and turn right. Walk by the tree and go straight to the lake. Play with a friend on the seesaw.* Using this same map, direct your child on other routes. Then, have your child direct you through the map.

Bird/Worm Pattern

146

Learn at Home, Grade 1

Subjects of Sentences

The **subject** of a sentence tells who or what does something.
Examples:
Polar bears love cold weather.
The bear's coat is thick.

Circle the subject of each sentence.

1. Polar bears live in the Arctic.

2. The Arctic is very cold.

3. The polar bear's coat is white.

4. The fur coat keeps the bear warm.

5. The bear has a layer of fat under its skin.

6. The fat is called blubber.

7. Blubber keeps the bear warm, too.

8. Polar bears eat seals.

9. A polar bear can sneak up on a seal.

10. The bear's white coat makes it hard to see.

Predicates of Sentences

The **predicate** of a sentence tells what the subject is or does.
Examples:
Parrots **are not all alike**.
Some parrots **can learn tricks**.

Circle the predicate of each sentence.

1. Parrots live in hot places.

2. Some macaws are three-feet long.

3. Macaws live in rainforests.

4. Other parrots build nests in desert cactuses.

5. Most parrots have long beaks.

6. They use their beaks for cracking nuts.

7. Some parrots cannot crack nuts.

8. They eat seeds and fruits instead.

9. Parrots are colorful birds.

10. These birds have loud voices.

Sentence Sequence

The words in a sentence must be in the correct order. **Cut out** and **glue** the words in the correct order to tell about each picture.

1.

2.

3.

1.	2.	3.
is going	We are taking	to swim
to the beach.	of food.	It's fun
My family	a basket	in the ocean.

Sneak a Peek!

Write the spelling words where they belong.

see
we he
me keep feel peek
bee

Nouns or Naming Words

_ _ _ _ _ _ _ _ _ _ _ _ _ _ _ _ _ _

_____

_ _ _ _ _ _ _ _ _ _ _ _ _ _ _ _ _ _

_____

_ _ _ _ _ _ _ _ _ _ _ _ _ _ _ _ _ _

_____

Verbs or Action Words

_ _ _ _ _ _ _ _ _ _ _ _ _ _ _ _ _ _

_____

_ _ _ _ _ _ _ _ _ _ _ _ _ _ _ _ _ _

_____

_ _ _ _ _ _ _ _ _ _ _ _ _ _ _ _ _ _

_____

Circle the misspelled spelling words. Then, **write** the sentence correctly on the lines.

1. Will ha pek inside?

_ _

_____

2. Kep that baa away!

_ _

_____

Learn at Home, Grade 1

Climbing Coins

penny	nickel	dime	quarter	half dollar

Balls of All Kinds

Color the **second** ball brown.

Color the **sixth** ball yellow.

Color the **fourth** ball orange.

Color the **first** ball black.

Color the **fifth** ball green.

Color the **seventh** ball purple.

Learn at Home, Grade 1

Let's Get Things in Order!

Help Mrs. Brown pick flowers in her garden. The flowers she wants are listed in the chart. Use the descriptions to **color** the flowers in her garden.

↓	→	Color it:
1st row	6th flower	red
2nd row	4th flower	blue
3rd row	1st flower	yellow
4th row	9th flower	pink
5th row	10th flower	orange
6th row	2nd flower	green
7th row	5th flower	black
8th row	7th flower	grey
9th row	8th flower	purple
10th row	3rd flower	brown

Flower Fun

Write plant words in the flower petals. Then, **cut out** the petals and **glue** them around the circle.

Example:

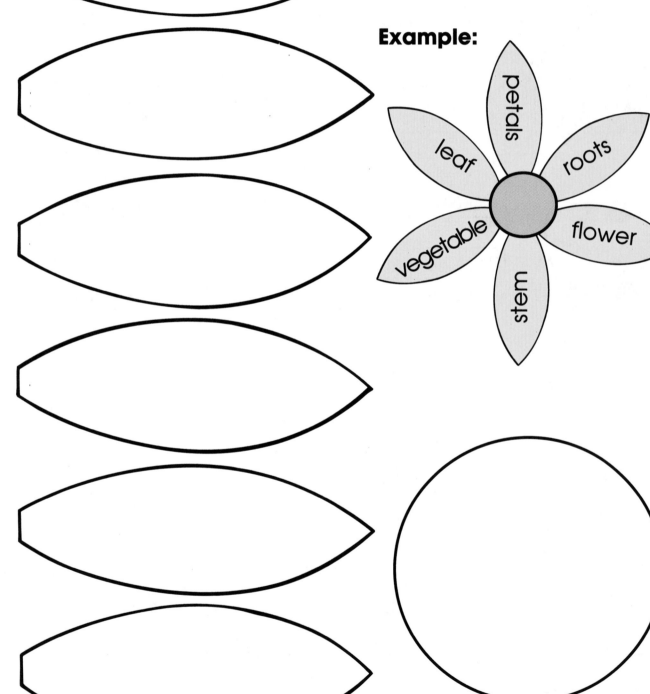

154

Learn at Home, Grade 1

Leaves

Leaves make food for trees. Leaves use sunlight to make food.
Leaves fall on the ground. You can find many shapes. Go outside.
Compare the leaves you found with the leaves on this paper.
Circle the leaves that look like the leaves you found. **Color** the
leaves on this page.

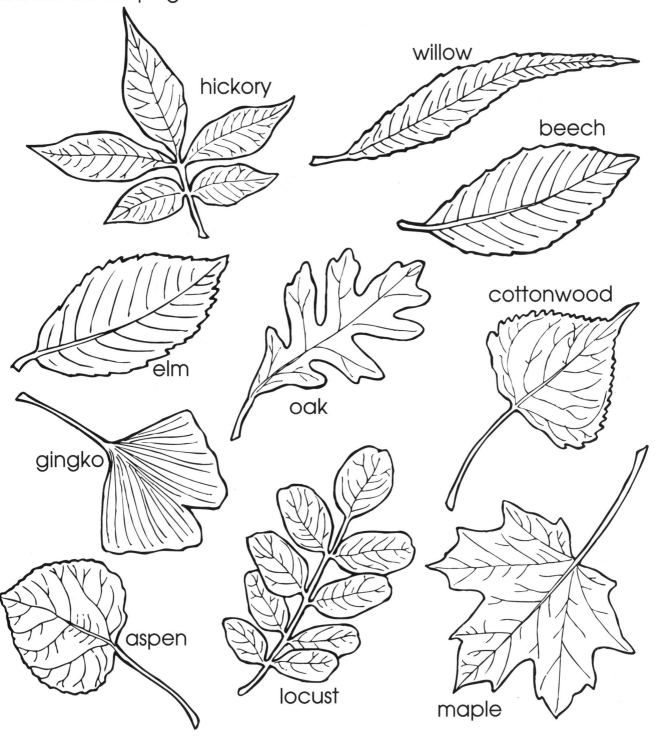

Nick's Neighborhood

Draw a line along the path Nick used to get home.

1. Nick left the library and stopped to play on the school swings.

2. Next, he looked at the puppies in the pet store window.

3. Nick watched as the fire truck raced out of the fire station.

4. Then, Nick ran home to get money to buy an ice-cream cone.

Learn at Home, Grade 1

Time to Go Home

This map shows ways the dinosaur can get to its cave. Use the key to find each symbol on the map. Then, follow the directions.

1. **Draw** a blue line that goes past the volcano.
2. **Draw** a yellow line that goes past the rocks.

Map Key

volcano   rocks   mountains   tree   dinosaur cave   plant   pond

Language Skills	Spelling	Reading

Monday
Statements and Questions
Write ten sentences. In each sentence, leave off the period. Have your child read each sentence and add the period.
	Pretest your child on these spelling words:
	    bite side
	    line hide
	    tie dive
	    wipe I
	Review the phonics skill of long *i* vowels.
		Read a book by Dr. Seuss to your child. Stop short of the final word in a rhyme. Have your child supply it. Find other books at the library with rhyming words. Read *The Cat in the Hat* by Dr. Seuss. Have your child substitute the final word in a rhyme with a different rhyming word.

Tuesday Write sentences without punctuation or capitalization, such as *the boy has a ball* and *his ball is blue.* Have your child read the sentences and add capitals and punctuation where appropriate. Have your child complete **Writing Sentences** (p. 162).	Have your child write the spelling words in sentences.	Have your child copy his/her favorite nursery rhyme or poem and illustrate it. Encourage him/her to practice reading the illustrated poem/rhyme.
Wednesday A sentence that tells something is called a *statement.* Provide examples of statements. Discuss the punctuation—the period tells you that the sentence is a statement. Have your child complete **Statements** (p. 163).	Have your child spell each word aloud while acting out the meaning of the word. Have your child complete **Shining Stars** (p. 166).	Help your child write another verse to "Humpty Dumpty" or to another nursery rhyme of his/her choice. The verse should tell what happens next to the characters. Encourage your child to use as many rhyming words as possible.

Thursday
An asking sentence is called a *question.* Provide examples of questions. Discuss the punctuation—the question mark tells you that the sentence is a question. Have your child complete **Questions I** (p. 164).
	Using white liquid glue, have your child write each spelling word in large letters on drawing paper. Then, have your child use thick yarn to form the letters, placing the yarn in the glue. When the words dry, your child can trace them with his/her finger while spelling the words.	Write pairs of rhyming words as your child names them.
		Examples: bug and rug fish and dish
		    log and dog night and kite
		    cat and bat big and pig
		For each rhyming pair, have your child draw a picture that illustrates both words. Then, he/she should write a sentence which combines both words. **For example**: I saw a green *kite* flying at *night* over the ghostly trees.

Friday Before reading a nonfiction book, encourage your child to think about what he/she would like to know about the topic. Then, work together to compose ten questions. Read the book and discuss the answers. If all the questions are not answered, find other books on the topic. Have your child write statements to answer the questions. Have your child complete **Questions II** (p. 165).	Give your child the final spelling test.	Introduce main idea to your child. Choose a small section of text such as a poem, a paragraph or page in a book. Read the selection and discuss the main idea. For guided practice, have your child describe the main idea on a different piece of text. *See* page 8 for a further exploration of **Main Idea**.

Learn at Home, Grade 1

Math	Science	Social Studies
Addition Facts to 18 Review the facts to 10 and introduce the facts to 18 to your child. Throughout the next few weeks (and over the next year), teach a variety of addition and subtraction strategies. Your child should have a repertoire of methods for finding sums and differences. *See* Math, Week 12, number 1. Have your child complete **Addition Grid** (p. 167) and find patterns.	Discuss the function of plant stems. Explain to your child that tree trunks, branches, twigs, cornstalks and flower stems are all examples of stems. *See* Science, Week 12, number 1.	Look at maps in a variety of books and atlases. Discuss the difference between land and water on a map. Notice the different colors used to show topography and water depth.
Present addition facts in a logical order. The goal is for your child to see the relationship between facts. Build the sense of *If I know what* 2 + 7 is, *then I know what* 3 + 7 *is*. *See* Math, Week 12, numbers 2 and 3.	Before reading *Jack and the Beanstalk*, tell your child you are going to tell him/her a story about a very tall stem. After reading, have your child retell the story orally and/or draw highlights of the story. Staple the pictures together in order to make a book. Have your child drink through straws of different lengths. Discuss his/her observations.	Teach your child how to represent water on a map. *See* Social Studies, Week 12, numbers 1 and 2.
Use flash cards to practice "counting on." Teach your child to state the larger number and count on the other amount. For the fact 8 + 3, your child should say, *8, 9, 10, 11*. It helps to tap while saying *9, 10, 11*. Some children count on fingers—a strategy to fall back on if a memorized fact is forgotten. Be sure to teach many strategies so that your child is not dependent on using his/her fingers.	Discuss the function of seeds. Explain that seeds are responsible for reproduction in most plants. Have your child draw and label the parts of a seed, including the hard outer shell or seed coat, the embryo and the food storage tissue. *See* Science, Week 12, numbers 2–4. Read *The Tiny Seed* by Eric Carle.	**Maps–Kinds and Uses:** Discuss different types of maps and their uses with your child. *See* Social Studies, Week 12, number 3.
Introduce the commutative property of addition with two colors of Unifix cubes. Start with the number 12. Have your child make several two-color trains of twelve blocks. For each train, have your child write an addition sentence. If your child builds 5 + 7 and 7 + 5, discuss the fact that they both total 12. Have your child pair up all the commutative property trains. *See* Math, Week 12, number 4. Have your child complete **It's All the Same** (p. 168).	**Field Trip:** Visit the produce section of a grocery store. Observe seeds in fruits. Purchase some to cut open to inspect the seeds. Have your child illustrate each fruit and its seeds.	Using the same maps as yesterday, have your child locate the key, the compass and the symbols on the map. Have your child mark your city on a state map. Have your child locate other cities that are north, south, east and west of your city.
On a sheet of drawing paper, have your child draw a picture of a forest. Pose story problems in the forest setting using addends of 0–9. Have your child place manipulatives on the drawing to model the story and solve the problem. Have your child make up stories. Then, have him/her practice addition strategies using the activities described in Math, Week 12, numbers 5 and 6. Have your child complete **How Many In All?** (p. 169).	**Art:** Have your child decorate a foam cup with a face. Have your child fill the cup with dirt and plant several grass seeds about 3/4" under the soil. Your child should water the plant as needed and keep it in a sunny spot. When the grass is 2"–3" high, draw a face on the cup. The grass will look like hair.	Ask your child to imagine how explorers in the time of Columbus managed without maps. Read and discuss **Traveling the World Through Maps** (p. 171).

TEACHING SUGGESTIONS AND ACTIVITIES

Math (Addition Facts to 18)

BACKGROUND

Addition facts to 18 are an extension of the addition facts to 10. Continue to provide your child with manipulatives and visual aids. A solid foundation with manipulatives gives your child images to refer to when doing more complex math. Many of the activities suggested in Weeks 4, 5 and 6 may be repeated in this section.

▶ 1. Make flash cards for addition facts with sums from 11 to 18. Keep them at a math center where your child may use them for practice. Use them in learning sessions with your child to reinforce skills.

▶ 2. Use blocks and flash cards to find relationships between facts. **Example:** *If five plus six equals eleven, what does five plus seven equal?* or *If eight plus two equals ten, what does eight plus four equal?*

▶ 3. Name a number. Have your child lay out all the flash cards that equal that number. Repeat this for several numbers. This activity can be used repeatedly in relation to the date. **Example:** On December 10, brainstorm all of the ways to make 10, such as 12 – 2, 8 + 2, 100 – 90 and 17 – 7. Let your child's imagination help him/her create a sense of 10.

▶ 4. Write 2 + 9 = 11 on the chalkboard or a large sheet of chart paper. Ask your child to write another addition sentence that is different but uses exactly the same numbers. Repeat with other pairs. Write some of the problems vertically. Guide your child into realizing that if 9 + 2 = 11, so does 2 + 9. Write several problems using the basic facts from 0 – 18.

▶ 5. Make cards that correspond to Cuisenaire rods. For example, draw a green rod (3) and a blue rod (9) in a line on a card. Write 12 on the back of the card. Make small cards with the sum of each picture card. Your child should match each picture card to its sum card. Your child can check the answers on the back.

▶ 6. Make a bingo grid five squares across and five squares down. Have your child write the numbers 11–19 in the boxes in random order, repeating as necessary. Hold up flash cards with the addition facts 10–18. Your child should cover the sum that corresponds to the card being held up.

Science (Plants)

Have your child check his/her plant and bean or corn growth and record his/her observations.

▶ 1. Have your child fill a half-pint jar three-fourths full of water. Instruct your child to put three drops of red food coloring into the water. Give your child a stalk of celery with leaves. Have him/her cut off the bottom of the stalk to create a 6" stem. Use the **Record Sheet** on page 170. Tell your child to draw a picture of the celery stalk in box number 1 before putting it into the jar. Have your child write the time the stalk was put into the jar. Your child should observe and draw the stalk every hour for three hours and write in the time. Discuss with your child what might have caused the red to rise up the stem. Ask: *What does this tell you about the function of the stem on a plant?* This experiment may be done with white carnations, asparagus or the stems of cauliflower and broccoli.

▶ 2. A seed may travel to a different location from the parent plant. Discuss modes of travel for seeds, such as wind, animals, people and water. Not all seeds grow into adult plants, so plants produce many seeds. In order for a seed to grow, the ground must contain the right nutrients and the seed must land in a spot with the correct amount of sunlight and water.

Learn at Home, Grade 1

3. Go on a seed walk and collect seeds. Look at the collection with your child and discuss how each seed might have traveled. Help your child identify the seeds. Tape the seeds onto a sheet of paper and write the names of the parent plants.

4. Give your child an apple to inspect. Have your child describe the outside of the apple. Cut open the apple and have your child describe the inside. If you cut an apple in half crosswise, the seeds form a star shape. Explain that some plants produce fruit that grows around and protects the seeds.

Social Studies (Mapping)

1. Write *ocean, lake* and *river* on the chalkboard. Ask your child what the three have in common. Ask: *What are the differences?* Ask your child to name other bodies of water.

2. Use a sandbox or put sand in a large rectangular roasting pan. Make a large depression in one corner. This represents one coast of an ocean. Scoop out two smaller areas to represent lakes. Make a long depression (river) to connect a lake with the ocean. Line each depression with plastic wrap. Fill the depressions with water. On a sheet of drawing paper, have your child make a map of the model landscape. Your child should use appropriate colors for the water and the land. Have your child label each body of water.

BACKGROUND
A map can show a part of the Earth. Locate your home on a variety of maps, including neighborhood, city, county, state and country. Also, gather maps that have different purposes, such as individual countries, world map, continents, nautical maps and contour maps. Maps may be used to help people travel from place to place, for political divisions or to learn the physical relationship of one place to another.

3. Provide a city map, state map and regional map with several states on it. Ask your child which map he/she would use if driving from his/her home to somewhere in the same city to another city in the state or to a nearby state. Help your child trace routes with his/her finger. Discuss how each map is the same and different.

Learn at Home, Grade 1

Writing Sentences

A **sentence** begins with a capital letter and ends with a period.
Read the two sentences on each line. **Draw** a line between the
two sentences. Then, **write** each sentence correctly.

i have a new bike   it is red

_____

- -

_____

- -

_____

we are twins   we look just alike

- -

_____

- -

_____

i have two tickets   let's go to the movies

- -

_____

- -

_____

the baby is crying   she wants a bottle

- -

_____

- -

_____

Learn at Home, Grade 1

Statements

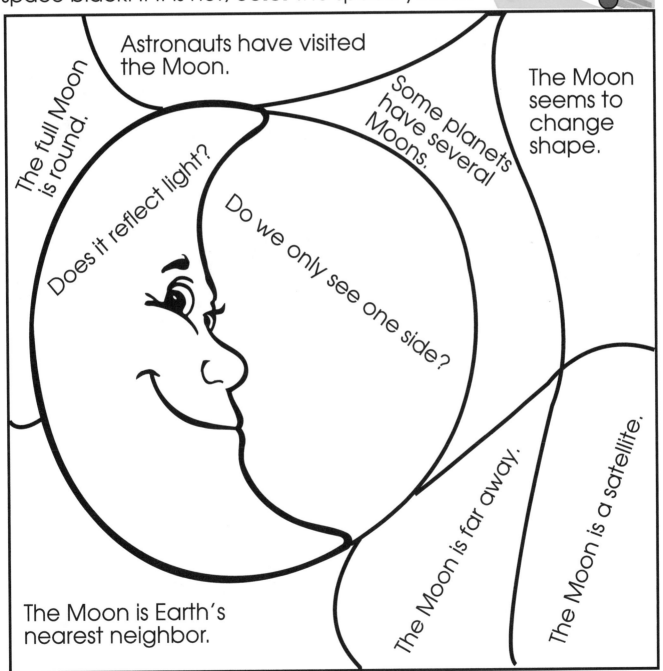

A **statement** is a sentence that tells something. It begins with a capital letter and ends with a period.
Example: The Moon orbits the Earth.

If the sentence is a statement, **color** the space black. If it is not, **color** the space yellow.

The full Moon is round.

Astronauts have visited the Moon.

Some planets have several Moons.

The Moon seems to change shape.

Does it reflect light?

Do we only see one side?

The Moon is far away.

The Moon is a satellite.

The Moon is Earth's nearest neighbor.

163

Questions I

A **question** is a sentence that asks something. It begins with a capital letter and ends with a question mark.
Example:
Have you ever visited a farm? What animals lived on the farm?

If the sentence is a question, put a **question mark** and **color** the barn red. If it is not, **draw** an **X** on the barn.

 1. I'm going to visit my grandma

 2. Would you like to go with me

 3. Will you ask your mother

 4. Did she say you could go

 5. What would you like to do first

 6. Do you want to see the ducks

 7. There are four of them on the pond

 8. We'll see the baby chicks next

 9. Are you glad you came with me

 10. Maybe you can come again

Learn at Home, Grade 1

Questions II

A **question** begins with a capital letter and ends with a question mark. Look at each picture of Panda. Ask Panda a question to go with each picture.

Shining Stars

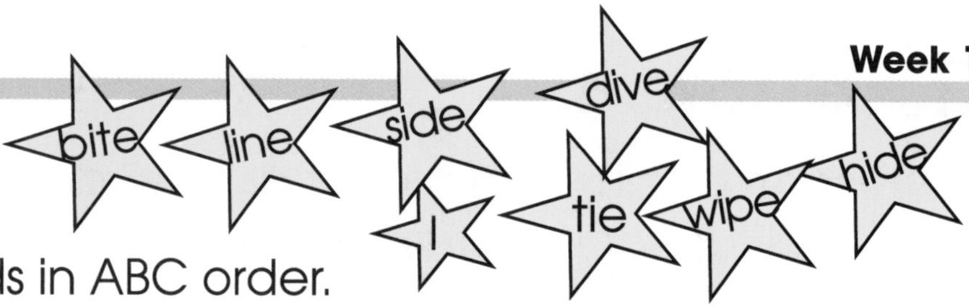

bite line side dive I tie wipe hide

Write the spelling words in ABC order.

1. _____

2. _____

3. _____

4. _____

5. _____

6. _____

7. _____

8. _____

Use the spelling words to complete the puzzle.

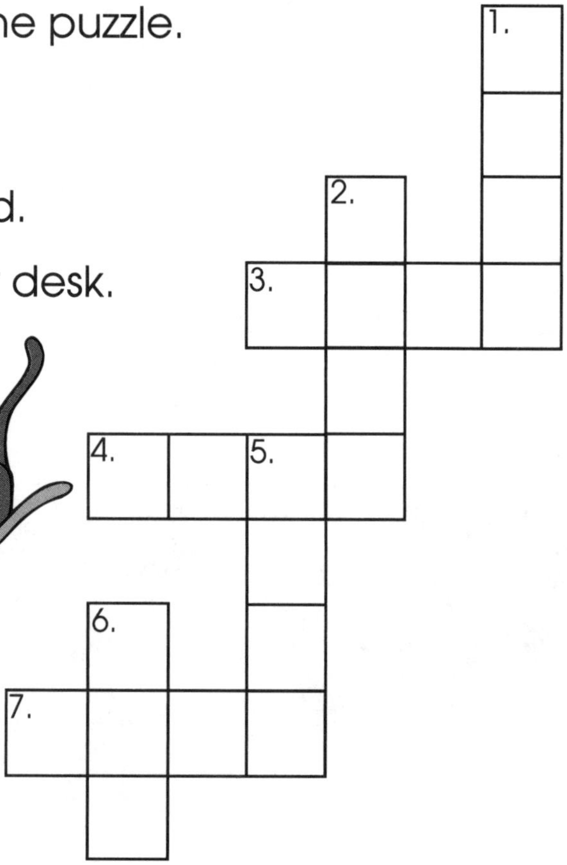

Across

3. The kitten likes to ___ under the bed.

4. Put the book on the left ___ of your desk.

7. Please ___ up the spilled milk.

Down

1. There was a long ___ at the bank.

2. Did the puppy ___ the slipper?

5. The seals will ___ off the rocks.

6. Can you ___ a ribbon on the gift?

166

Learn at Home, Grade 1

Addition Grid

Write the sums where the columns and rows meet. The first one shows you what to do.

+	1	2	3	4	5	6	7	8	9
1	2								
2									
3									
4									
5									
6									
7									
8									
9									

It's All the Same

Count the objects and **fill in** the blanks. Then, switch the addends and **write** another addition sentence.

Example:

If __3__ + __8__ = __11__ , so does __8__ + __3__ .

If _____ + _____ = _____ , so does _____ + _____ .

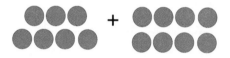

If _____ + _____ = _____ , so does _____ + _____ .

If _____ + _____ = _____ , so does _____ + _____ .

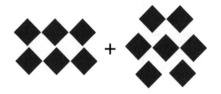

If _____ + _____ = _____ , so does _____ + _____ .

If _____ + _____ = _____ , so does _____ + _____ .

Learn at Home, Grade 1

How Many in All?

Count the number in each group and write the number on the line. Then, add the groups together and write the sum.

 _____ strawberries

 _____ strawberries

How many in all? _____

 _____ cookies

 _____ cookies

How many in all? _____

 _____ shoes

 _____ shoes

How many in all? _____

 _____ balloons

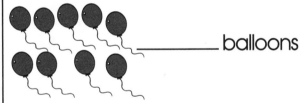 _____ balloons

How many in all? _____

 _____ balls

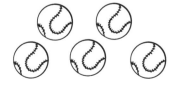 _____ balls

How many in all? _____

 _____ flowers

 _____ flowers

How many in all? _____

Record Sheet

Time:	Time:	Time:	Time:
1. Before putting in water	2. Then	3. Next	4. Finally

Learn at Home, Grade 1

Traveling the World Through Maps

Pretend that you are an explorer traveling around the world. What is one of the first things you will need? A map of the Earth, of course! A map is a group of carefully drawn pictures. It can be of the world, your city or your neighborhood. Maps have been used for a long time by people all over the world. The very first maps were made from dirt, sand or clay. The Chinese painted maps on silk. Why do people need maps?
Write on the lines below.

Language Skills	Spelling	Reading

Monday
 	
Questions
Make a mystery box out of a shoe box decorated with question marks. Secretly hide a familiar object in the box. Have your child ask questions to determine the contents. Write each of your child's questions on a chart or chalkboard. When your child guesses correctly, open the box. *See* Language Skills, Week 13, number 1.
	Pretest your child on these spelling words:
	
	   home go
	   hope so
	   hole no
	   note rope
	
	Review the phonics skill of long *o* vowels.
		Compound Words
		Introduce compound words. Begin by asking what a ball of snow is called. Write *ball of snow* as you say it. When your child responds, write *snowball*. Repeat with *work done at home* (homework), *walk at the side of the road* (sidewalk), *boat that you row* (rowboat) and others. Tell your child that these new words are called *compound words*. Challenge your child to define *compound word*.

Tuesday Choose an activity that your child would like to learn to do, such as bake a cake, go fishing, sew or play a game. Guide your child to formulate questions that will help him/her complete the activity. *See* Language Skills, Week 13, number 2.	Have your child write the spelling words in sentences.	Read *A House Is a House for Me* by Mary Ann Hoberman. Discuss the main idea of the book. Look through the book and have your child list any compound words he/she found there. Have your child complete **Two Words in One** (p. 179).
Wednesday **Game:** Play "Twenty Questions" with your child. Have him/her generate questions that may only be answered *yes* or *no* in order to discover a person, place or thing that you are thinking of.	Have your child spell each word aloud. Have him/her jump on two feet while saying the consonants and jump on one foot while saying the vowels. Have your child complete **Noticeable Notes** (p. 178).	Brainstorm with your child a list of other things that can be considered houses according to the philosophy of *A House Is a House for Me*. Have your child draw a picture of at least three of the "houses" brainstormed, then write a sentence about each picture following the pattern of the story.
Thursday Teach your child how to change simple statements into questions by changing word order. Have your child complete **Changing Sentences** (p. 176).	Make two large cube-shaped blocks by folding paper. Before folding, write a spelling word on each side. Have your child throw the blocks, read the two words that are faceup and write a sentence using the two words spelled correctly.	**Game/Center:** Write compound words on index cards. Cut the cards in half, separating the word into two individual words. Have your child read each individual word, match the two words that form a compound word and write the compound words.
Friday Have your child write a sentence about something he/she has done. Then, encourage your child to add a sentence telling what happened next or including more details. Have your child complete a copy of **Sentence Building** (p. 177).	Give your child the final spelling test.	Using words from *A House Is a House for Me*, teach classification skills. Help your child sort words and invent category names for classifying them. *See* page 12 for a further exploration of **Classification.**

Learn at Home, Grade 1

Math	Science	Social Studies
Review subtraction facts with minuends from 1–10 and introduce facts with minuends from 11–18. Teach the facts in groups that help your child become aware of patterns and relationships between different facts. *See* Math, Week 13, number 1.	Introduce mushrooms. Mushrooms are not plants, but they are living things. *See* Science, Week 13, number 1.	**You and the World** Show your child a world map from an atlas. Find your state or province. Discuss the size of the world compared to your state or province. Teach your child the names of the continents and oceans. *See* Social Studies, Week 13, numbers 1 and 2.
Have your child build and answer subtraction problems (11–18) using blocks and a grid of ten squares. *See* Math, Week 13, numbers 2 and 3.	Write *Stem, Leaf, Root, Seed* and *Fruit* across the top of a large sheet of paper. Gather a variety of fruits and vegetables, such as carrots, celery, radishes, apples, peanuts, corn, lettuce, oranges and peas in a pod. (You may also use pictures of the foods.) Work with your child to sort each food into the proper category.	Make two copies of **Our World** (p. 180). Have your child complete **Our World**.
Present subtraction facts using related addition facts and the commutative property. This is also known as "fact families": (5 + 7 = 12, 7 + 5 = 12, 12 – 5 = 7, 12 – 7 = 5). *See* Math, Week 13, numbers 4 and 5.	**Music:** Make up songs about plants using the tune "Are You Sleeping?" *See* Science, Week 13, number 2. Have your child draw pictures to go along with the verses of the songs.	Look at the **Our World** map with your child. Help your child outline his/her country. Make a copy of **Our Country** (p. 181). Have your child follow the directions to complete the page.
Give your child practice constructing fact families by giving him/her three numbers to use (8, 9, 17). Give your child a domino to study. Have him/her count the dots on each side and the total number of dots. Have him/her then write two addition and two subtraction facts using the domino as a model. Repeat with six other dominos, each with at least eleven total dots.	**Art:** Gather beans and seeds of several different sizes and colors. Give your child a 9" x 12" piece of cardboard and glue. Instruct your child to make a picture using only beans and seeds. Your child should plan the picture first and then glue each seed on individually.	Show your child maps of the continents, one at a time. Name some countries on each. Point out the difference between a country, province and state.
Center/Game: Continue to give your child practice with subtraction facts using manipulatives and flash cards. *See* Math, Week 13, numbers 6 and 7.	Be creative with fruits and vegetables. *See* Science, Week 13, number 3. Use carrots, celery, turnips, potatoes, onions, beets, lettuce, parsley, radishes, spinach, asparagus, pea pods and beans.	Make a puzzle of **Our World** (p. 180). Cut out each continent, leaving the water intact. Write the name of each continent on a small card. Have your child assemble the puzzle and place the name of each continent on the correct continent.

TEACHING SUGGESTIONS AND ACTIVITIES

Language Skills (Questions)

▶ 1. **Mystery box:** If your child's questions are not leading to discovery, review the previous questions and ask your child to state what he/she already knows about the object in the box. After your child has discovered what is in the box, reread each question your child asked. Draw a line under the first word of each question. Many of the questions probably begin with *what, how, why, where* and *when.* Discuss which clues helped your child figure out the mystery.

▶ 2. Write your child's questions on lined paper. Answer each question orally or in writing. When your child has no more questions, allow him/her to complete the activity. Encourage further questioning as the need arises. Discuss what makes a good question and the value of asking questions.

Math (Subtraction Facts to 18)

BACKGROUND
Subtraction facts to 18 is an extension of the subtraction facts to 10. Continue to use manipulatives and visual aids to build a solid foundation for your child. Many of the activities suggested in Weeks 7 and 8 may be extended for these facts.

▶ 1. Review subtraction facts from 10 using flash cards. Make subtraction cards for facts from 18. Introduce the facts in order. Teach all facts with 11 as the minuend. Have your child use blocks to build the facts in order (11 – 1, 11 – 2, 11 – 3, etc.). Then, mix up the cards and have your child put them in order and read the equations. When all of the minuends through 18 have been taught, mix them up and have your child practice giving the answer.

▶ 2. Study the **Addition Grid** (p. 167) with your child. Find 11 on it. Tell your child to think of 11 as the minuend. Show your child how to find the subtrahend and the difference on the edges of the grid. Have your child find all the minuends through 18.

▶ 3. Write numbers in order to serve as minuends. Subtract the same number from each one. Have your child find the answer, using blocks. Discuss the pattern he/she found.

▶ 4. Use blocks and a folded page to teach the commutative property of addition. On one-half of the page, place nine blocks. Place two on the other half. Have your child count the total and write the two addition equations (2 + 9 = 11 and 9 + 2 = 11). Ask: *How many blocks in all?* Cover half of the page and one set of blocks. Ask your child how many are hidden. Have your child write a subtraction fact. Hide the other half and have your child write the other subtraction fact (11 – 9 = 2 and 11 – 2 = 9). Say: *If you know one fact, you actually know four facts.* This demonstrates the inverse property of addition and subtraction and the commutative property of addition. Do this activity repeatedly for other facts through 18.

▶ 5. Give your child a sheet of 9" x 12" drawing paper. Tell him/her to fold it into fourths. This activity may be done in one of two ways:

   a. Write four unrelated addition facts on the chalkboard or on a chart. Instruct your child to copy one problem in each section. In each section, your child should write the addition fact that shows the commutative property and the two subtraction problems that are the inverse of the addition facts.

   b. Write four unrelated subtraction facts for your child to copy in each section. In each section, your child should write the related subtraction fact and the two inverse addition facts.

Learn at Home, Grade 1

► 6. Leave subtraction flash cards in the math center where your child may use them to practice his/her facts.

► 7. **Game:** Start with ten familiar objects. Put them on a tray. Have your child look at the tray for half a minute. Then, take away the tray and remove some of the objects. When your child looks at the tray again, have him/her tell a subtraction problem describing how many were taken away and how many are left.

Example: *There were ten objects on the tray. Six were taken away and four are left.* Repeat several times with different numbers of objects.

Science (Plants)

Have your child check his/her plant and bean or corn growth and record the observations.

► 1. Take your child outside to look for and draw pictures of mushrooms. Mushrooms can be very colorful. **Warning:** Tell your child not to eat mushrooms found in the yard or woods.

► 2. **Music/Art:** Sing the verses below to the tune of "Are You Sleeping?" Your child may make up more verses about plants. Your child may also enjoy illustrating the verses.

Watermelon, watermelon
See how it drips! See how it drips!
Up and down your elbows, up and
  down your elbows!
Spit out the pits! Spit out the pits!

Big green apple, big green apple
Hear it crunch! Hear it crunch!
It is very tasty! It is very tasty!
Time to munch! Time to munch!

► 3. Choose a variety of fruits and vegetables and have your child complete one or all of the following activities:
Have your child classify each food as a root, stem or leaf.
Prepare and eat a new vegetable or fruit.
Make vegetable soup after reading *Stone Soup* (Versions by Marcia Brown, Tony Ross, etc.).
Make a vegetable dip. Mix sour cream, a little mayonnaise, worcestershire sauce and dill weed. Dunk washed raw vegetables in the dip and enjoy.
Use different vegetables and fruits to form the head, body and limbs of a person. Use cream cheese and toothpicks to hold the body parts together.

Social Studies (You and the World)

BACKGROUND
Although the size of the world is difficult to conceive, your child will enjoy learning the names of the continents and seeing his/her state in relation to the whole world. Later, your child will learn about children from other countries.

► 1. Study a map of the world. Ask your child what he/she sees more of—land or water. Explain that water covers 70% of Earth, and that is why when one looks at a map of the world, the main color is blue. Ask your child to name the colors that represent land. Explain that the varied colors represent different types of terrain, such as mountains, deserts and grasslands.

► 2. Try to find a map that shows each continent in a different color. Teach the names of the seven continents. Read each name over with your child. Point to your home and have your child identify the continent on which you live. Teach your child the names and locations of the four oceans. Which ocean is closest to where you live?

Changing Sentences

The order of words can change a sentence. Read each telling sentence. Change the order of the words to make an asking sentence. **Example:**

The clown is happy.

Is the clown happy?

The boy can swim.

_ _

The bell will ring.

_ _

The popcorn is hot.

_ _

The flowers are lovely.

_ _

Learn at Home, Grade 1

Sentence Building

Sentences can tell a story. Read each sentence. **Cut out** and **glue** the sentence that tells what happened next. **Write** a sentence that tells what could happen after that.

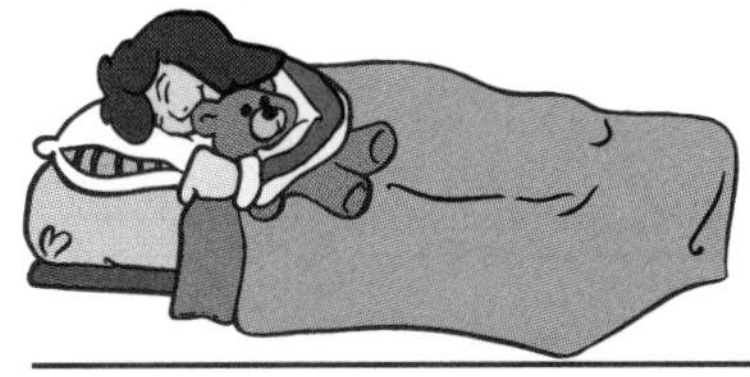

Mary went to bed and quickly fell asleep.

Glue

Brad saw something shiny in the grass.

Glue

Sally wanted a pet for her birthday.

Glue

He bent down to see what it was.

Her mom took her to the pet store.

She began to have an amazing dream.

Noticeable Notes

Read each clue. **Write** the correct spelling word. It begins with the sound of . . .

| home | hope | go | hole | so | note | rope | no |

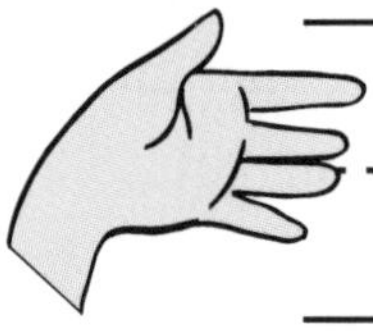

_ _ _ _ _ _ _ _ _ _ _ _ _ _

_ _ _ _ _ _ _ _ _ _ _ _ _ _

_ _ _ _ _ _ _ _ _ _ _ _ _ _

_ _ _ _ _ _ _ _ _ _ _ _ _ _

_ _ _ _ _ _ _ _ _ _ _ _ _ _

_ _ _ _ _ _ _ _ _ _ _ _ _ _

Write the missing spelling words in the boxes.

1. May we ___ to the store later?

2. Robin wrote a ___ to his dad.

3. It is ___ cold that there is ice on the street.

4. We ___ that we can go on a trip.

5. There is ___ other way to get ___.

6. The workmen dropped the ___ into the ___.

Learn at Home, Grade 1

Two Words in One

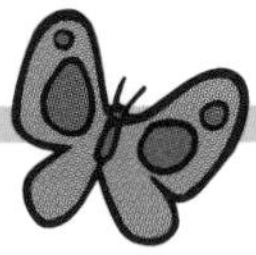

Write the two words that make up each compound word below.

snowball 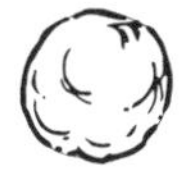

raincoat 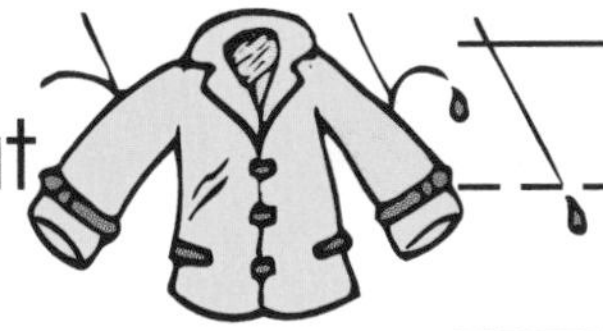

airplane 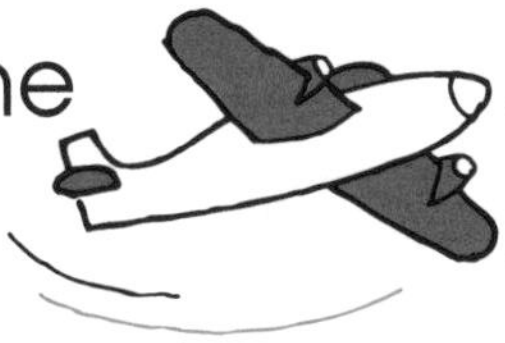

watermelon 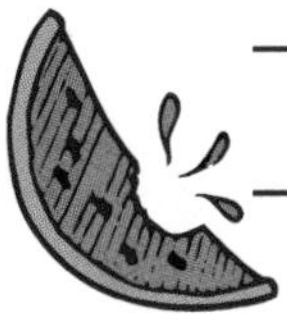

haircut 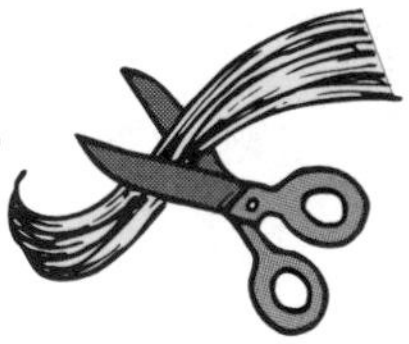

football 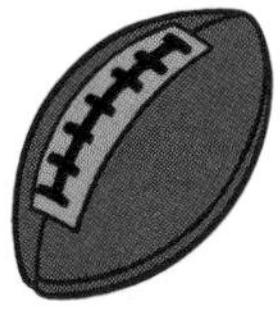

sunshine 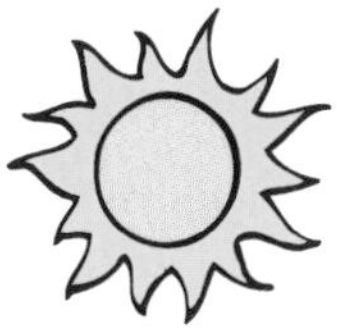

Our World

Color the water blue. **Color** the land green or brown. **Label** North America.

180

Learn at Home, Grade 1

Our Country

1. **Color** your state blue. **Draw** an **X** where you live.
2. **Color** the rest of the map yellow.
3. **Trace** the sentence at the bottom with pencil.

This is our country.

	Language Skills	**Spelling**	**Reading**

Monday	**Sentence Building**
	Write a factual sentence, such as *We live in Centerville.* Ask your child to create a second sentence that gives more details, such as *Centerville is in Utah.* Add more sentences until your child can think of no more. Read the story together.
	Have your child complete **Making Sentences** (p. 186).
		Blends
		Pretest your child on these spelling words:
		    snap stove
		    sled spin
		    smell snail
		    sleep skip
		Teach the phonics skill of beginning consonant blends. *See* Spelling, Week 14.
			Explore the literal meanings of compound words. *See* Reading, Week 14, number 1. Read *King Bidgood's in the Bathtub* by Audrey Wood.

Tuesday	Draw a picture of a big dog. Have your child write about the dog in a sentence, such as *The dog is big.* Have your child write a sentence about the dog's name, such as *The dog's name is Toto.* Teach your child how to join two sentences into one, such as *The dog is big and its name is Toto.* Give your child other pairs of sentences to join.	Have your child write the spelling words in sentences.	Teach the story elements: *setting, characters, problem, events* and *solution.* Work with your child to identify each element in *King Bidgood's in the Bathtub.* To add interest, write the title of the story on a picture of a bathtub and write each story element in individual soap bubbles floating in and above the tub. *See* page 9 for a further exploration of **Story Elements.**
Wednesday	Look at the sentences created yesterday. Have your child rewrite each sentence, changing word order but maintaining the meaning. **Example:** *The dog is big and named Toto* can be rewritten as *The big dog is named Toto.*	Have your child spell each word aloud while walking in a circle. Have him/her step once for each letter. Have your child complete **Slippery Slopes** (p. 187).	Have your child write an original story based on *King Bidgood's in the Bathtub.* Have him/her replace the setting and characters of the story with a familiar setting and characters such as family members. **Example:** "Help! Help!" cried the baby when the sun came up. "Mommy's on the lounge chair and she won't get off! Oh, who knows what to do?" "I do!" cried the cat when the sun came up. "Get off! It's time to wash!" "Come on!" cried Mommy....
Thursday	Teach your child to add details to a sentence. *See* Language Skills, Week 14, number 1.	Have your child write each spelling word on an index card with a black marker. Using a different color crayon or marker to write the word again, have him/her "shadow" the first spelling. He/she should then use a third color to trace the word again. Your child should repeat this several times, creating a "rainbow" effect. Have him/her repeat this with each of the remaining spelling words.	Choose one picture from the book with a lot of detail. Have your child write a list of nouns found in the picture and an adjective for each one. Have your child edit the list for spelling. Then, encourage your child to practice reading the words and using them in written sentences.

Friday	Write the sentence parts below for your child. Have him/her write a word on each of the lines. Then, have him/her draw a picture of the last sentence.
	    I found my _____ .
	    I found my _____ in the _____ .
	    I found my _____ _____ in the _____ .
	    I found my _____ _____ in the _____
	      under the big _____ .
		Give your child the final spelling test.	Teach story sequence. Draw the Sun and Moon in the various stages listed throughout *King Bidgood's in the Bathtub.* Have your child retell the events of the story in sequential order as they correspond to the progression of the day. *See* page 10 for a further exploration of **Sequence.**

Learn at Home, Grade 1

Math	**Science**	**Social Studies**
Addition and Subtraction to 18 Teach your child "doubles" facts (3 + 3, 7 + 7, etc.). Encourage your child to look for doubles in familiar places. For example, an electrical outlet is a double 3 and an egg carton is a double 6. Also, use blocks to help your child visualize numbers in pairs. When addition doubles are memorized, the subtraction doubles are easy to spot: 9 + 9 = 18, 18 − 9 = 9	**Animals** Prepare an insect home in a jar with holes in the lid. Allow your child to collect insects (and food and bedding from their environment) to fill the jar. Encourage your child to observe and discuss the insects. What do they have in common? What do they eat? Identify the insects, if possible. *See* Science, Week 14, number 1.	**Around the World** Study a globe with your child. *See* Social Studies, Week 14, numbers 1 and 2.
Have your child draw and color a picture of a circus or zoo to use as a background for telling story problems. Discuss clue words for addition and subtraction. Have your child write a series of story problems related to the picture he/she drew. Have your child complete **Crayon Count** (p. 188).	Read about insects with your child. Ask your child to write an insect story, including facts from the books you read together. Have your child add illustrations to his/her story and publish it. Have your child complete **Crawling With Insects** (p. 190).	Help your child develop an awareness of other cultures by providing opportunities to taste food from other countries. *See* Social Studies, Week 14, number 3.
Teach this strategy for subtraction: If the subtraction sentence is 16 − 7, start with 16 and subtract 6 first to get to 10, then subtract one more. Teach your child to use 10 as a bridge, taking away 7 in two parts. Have your child use the new strategy to solve these problems: 15 − 6 = 13 − 5 = 17 − 8 = 18 − 9 = 16 − 7 = 17 − 9 = 16 − 8 = 14 − 5 = 12 − 3 = 14 − 6 = 11 − 2 = 15 − 7 = 12 − 4 = 13 − 4 = 11 − 3 =	Go for an insect walk in the woods, a field or the yard. Encourage your child to look for insects under rocks, logs and leaves and on flowers and tree trunks. Take along insect books for identification. Have your child observe insects' movements and try to guess what they are doing. Back at home, have your child dictate sentences describing what he/she saw on the walk.	**Field Trip:** Take your child to a large grocery store. Look at foods in the international aisle and make a list of several foods and the countries where they were made. After returning home, have your child write the food names on small cards and pin them to a map near the appropriate country.
Pose a familiar problem, such as *My rock collection contains 15 rocks. There are only 7 in my box. How many are missing?* The problem could be solved using the equations 15 − __ = 7 or 7 + ○ = 15. Have your child use rocks to demonstrate. Discuss the appropriate time to write equations in this manner. Pose more story problems for guided practice. *See* Math, Week 14, numbers 1 and 2.	Observe a spider (not an insect) on its web. Discuss the spider's activity, appearance and food. Ask your child to compare the spider to an ant. *See* Science, Week 14, number 2. Sing "The Eensy, Weensy Spider" and do finger movements with it. Make a spider web using white glue on wax paper. When the glue is dry, peel off the wax paper and mount the glue web on black construction paper.	With your child, study several countries around the world. Go to the library for books, magazines and encyclopedias. Encourage your child to choose a country from each continent (except Antarctica). Choose countries for which you are able to find the most resources. *See* Social Studies, Week 14, number 4 for activity suggestions. Save your child's completed pages in this study in the *Around the World* folder. This project will take about eight days.
Continue to provide your child practice with addition and subtraction. Play math games with your child to reinforce learning. *See* Math, Week 14, number 3. Have your child complete **Be a Good Detective** (p. 189).	Prepare a temporary home for earthworms in a terrarium-like container. Provide the worms with moist dirt, leaves and dead plant material. Look for worms in the garden, after a rain or at night. *See* Science, Week 14, number 3.	Continue the project begun on Thursday.

TEACHING SUGGESTIONS AND ACTIVITIES

Language Skills (Sentence Building)

▶ 1. Teach your child to add details to sentences. Show your child a picture with a lot of detail, such as a brown dog running fast on the sidewalk, chasing a ball. Write a simple sentence leaving out an adjective. **Example:** *I see a dog.* Have your child fill in the missing word. Build the sentence by adding another detail, but leaving off a word for your child to fill in. **Example:** *I see a brown dog running.* Continue building the sentence, as in the following examples: *I see a brown dog running fast on_____. I see a brown dog running fast on the sidewalk after _____.* Discuss how the sentence told more and more information each time. Repeat this sentence-building activity with another picture.

Spelling (Blends)

BACKGROUND
A blend is made up of two consonants that join together to form a single sound. Each letter can be heard in the blend. Blends include *bl, sm, cl, br, sn, cr, fl, pl, dr, gr, tr, st, sc, sl* and *gl*. Do not confuse blends with digraphs. When a digraph is formed, the two consonants create a new sound as in *sh, th, ch* and *kn*.

Reading (Compound Words)

▶ 1. Draw a picture of a stick of butter with wings. Ask your child to name the compound word it illustrates. Explain to your child that some compound words mean just what they say and some seem silly if you think of the meaning of each individual word. Tell your child to draw pictures of some compound words showing the literal meaning of each individual word. Write these suggestions: *doghouse, armchair, rainbow, ballroom, highway, horsefly, bookworm, ladybug, horseshoe, firehouse, football* and *earthworm.* Give your child a sheet of drawing paper. Tell your child to fold it in half and draw the actual meaning of a compound word on the left side and a literal interpretation on the right side. Write the compound word at the top of the page.

Math (Addition and Subtraction to 18)

Many of the activities suggested in this week are extensions of things done in past weeks. If you feel more time is needed for your child to understand and internalize last week's concepts, spend time repeating what was taught during Week 13. A solid understanding of the "basics" makes learning future concepts easier.

▶ 1. Write $\square$ – 6 = 7 on the chalkboard. Give your child twenty blocks and ask him/her how to solve this equation. Through trial and error, your child should figure it out. Provide several similar equations and lead your child to discover that by adding 6 and 7 (as in the case above), he/she can find the missing number.

▶ 2. Write 13 – ___ = 7. Allow your child to discover the process for finding the answer. Ask for a verbal explanation. Lead your child to understand that it can be found by subtracting the known numbers, 13 and 7. Provide several equations for your child to practice and become familiar with the process.

▶ 3. **Physical Activity/Game:** Use the floor graph from Math, Week 10, number 1. Place a flash card with a missing addend or subtrahend in each square of the grid. Write the answer to each problem on a separate card. On the back of the card, write *jump, hop* or *clap.*

    Game Directions: Have your child throw a beanbag onto a problem, then find the answer card to go with the problem. He/she must follow the command on the back of card before covering the flash card with the answer card.

Learn at Home, Grade 1

Science (Animals)

▶ 1. Look at pictures of insects with your child and discuss their characteristics: All insects have six legs, three body parts and an external skeleton. Most insects have antennae and two pairs of wings. Find each of these parts on the insects you observe.

▶ 2. Help your child make an anthill by filling a box with loose, fine soil mixed with sand. Capture a few ants and put them in the prepared soil mixture for closer observation. Your child should supply crumbs for the ants' food. Cover the box securely with a screen.

▶ 3. Help your child create a temporary home for earthworms. Encourage your child to observe the worms in their new home. Have your child count how many worms are in the jar. Have him/her observe and describe the worms' movement, appearance and environment. Discuss how worms are beneficial to farmers and gardeners. Worms swallow soil in the process of eating decayed organic matter and produce castings that enrich the soil. After your child has observed the worms for a period of time, have him/her release the worms to their natural home.

Social Studies (Around the World)

▶ 1. Draw a large map of the world and hang it up in the classroom. Allow your child to study a globe. Discuss how the globe is alike and different from a map. Have your child notice how much of the world can be seen while looking at one side of the globe.

▶ 2. Fold a sheet of 12" x 18" construction paper in half, forming a folder. Using a compass, draw a large circle on each side of the folder. Have your child draw and color one half of the world on each circle. Give your child a black marker to write *Around the World* on the front of the folder. All papers completed during this unit will go into this folder.

▶ 3. Prepare and eat an "international" breakfast or lunch. Some options for breakfast include huevos rancheros (Mexico), a croissant (France), a scone (England), cheese and/or a slice of a small salami (Europe). Options for lunch include borscht (Russia), goulash (Hungary) and trifle (England). Look through your cookbooks for other international recipes. Have your child draw pictures of the foods prepared on small cards. Pin each card on the map over the country from which it came.

▶ 4. You will need to work with your child on this first research project. Ask questions, spark interest and read aloud resource books. Some suggested activities are given below.

   a. Trace the outline of the country. Write the name in the outline. Below the country, write a sentence telling where the country is located. **Example:** _____ (country) is in _____ (continent).

   b. Teach some words in the language, of the chosen country, such as *hello, good-bye, yes, no* and the counting words. Write the words on cards.

   c. Find a picture of the country's flag. Have your child make a copy of it using markers on a 3" x 5" card. Put it on the wall map.

   d. Read a book about the children living in the country. Have your child complete *A Family Living In* _____ (p. 191).

Making Sentences

A sentence can tell about you. **Write** a word to complete each sentence.

My name is _____

_ _

_____.

My eyes are _____

_ _

_____.

My hair is _____

_ _

_____.

My favorite colors are _____

_ _

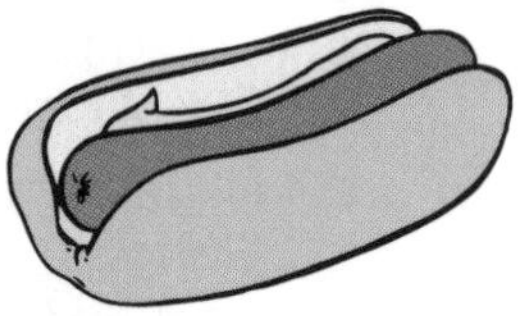

_____.

My favorite foods are _____

_ _

_____.

Learn at Home, Grade 1

Slippery Slopes

Use the spelling words to complete the puzzle.

snap snail skip sled
smell sleep stove spin

Across

2. You can play on this in the snow.
4. Can you ___ across the floor?
5. You do this with your nose.
6. The tires ___ when you ride your bike.

Down

1. You ___ in a bed.
3. You use this when you cook.
4. A ___ has a shell and moves very slowly.
5. Can you ___ your fingers?

Crayon Count

Solve the problems on each box.
Count the crayons. **Write** the number on the blank. **Circle** the problems that equal the answer.

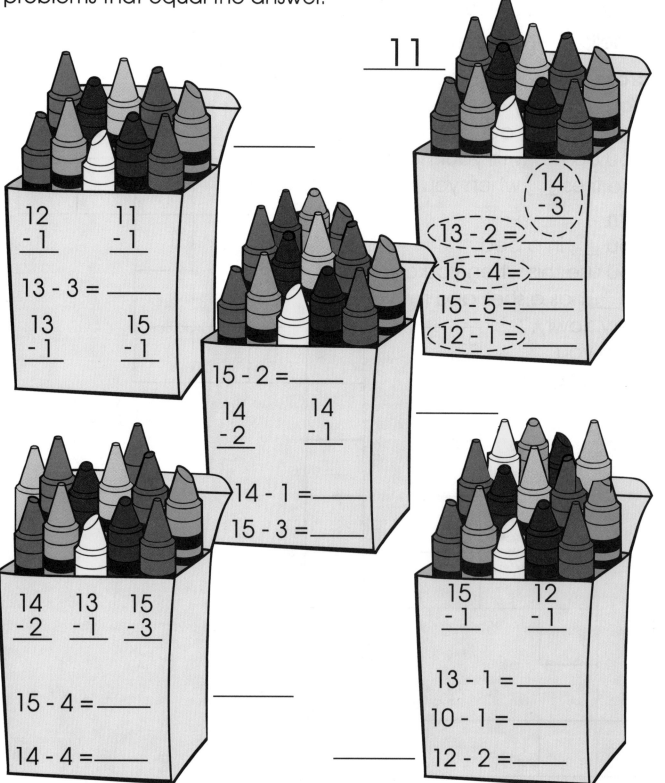

11

12   11
-1   -1

13 - 3 = _____

13   15
-1   -1

15 - 2 = _____

14   14
-2   -1

14 - 1 = _____

15 - 3 = _____

14
-3

13 - 2 = _____

15 - 4 = _____

15 - 5 = _____

12 - 1 = _____

14   13   15
-2   -1   -3

15 - 4 = _____

14 - 4 = _____

15   12
-1   -1

13 - 1 = _____

10 - 1 = _____

12 - 2 = _____

Learn at Home, Grade 1

A Family Living In

Describe what this country looks like.

_____

_____

_____

_____

Name some foods the people of this country like to eat.

_____

_____

_____

Draw a picture of a person from this country in the box above.

What are the schools like in this country?

_____

_____

_____

Write some words in this country's language.

_____

_____

_____

	Language Skills	**Spelling**	**Reading**

Monday	**Past and Present Tense**
	Teach your child about present-tense verbs by asking him/her to describe what he/she is doing right now. As you change activities, ask the same question again. Have your child brainstorm a list of present-tense verbs.
	Have your child complete **Present-Tense Verbs** (p. 196).
		Pretest your child on these spelling words:
		  free prize
		  drive cross
		  grass frog
		  train grade
		Review the phonics skill of *r* blends.
			Read *We're Going on a Bear Hunt*, retold by Michael Rosen. On the first reading, read the book all the way through, modeling rhythm and expression. On subsequent rereadings, read with your child, enjoying the story and language. Eventually, remove your voice so that your child is reading independently. Have your child create hand motions to go along with the text.

Tuesday	Give your child experience forming complete sentences. Fold a paper in thirds, forming three columns. In the first column, brainstorm a list of subjects (persons or animals). In the second, write a list of present-tense verbs. In the third, list several prepositional phrases. Have your child mix phrases from each column, forming sentences that make sense. **Examples:** Mother plays in the dirt. The cat scratches by the lake. Gretchen runs with the boys.	Have your child write the spelling words in sentences.	Teach location words such as *over, under, in, out, through, on, above* and *below*. Play a game of "Follow the Leader" and use the location language to describe your actions. Write a book with your child in which you describe where you went. **Example**: *We played **on** the swings; We walked **through** the woods* and *We ran **under** the branches*. Have your child illustrate each action.
Wednesday	Teach your child about past-tense verbs by asking him/her to list actions he/she performed yesterday. Point out how many of the words end in *ed*. Have your child write several present-tense verbs. Ask your child to add *ed* to each of the words, then have him/her read and use the new words in sentences.	Have your child spell each word aloud, using a different silly voice each time. Have your child complete **Cracker Crunchers** (p. 199).	Discuss words that imitate sounds—*onomatopoeia*. Copy the onomatopoeia from the book *We're Going on a Bear Hunt*. Have your child read the words with expression. Brainstorm other words that imitate sounds, such as *buzz*. Read *Buzz Said the Bee* by Wendy Lewison.
Thursday	Have your child complete **Past-Tense Verbs I** (p. 197).	Have your child bend pipe cleaners to form the letters of each spelling word.	Have your child make up other obstacles that the bear hunting family must go through. Write additional pages for the book following the same pattern. **Art:** Have your child draw a picture of his/her family going on some kind of hunt. Have him/her use watercolors.
Friday	Have your child pick an activity he/she likes to do. Then, have him/her write two short stories about it—one in the present and one in the past. Have him/her underline the verbs. Make a chart with two columns: *Past-Tense Verbs* and *Present-Tense Verbs*. Have your child put each verb in the correct column. Have your child complete **Past-Tense Verbs II** (p. 198).	Give your child the final spelling test.	Discuss whether the story *We're Going on a Bear Hunt* could really have happened. Ask your child to provide supporting arguments for his/her position. *See* page 11 for a further exploration of **Fantasy and Reality**. Discuss books familiar to your your child and decide whether they are fantasy or reality.

192

Learn at Home, Grade 1

Math	Science	Social Studies
Place Value Have your child count and group into tens several sets of objects (toothpicks, washers, dried beans, Unifix cubes). When ten objects are grouped, call the group "a ten." *See* Math, Week 15, number 1 (step 1).	**Animal Habitats** Brainstorm with your child a list of animals. Write each animal name on an index card. Allow your child to sort the animals into groups. Have your child explain his/her sorting rule, then sort them into different groups.	Read poetry from other countries. Here are some to get you started: "The Train to Glasgow" by Wilma Horsburgh in *Once Upon a Rhyme.* "London Rain" by Nancy Byrd Turner in *All the Silver Pennies.* "Kangaroo and Kiwi" in *To the Moon and Back* compiled by Nancy Larrick.
Using Monday's procedure, ask your child to count to 15, then 22. If he/she seems confident, move on to Step 2. Have your child count and group into tens several sets of objects and match them to written numerals. *See* Math, Week 15, number 2.	Discuss different environments in which animals may live, such as woodland, grassland, jungle, rainforest, desert, pond, ocean, backyard, farm and arctic. You can find this information in an encyclopedia or other books about animals. Over the next ten days, have your child make one page per day of an animal habitat book. *See* Science, Week 15, number 1.	Have your child write a four-line poem about a specific country's weather.
See Math, Week 15, number 2. Place the blue 2 card over the tens column and the white 3 over the ones column. Have your child "build" the number with manipulatives. Repeat with a different set of numbers. If your child is confident, move on to Step 3. Have your child count and group into tens several sets of objects. Then, have your child write the numerals in order on lined paper. *See* Math, Week 15, number 3.	Have your child draw and label animals living in a grassland community for his/her habitat book. **Physical Activity:** Name an animal. Have your child move like that animal moves.	Recite "Pussy Cat, Pussy Cat, Where Have You Been?" Then, have your child say the response lines. Help your child rewrite the poem to go with a selected country.
Have your child roll two dice. The number on one die tells your child what number to "build" in the ones place. Have him/her then "build" the number of tens rolled on the other die. He/she should read the resulting number from the place-value board, then count the manipulatives by ones. Have your child complete **Table Time** (p. 200).	Have your child draw and label animals living in a jungle for his/her habitat book. **Art:** Make an accordion animal. *See* Science, Week 15, number 2.	Teach some songs from or about foreign countries. Songbooks include *A Fiesta of Folk Songs from Spain and Latin America* edited by Henrietta Yurchenko and *Lullabies from Around the World,* edited by Lynn Knudson. Then, teach "Frere Jacques" in English and French.
Reinforce place value using the activities described in Math, Week 15, numbers 4–6. Have your child complete **Place Value** (p. 201).	Have your child draw and label animals living in a rainforest for his/her habitat book.	Make finger puppets out of felt. Sew the pieces together close to the edge, leaving an opening at the bottom. Have your child cut out or draw eyes, hair and a mouth from fabric scraps and glue them into place. Help your child decorate the puppet to reflect the native dress of the country it represents. Have the puppet "tell" facts about the country.

Learn at Home, Grade 1

TEACHING SUGGESTIONS AND ACTIVITIES

Math (Place Value)

BACKGROUND

When your child understands that the number 36 means 3 tens 6 ones, he/she is working with the concept of place value. To understand place value, your child must learn to see a group of ten objects as "one ten," a unit. This is a difficult concept that is built up with hands-on experience grouping a variety of manipulatives and repeated counting of objects by ones as well as by tens and ones. To make a place-value board, fold an 12" x 18" sheet of paper in half lengthwise and label it as shown below. Have your child color the tens side with a blue crayon.

▶ 1. **Step 1:** Provide about 25 toothpicks, straws or craft sticks. As your child counts them aloud, have him/her place them on the ones side of the place-value board. Have your child count them again, but this time when he/she counts 10, have him/her wrap all 10 in a rubber band and put them on the tens side. Say, *There's a ten.* Then, ask: *How many are in that bundle?* (10) Have your child continue until he/she gets another ten. He/she should bundle this ten as well and put it on the tens side. Ask: *How many tens are there now?* (2) Have your child finish counting. He/she should put the five single sticks on the ones side of the board. Ask your child: *How many are there?* Have your child count along with you: *One ten, two tens. . . two tens and five.* Write *25* as you say, *Two tens, five ones, 25.* Repeat the above activity with varying amounts and different objects. When using small manipulatives, such as washers, dried beans or cereal, place ten in a small souffle cup and call it "a ten." It is important to do this several times before moving to the next step.

TENS	ONES

▶ 2. **Step 2:** Make two sets of cards 0–9. Write one set on white card stock, the other on blue card stock. Repeat Step 1, but while counting, place the matching white cards above the ones place of the place-value board. Place the blue zero above the tens place. When your child reaches 10, ask: *How many are in the ones place?* (10) Have your child put the white zero card above the ones place. Ask how many bundles of ten there are. Place the blue one card above the tens place. (If your child doesn't put a bundle in the tens column, you will have to guide him/her into bundling ten ones into one ten.) Continue counting and placing the number cards. Repeat with a variety of manipulatives.

▶ 3. **Step 3:** Repeat Step 2. Each time your child places a toothpick (or other object), he/she should also write the number. It is helpful to draw a vertical line on the lined recording paper. Have your child write the number of tens to the left of the vertical line and the ones to the right (see illustration at right).

tens	ones
0	0
0	1
0	2
0	3
0	4
0	5
0	6
0	7
0	8
0	9
1	0

▶ 4. Say a number between 0 and 19. Have your child make the number with Unifix cubes on the place-value board. When your child reaches ten cubes, have him/her snap them together to form "one ten."

▶ 5. Arrange a number between 1 and 19 with paper clips on the place-value board. Have your child count and write how many paper clips are in your arrangement.

▶ 6. Repeat Step 3 above with one exception: each time, have your child add two toothpicks instead of one. The record sheet will reflect that by counting by 2's. For a challenge, have your child count by 3's, 4's or 5's.

Learn at Home, Grade 1

Science (Animal Habitats)

▶ 1. This week, have your child use a sheet of 9" x 12" paper to draw pictures of animals in different habitats. Provide several books for your child's reference. Start with woodland animals. Have your child draw and color animals that live in a woodland community and label the page *Woodland Animals.* When your child finishes, write each animal's name with a felt-tip black pen. Staple the pages from each habitat into your child's book.

▶ 2. **Art:** Give your child a strip of white 6" x 18" paper. Teach your child to fold the paper like an accordion. Have your child make an animal's head and back end out of construction paper and glue them to either end of the accordion.

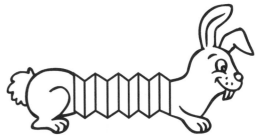

195

Present-Tense Verbs

Week 15

A **present-tense verb** tells about action that is happening **now**.
Example: Dad **works**. The children **help**.

Write a verb that tells about what is happening now to complete each sentence.

raked	weeded	planted
watered	mowed	picked

1. The kids _____.

2. Dave _____.

3. Suzie _____.

4. Troy _____.

5. Mother _____.

6. Jane _____.

Learn at Home, Grade 1

Past-Tense Verbs I

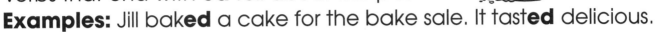

Some verbs tell what happened in the **past**.
Verbs that end with **ed** tell about the past.
Examples: Jill bak**ed** a cake for the bake sale. It tast**ed** delicious.

Write the verb that tells what happened in the past. **Write** it in the blank. _____

1. First, Jill _____ the flour.
   (measured, measures)

2. She _____ some baking powder and salt.
   (adds, added)

3. Next, she_____ the sugar and the butter.
   (mixed, mixes)

4. She_____ an egg into the bowl.
   (cracked, cracks)

5. She_____ in a little milk and vanilla.
   (pours, poured)

6. Jill _____ the batter into a cake pan.
   (spooned, spoons)

7. She_____ it for 35 minutes.
   (bakes, baked)

Past-Tense Verbs II

A **past-tense verb** tells about action that has already happened.
Add **ed** to most verbs to show the past tense.
Example: We paint**ed** in art class yesterday. I finish**ed** my picture on time.

Write the past tense of the verb in the blank.

1. Ms. Lewis _____ out the paper.
   (passes, passed)

2. I _____ my name.
   (printed, print)

3. We _____ to the directions.
   (listen, listened)

4. We _____ water to the paint.
   (added, add)

5. I _____ yellow and blue.
   (mixed, mix)

6. I _____ a stem.
   (painted, paint)

7. I _____ my brush.
   (clean, cleaned)

Learn at Home, Grade 1

Cracker Crunchers

Look at each clue. **Write** the correct spelling word.
It begins like...

_ _

_ _

_ _

Circle the spelling words that are not spelled correctly. Then,
write them correctly on the lines.

1. Look both ways before you kros the
   street.

   _ _ _ _ _ _ _ _ _ _ _ _ _ _ _ _ _

2. My sister is in the first jraid.

   _ _ _ _ _ _ _ _ _ _ _ _ _ _ _ _ _

3. A butterfly landed on the blade
   of graz.

   _ _ _ _ _ _ _ _ _ _ _ _ _ _ _ _ _

4. A little froj jumped into the pond.

   _ _ _ _ _ _ _ _ _ _ _ _ _ _ _ _ _

5. They rode the little chrain around
   the zoo.

   _ _ _ _ _ _ _ _ _ _ _ _ _ _ _ _ _

6. Gus won the grand prise in the
   spelling contest.

   _ _ _ _ _ _ _ _ _ _ _ _ _ _ _ _ _

Table Time

Use a place-value board to build each number. **Write** the numbers in the tables.

tens	ones

34

tens	ones

19

tens	ones

27

tens	ones

42

tens	ones

50

tens	ones

65

tens	ones

4

tens	ones

23

Learn at Home, Grade 1

Place Value

Write the value of each number below.

35 _____ tens _____ ones

19 _____ tens _____ ones

8 _____ tens _____ ones

26 _____ tens _____ ones

49 _____ tens _____ ones

10 _____ tens _____ ones

Write the number below.

4 tens 6 ones _____   3 tens 2 ones _____

2 tens 9 ones _____   4 tens 0 ones _____

1 ten 4 ones _____   0 tens 6 ones _____

2 tens 1 one _____   4 tens 7 ones _____

3 tens 3 ones _____   1 ten 1 one _____

	Language Skills	**Spelling**	**Reading**
Monday	**Irregular Verbs** Review regular verbs and introduce irregular verbs. *See* Language Skills, Week 16, number 1.	Pretest your child on these spelling words: 　　plus　　　place 　　plane　　float 　　flat　　　clap 　　fly　　　　glide Review the phonics skill of *l* blends.	**Contractions** Introduce contractions to your child. It is helpful to think of contractions as shortcuts in speaking and writing some words. *See* Reading, Week 16, number 1. Read *Heckedy Peg* by Audrey Wood aloud to your child. Ask questions to assess your child's comprehension. *See* page 8 for a further exploration of **Comprehension.**
Tuesday	Play a matching game. Write past- and present-tense verbs on individual index cards. Use regular and irregular verbs. Your child can mix and match cards or play a game of "Memory."	Have your child write the spelling words in sentences.	Have your child look through *Heckedy Peg* for contractions. Help your child read each contraction and determine the words which make it up. Write the contractions and the two words each is made from on a reference chart. Encourage your child to add to the list during the study of contractions.
Wednesday	**Game/Physical Activity:** Play a game that tests your child's mastery of present- and past-tense verbs. *See* Language Skills, Week 16, number 2.	Have your child spell each word aloud and act out the meaning. Have your child complete **Fluffy Flapjacks** (p. 207).	Make a set of matching contraction cards. Play a memory game with your child in which he/she tries to find pairs made up of a contraction and the two words from which it was made. Scramble and turn over all the cards. Arrange them in rows and columns. Have your child turn over any two cards on each turn. If the cards match, your child keeps the cards and takes another turn. If they do not match, both cards are turned over and the next player selects two cards.
Thursday	Make two columns titled *Present* and *Past.* Write a list of present-tense verbs, skipping a line between each word. Make a list of past-tense verbs, starting on the second line and skipping lines. Your child should write the missing tense of each verb and underline the irregular verbs. **PRESENT　　　PAST** 　guess 　　　　　　　went 　　　　　　　found	Using his/her finger as a pencil, have your child write each of his/her spelling words on a textured surface. Possible surfaces include sandpaper, a tablecloth, flour or sand in a baking pan, or a computer mouse pad.	**Center:** Use **Neighborly Words** (p. 208) to create a center activity or interactive bulletin board. Have your child practice writing contractions on lined paper.
Friday	Have your child complete **Irregular Verbs** (p. 206).	Give your child the final spelling test.	Discuss the children's behavior in *Heckedy Peg*. Have your child evaluate their behavior and suggest a way they could have handled the witch better from the start. **Art:** Give your child an old hat to decorate. Provide plenty of art supplies. Tell your child to be creative while designing a hat for Heckedy Peg or one of the children in *Heckedy Peg*.

Learn at Home, Grade 1

Math	Science	Social Studies
Draw a simple place-value board on drawing paper. Pick a number between 11 and 39 for your child to model in groups of tens and ones by drawing that number of objects on the place-value board. Objects that are simple to draw in groups include marbles, beads, cookies and pencils.	Help your child describe attributes common to birds. *See* Science, Week 16, number 1. Have your child draw and label animals living in a desert for his/her habitat book.	**Field Trip:** Arrange to visit a nearby ethnic neighborhood. Eat a meal in a restaurant, visit a church and meet and talk with some of the people. Notice the homes, dress of the people, the stores and foods for sale. Look at street names to see if they reflect the ethnicity of the area.
Fold drawing paper into fourths and write a 2-digit number in each fourth. Have your child draw a picture modeling that number using groups of ten. *See* Math, Week 16, numbers 1 and 2.	Go on a bird walk. Take bird identification books and **My Bird List** (p. 209) with you. When a bird is spotted, help your child look it up in the bird book. Fill in information about it on the activity sheet. Have your child draw and label animals living in a pond for his/her habitat book.	Teach your child that America is a mixture of cultures. Discuss yesterday's trip. Discuss how many of America's families originally came from other countries. Arrange to have your child talk to friends and neighbors about their family's origin. Ask if their family still carries on any of the old country's traditions. Show your child pictures of the Statue of Liberty and discuss: *What does the statue symbolize to many people?*
In each of several jars, place between 15 and 99 objects. Place blocks in one jar, paper clips, cotton balls, dried lima beans, spare keys and so on in other jars. Have your child estimate the number of objects before counting them on the place-value board and grouping tens in paper cups. On lined paper, have your child name the object and record both his/her estimate and the actual number of objects counted.	Examine the bills of a variety of birds. *See* Science, Week 16, number 2. Have your child draw and label animals living in an ocean for his/her habitat book.	Obtain pictures of famous buildings and monuments around the world, such as the Eiffel Tower, Buckingham Palace, St. Basil's Cathedral and the Sphinx. Display the pictures on the map. Have your child draw each and write a sentence about it. **Variation:** Explore famous art pieces from around the world.
Have your child study patterns on the **Hundred Chart** (p. 31). Point out that the tens change place as you scan down the chart. The ones increase as you scan across the chart. *See* Math, Week 16, number 3. Have your child circle any patterns he/she notices on the **Hundred Chart.**	Have your child observe fish in a fish tank and compare them to illustrations in books or the encyclopedia. Point out the gills, fins and scales and discuss the function of each. If possible, visit a pet store. Have your child draw and label animals living in an arctic environment for his/her habitat book.	Look in newspapers and magazines for articles and/or pictures of things happening around the world. Cut them out, discuss them and put them on the world map. Repeat this activity daily for several days.
Provide your child manipulatives to use to count to 100. *See* Math, Week 16, number 4.	Check out reptile books from the library, and help your child look up reptiles in the encyclopedia. He/she should use the information to answer the questions on **I Slither and Crawl** (p. 210). Have your child complete **A Reptile Riddle** (p. 211).	**Music/Physical Activity:** Check out recorded music or videos of folk dances from other nations from the library. Encourage your child to dance along with the tape or video.

TEACHING SUGGESTIONS AND ACTIVITIES

Language Skills (Irregular Verbs)

▶ 1. The verbs studied last week are called regular verbs because the past tense is formed by adding *ed*. The past tense of irregular verbs usually looks different from the present tense and is different in spelling.

Examples:	sing	*sang*	say	*said*
	hide	*hid*	go	*went*
	is	*was*	hold	*held*
	catch	*caught*	drink	*drank*

▶ 2. **Game/Physical Activity:** Have your child stand in the middle of a large room facing one wall. Read one word at a time from yesterday's cards. When your child repeats the word, he/she should take one of the following actions: If the word is in the present tense, he/should take two steps or jumps forward. If the word is in the past tense, he/she should take a giant step backward. Play stops when your child reaches the wall he/she is facing. If your child's action is incorrect, he/she must return to his/her position at the beginning of that turn.

Reading (Contractions)

▶ 1. Write a pair of words (see below). Have your child read the pair and name the contraction formed by them. Write the contraction next to the pair on your child's paper. Repeat with several other pairs.

Examples:	is not	are not	do not	did not
	I will	I am	I have	I would
	has not	was not	should not	will not
	they are	we are	you are	that is
	what is	who is	there is	have not
	it is	would not	she would	does not
	he is	could not	let us	had not

Math (Place Value)

▶ 1. Prior to this activity, prepare nine bundles of ten toothpicks. Put them in a small box along with ten single sticks. Have your child set up a number such as 19 on the place-value board. Discuss the meaning of nineteen. Have your child count the toothpicks by ones. Then, have your child add one stick. Ask how many sticks there are now. Discuss what "twenty" means. Have your child count by ones again. If your child hasn't already done it, have him/her exchange the ten single sticks for a bundle of ten and put the bundle in the tens column. Ask your child to explain why this shows twenty. Repeat, calling out random numbers for your child to build, then count on one or two numbers.

▶ 2. Go for a number walk. Look for numbers on signs and have your child tell you how many tens and ones each one represents.

▶ 3. Study a hundred chart with your child. Point to the numbers 1, 11, 21, 31 and 41. Ask your child to describe how the numbers are related. **Example:** The tens place increases in counting order while the ones place stays the same. Give your child small cards with the numbers 1–30. Have him/her use the cards to form a grid with fewer than ten across. Then, discuss with your child any patterns he/she sees.

▶ 4. Encourage your child to count to 100 using manipulatives. Have your child record each number as he/she places the manipulatives on the place-value board.

Science (Animals)

▶ 1. Draw a picture of a bird on a sheet of drawing paper. Help your child label its wings, feet, bill, feathers and tail. Discuss the function of each part. Show pictures of a variety of birds. Ask your child to think about why birds have different-shaped bills, long and short legs and come in widely varying colors.

▶ 2. While looking at pictures of birds in books and in the encyclopedia, have your child draw three very different bills in a chart similar to the one below. Ask your child to imagine the function of each of the bills he/she drew. Provide samples of the types of foods birds eat, such as seeds, insects, flower nectar and meat (small animals). Ask your child to guess which bill seems adapted to eat each food. Use a bird guide to verify your child's predictions. Fill in the type of food the bird eats under the picture of the bill on the chart. Provide samples of the types of tools the bills resemble, such as the claw end of a hammer, a straw and pliers, etc. Write the name of the tool under the appropriate bird's bill on the chart.

Shape			
Food			
Tool			

A verb that does not show past-tense by adding **ed** is called an **irregular verb**.

Example: run, **ran**   dig, **dug**   ride, **rode**   come, **came**

Draw a line to match each present-tense verb with the past-tense verb.

1. go   sat   4. take   took

2. sit   slept   5. say   made

3. sleep   went   6. make   said

Write the past tense of the irregular verb in each blank.

1. Kara _____ to Margo's to sleep overnight.
         (goes, went)

2. She _____ some games with her.
        (took, takes)

3. Margo's mom _____ pizza.
                (made, makes)

4. They _____ late.
         (slept, sleep)

5. Kara _____ she had a great time.
        (says, said)

Learn at Home, Grade 1

Fluffy Flapjacks

plus   float   fly   plane   place   glide   flat   clap

Unscramble the letters on each flapjack below. **Write** the spelling words correctly in the boxes.

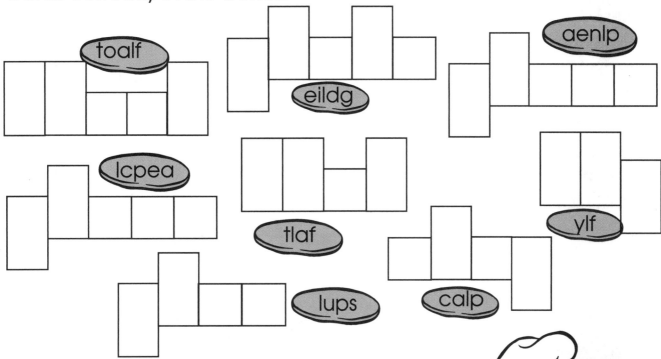

toalf

eildg

aenlp

lcpea

tlaf

ylf

lups

calp

Write the missing spelling words on the lines.

1. Two ___ ___ ___ ___ two will equal four.

2. A toy boat will ___ ___ ___ ___ ___ in the pond.

3. Glen's bike has a ___ ___ ___ ___ tire.

4. The little bird cannot ___ ___ ___ yet.

5. Our new sled will ___ ___ ___ ___ ___ down the hill.

6. They waited for the ___ ___ ___ ___ ___ to land.

7. We can ___ ___ ___ ___ along while they sing the song.

8. This is the best ___ ___ ___ ___ ___ to eat tacos.

Neighborly Words

Use the pattern below to make houses from construction paper.

1. **Cut out** the house pattern below.
2. **Fold** on the dotted lines.
3. On each outside flap, **write** two words that make a contraction. (**Example:** is not = isn't.)
4. Then, open the flaps and **write** the matching contraction inside.

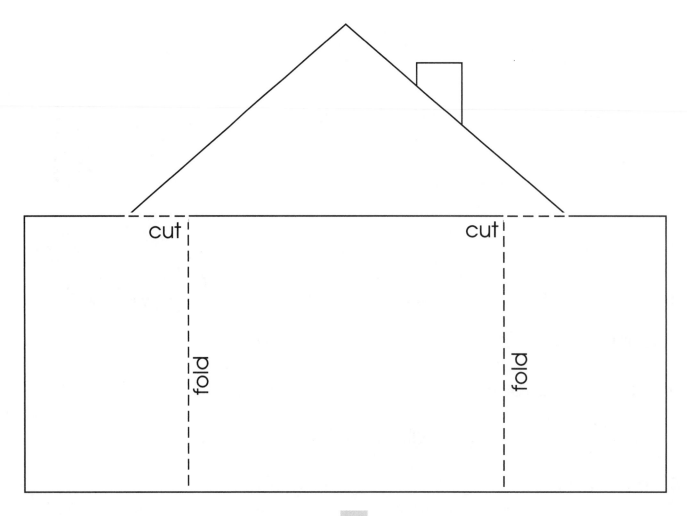

208

Learn at Home, Grade 1

My Bird List

Bird watchers keep a list of all the different kinds of birds they have seen. They also keep track of the date and location. Keep a list of your own using the chart below.

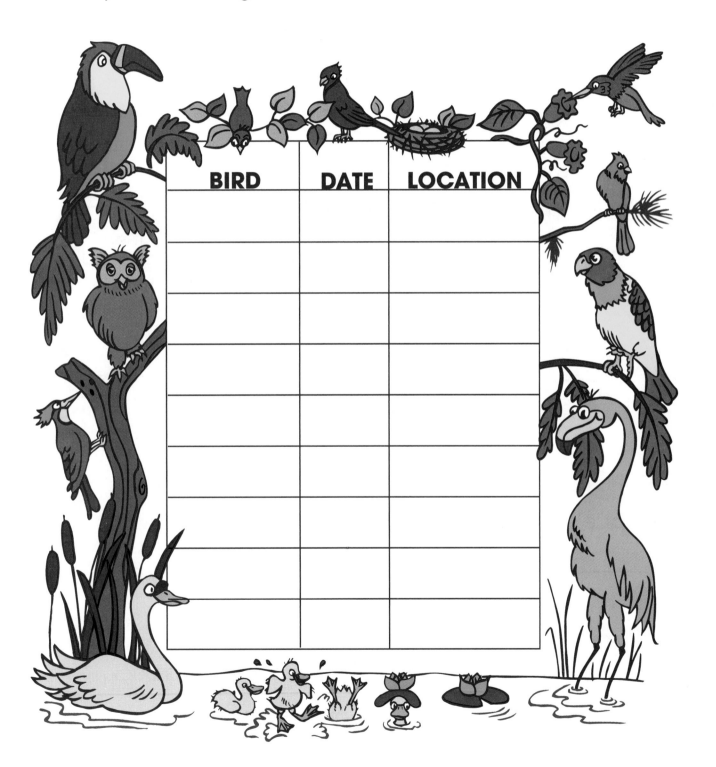

BIRD	DATE	LOCATION

209

I Slither and Crawl

Do the puzzle about reptiles. **Color** only the reptiles.

eggs   cold   scales   snake   turtle

Across

2. A reptile's skin has _____ .

5. A _____ is a reptile with no legs.

Down

1. A_____ is a reptile with a hard shell on its back.

3. Reptiles are _____ -blooded animals.

4. Baby reptiles hatch from_____.

Learn at Home, Grade 1

A Reptile Riddle

Circle the animal that does not belong in the group. **Write** the letters beside the circled words in the spaces below to find the answer to the riddle.

Birds
1. L robin
   N bluebird
   I cow
   J crow

Insects
2. L snake
   A ladybug
   N wasp
   T bee

Dog
3. B collie
   I beagle
   S shepherd
   L ox

Reptiles
4. R snake
   I horse
   G turtle
   W alligator

Farm Animals
5. G tigers
   K pig
   O cow
   Y hen

Jungle Animals
6. J lion
   B cheetah
   U tiger
   A rat

Zoo Animals
7. M bear
   O giraffe
   T dog
   F zebra

Ocean Animals
8. H octopus
   T whale
   K shark
   O camel

Fish
9. R raccoon
   I perch
   V catfish
   L tuna

Riddle:
What do you call a sick crocodile?

An . . .

_____ _____ _____ _____ _____ _____ _____ _____ _____
  1   2   3   4   5   6   7   8   9

211

	Language Skills	**Spelling**	**Reading**
Monday	**Linking and Helping Verbs** The verbs *is* and *are* are not like other verbs because they do not express an action. Both are present-tense and are used to link two like things or a noun and an adjective. Use *is* with one person, place or thing and *are* with more than one. **Examples:** *My pet is a poodle.* *The rocks are heavy. The dog is friendly.* *The carrots are orange.*	Pretest your child on these spelling words: <table><tr><td>ant</td><td>land</td></tr><tr><td>cost</td><td>milk</td></tr><tr><td>desk</td><td>wasp</td></tr><tr><td>left</td><td>pest</td></tr></table>Call your child's attention to the double consonant at the end of each word.	Write ten sentences, each containing two words that can be changed to a contraction. **Example:** *Jane did not come to the party.* Have your child circle the two words (did not) and rewrite the sentence, replacing the two words with a contraction. *See* Reading, Week 17, numbers 1 and 2. **Spelling:** Include some contractions on your child's spelling list.
Tuesday	In the past tense, *was* and *were* are used just as *is* and *are*. Use *was* with singular subjects and *were* with plural subjects. **Examples:** *They were friends. The play was funny. Football was my favorite sport. My cousins were baseball champs. See* Language Skills, Week 17, number 1.	Have your child write the spelling words in sentences.	Read *The Very Hungry Caterpillar* by Eric Carle. Then, have your child sequence the story following the life cycle of a butterfly.
Wednesday	The verbs *is, are, was* and *were* also act as helping verbs. A helping verbs helps an action verb express a clearer meaning. **Examples:** *Saul is going to the party.* *Sally and Dick are shaking hands.* *The dogs were walking in the park.* Write sentences for your child to fill in the missing helping verbs.	Have your child complete **Seeing Double** (p. 216).	**Art:** Have your child use paints to create a large butterfly. Then, have him/her write a description of the butterfly.
Thursday	Have your child write a paragraph describing a magazine or book picture. Then, have him/her underline any linking or helping verbs used in the paragraph.	Have your child make a patty out of modeling clay. Using a clay tool, have him/her write each spelling word in the clay. He/she should use his/her finger to smooth the surface and erase the writing between each word.	Teach your child about cause and effect. Think of some cause-and-effect relationships in the story and ask questions that help your child identify them. **Examples:** What caused the caterpillar to eat the apple? What was the effect of eating all week? *See* page 10 for a further exploration of **Cause and Effect.**
Friday	Write several sentences, omitting the words *is, are, was* and *were* in each one. Have your child fill in the missing verb. **Sample sentences:** *The boy ___ sitting now.* *Last night, my cat ___ stuck in a tree.* *We ___ going to the zoo today, but it started to rain.* *After dinner, the sky ___ dark.*	Give your child the final spelling test.	Have your child reread *The Very Hungry Caterpillar*. Then, have him/her create his/her own book called *The Very Hungry _____ (your child's name)*, modeled after Carle's story.

Learn at Home, Grade 1

Math	**Science**	**Social Studies**
Place Value and 2-Digit Addition (No Regrouping) Using blocks, place 4 tens and 6 ones on a place-value board for your child to identify. If your child says *46* without counting by ones, he/she may be ready for 2-digit addition. Have your child build 32 with toothpicks or other manipulatives, then roll a die to determine the number of toothpicks to add. Then, have him/her add and count.	Have your child draw and label farm animals for his/her habitat book. He/she should then make a cover and staple the pages inside.	Over the next three days, write a story about taking a trip around the world. Details should be based upon what your child has learned. *See* Tuesday and Wednesday of this week for more details.

Have your child build the number 23 with Unifix cubes or other manipulatives. After recording *23* on lined paper, have your child roll a die to determine the number of toothpicks to add. He/she should write that number below 23, then add and count the cubes.
 Example:
 $$\begin{array}{r} 2\,3 \\ +\ 4 \\ \hline 2\,7 \end{array}$$
 See Math, Week 17, numbers 1 and 2.
	Teach your child the characteristics of amphibians. *See* Science, Week 17, number 1. Have your child finish the sentence beginning, *If I were an amphibian, I would....*
	 Have your child complete **I'm Slippery and Cold** (p. 218).
		Encourage your child to use this outline in telling the story:
		 I. Getting ready
		 II. Types of transportation
		 III. Countries visited
		    A. Arrival
		    B. Sights
		    C. People
		    D. Special experiences (food, dance)
		    E. Departure
		 IV. Home

Write a 2-digit addition problem that does not require regrouping. Have your child build each number with toothpicks, then combine all the ones at the bottom of the ones column. Have him/her record the total. Then, he/she should combine all the tens at the bottom of the tens column and record the total. Repeat with different numbers. *See* Math, Week 17, number 3.	Teach your child the characteristics of mammals. Mammals are warm-blooded, covered with fur or hair and are born alive. Mammals breathe with lungs, and they drink their mother's milk. *See* Science, Week 17, number 2. Have your child complete **From Mice to Whales** (p. 219).	Have your child illustrate his/her story and make it into a book.
Make a page of 2-digit addition problems that do not require regrouping. Have your child use cereal or other small manipulatives to solve the problems. *See* Math, Week 17, number 4.	**Cooking:** Make some animal treats. *See* Science, Week 17, number 3.	Obtain *The Usborne 'Round the World Cookbook* by Caroline Young. Read recipes for traditional foreign dishes and plan a menu with your child for a meal. Make a shopping list for the necessary ingredients. Go to the store with your child to purchase them. Decorate your dining area.
Provide your child with practice adding ten. Have your child build any 2-digit number with cubes. Direct your child to add a stack of ten cubes and state the total out loud. Have him/her add additional stacks and continue counting by tens. Repeat, starting with a different 2-digit number. Then, have your child compare his/her results to a hundred chart. Have your child complete **Picture This** (p. 217).	Invite a friend over to enjoy your child's animal treats and have your child share his/her completed book with his/her friend.	Prepare the meal with your child and serve it for lunch or dinner. Measuring for the recipe and timing make this a valuable math lesson as well.

TEACHING SUGGESTIONS AND ACTIVITIES

Language Skills (Linking and Helping Verbs)

▶ 1. Make four cards for your child with the words *is, are, was* and *were* written on them. Write ten sentences with the linking verb missing. Read each sentence with your child. Have your child choose the card (verb) that fits the sentence. Then, have him/her read the complete sentence.

Reading (Contractions)

▶ 1. Write five sentences that contain contractions. In each sentence, replace the contraction with a blank space. Write the missing contractions, out of order, along the bottom of the page. Have your child read the sentences and write the correct contraction in each space.

▶ 2. **Game:** Play a game like "Bingo" with contractions. To prepare for the game, write a contraction in each of the 25 boxes of a five-by-five grid. Write the two words that make up each contraction on individual index cards. To play the game, choose one card and state the two words. Have your child place a block or bingo chip on the box containing the matching contraction. Continue play until your child covers five boxes in a row, column or diagonal.

Math (Place Value and 2-Digit Addition, No Regrouping)

BACKGROUND
Your child must have a good understanding of the structure of 2-digit numbers before addition of such numbers will make sense. Work another week with your child on the concept of place-value rather than take him/her into addition of these numbers too soon. The goal of these activities is to provide your child with concrete experience that will give him/her a foundation on which to build more complex mathematical skills.

▶ 1. Have your child use available manipulatives (toothpicks or Unifix cubes) to build a number you write on the board.

▶ 2. Repeat number 1 above but build the numbers in pairs. Make sure there is no regrouping involved and that the total will not exceed 49. Write the first number on the chalkboard. Instruct your child to build the number using manipulatives. Write the second number under the first number on the chalkboard, and have your child build the number just under the first number. Have your child count how many ones he/she has in all. Then, ask how many tens there are in all. Lead your child to understand that the two numbers are being added. As your child comes to this realization, draw a line under the two numbers, put a plus sign to the left of the bottom number and write the total below. Review with your child what happened. Repeat this activity several times.

▶ 3. Construct two numbers using manipulatives. Build the first number on a place-value board. Draw a place-value frame on the chalkboard. Have your child write the number on the board. Be sure that your child places the numerals in their correct columns. Construct a second number and have your child write the number it represents under the first number on the board. Tell your child to draw a line under the two numbers and to make a plus sign to the left of the bottom number. Referring to the constructed numbers, ask how many ones there are. When your child responds correctly, instruct him/her to write that number in the ones column. Have your child count the number of tens and write the amount in the tens column. Ask your child which was added first, the ones or the tens. Point out that this is always true in math.

Learn at Home, Grade 1

4. Write *3 tens and 2 ones*. Under it write *+1 ten and 5 ones*. Draw a line under it. Ask your child what should be added first. Have your child add the ones and write *7 ones* under the problem in the correct place. Then, have your child add the tens and write *4 tens* under the problem in the correct place. Ask your child another name for 4 tens and 7 ones. Write *47*. Repeat this activity several times with different numbers.

Science (Animals)

1. Amphibians have a very unusual feature—they can live on land and in water. Ask if your child knows of any such animals. Show your child a book of amphibians. From the book, make a list of animals in this class. Amphibians are like reptiles and fish because they are cold-blooded and they hatch from eggs, but they don't have scales on their skin.

2. **Game:** Give your child cards with an animal listed on each. Instruct your child to group the animals and explain his/her groupings to you. Discuss how the groupings have changed since the beginning of the unit.

3. **Cooking:** Make the following edible science projects with your child:

   a. **A Ladybug Lunch**
      Ingredients: 1 apple cut in half   2 tablespoons peanut butter
                         20 seedless grapes   6 raisins
                         2 lettuce leaves   7 toothpicks

   Wash and pat dry the fruit and lettuce. Set the lettuce on a plate. Put half an apple on top of it, skin side up. Use peanut butter to stick raisins on the ladybug's back so they look like its spots. Using toothpicks, attach a grape to one end of the apple to look like its head, and attach three grapes on each side for legs.

   b. **Tasty Bird Nests**
      Ingredients: 1 bag butterscotch or chocolate chips   1 cup peanuts
                         1 5-oz. can chow mien noodles   1 bag small jellybeans

   Melt the chips over low heat in a double boiler. Stir in the noodles and peanuts. Drop the mixture by spoonfuls onto wax paper. Have your child mold the mixture into "nest" shapes. Add jelly bean "eggs" and chill for 15 minutes.

Seeing Double

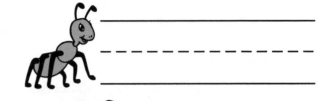

Write each spelling word next to its picture.

| ant cost desk left milk |
| land wasp pest |

_____

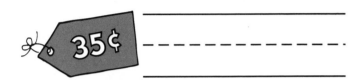
_____

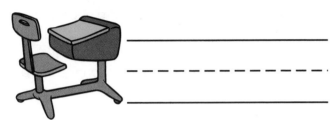
_____

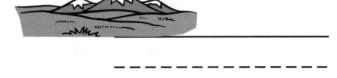
_____

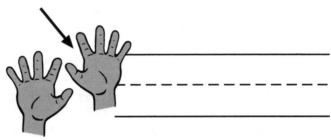
_____

Write the missing spelling words.

_____

_____.

1. How much does this toy _____ ?

_____

_____

2. My little sister sometimes acts like a _____ .

_____

_____

3. I'd like a glass of _____ with my cookies.

_____

_____

4. I was stung by a _____ .

216

Learn at Home, Grade 1

Picture This

Add the ones and then the tens in each problem. Then, **write** the sum in the blank.

Example:

```
  2 tens  and  6 ones
+ 1 ten   and  3 ones
_____
  3 tens  and  9 ones = 39
```

```
  1 ten   and  4 ones
+ 3 tens  and  3 ones
_____
      tens  and      ones = ___
```

```
  1 ten   and  6 ones
+ 2 tens  and  3 ones
_____
      tens  and      ones = ___
```

```
  1 ten   and  6 ones
+ 3 tens  and  1 one
_____
      tens  and      ones = ___
```

```
  1 ten   and  3 ones
+ 1 ten   and  1 one
_____
      tens  and      ones = ___
```

```
  2 tens  and  5 ones
+ 2 tens  and  0 ones
_____
      tens  and      ones = ___
```

```
  1 ten   and  5 ones
+ 2 tens  and  4 ones
_____
      tens  and      ones = ___
```

```
  2 tens  and  3 ones
+ 2 tens  and  2 ones
_____
      tens  and      ones = ___
```

Learn at Home, Grade 1

I'm Slippery and Cold

Do the puzzle about amphibians. **Color** only the amphibians.

land   gills   skin   eggs   cold

Across

3. Amphibian babies breathe with either lungs or _____.

5. Amphibians live in the water and on _____.

Down

1. Amphibian babies usually hatch from _____.

2. Amphibians are _____ -blooded animals.

4. Amphibians often have smooth, moist _____.

218

From Mice to Whales

Do the puzzle about mammals. **Color** only the mammals.

hair   babies   lungs   milk   warm

Across

2. A mammal's body is usually covered with _____ .

3. Mother mammals feed _____ to their babies.

5. Mammals' _____ are born alive.

Down

1. Mammals are _____ -blooded.

4. Mammals breathe with _____ .

Language Skills	**Spelling**	**Reading**
Monday **Review Week** Review sentences with your child. Write ten sentences and partial sentences on the chalkboard. Have your child circle each complete sentence. On writing paper, have your child rewrite each partial sentence as a complete sentence.	**Review Week** Review long vowels with your child. Make a list of words from Weeks 10–13 for your child to record on tape. Record your child reading a word, counting silently to ten, spelling the word slowly, then repeating the word. Have him/her repeat this procedure with each word. Have your child play the tape back and spell the word aloud in the 10-second pause.	**Review Week** Review nouns and verbs with your child. On index cards, write ten singular nouns and ten present-tense verbs. Have your child determine how to sort the words into two groups (nouns and verbs). Have your child write each word on lined paper, add an ending, then use the new word form in a written sentence. *See* Reading, Week 18, number 1.
Tuesday Review statements and questions. Write five statements and five questions on lined paper. Ask your child to turn each question into a statement and each statement into a question. Your child should include correct punctuation. Have your child complete **Review of Sentences** (p. 224).	Have your child complete **Extensions** (p. 225).	Review rhyming words. With your child, make an alphabetical string of rhymes. Think of a word that begins with *a*, add a rhyming word that begins with *b* and continue until your child is stuck. For that letter, think of a near rhyme or at least a word that shares a sound and continue a new string of rhyming words. **Example**: *air, bear, care, dare, ear, fear, gear, hear*, etc.
Wednesday Review sentence sense with your child. Write several sentences in nonsensical order, such as *The cat in the sun sleeping was.* Have your child rewrite the sentences so they make sense.	**Game:** Play the "Spelling Bee" game. *See* Spelling, Week 18, number 1.	Review compound words. Discuss how compound words and contractions are alike and different.
Thursday Review building sentences with your child. Begin with a simple sentence and have your child build the sentence with details. **Example:** *Tom bought a hat.* *Tom bought a new hat.* *Tom bought a new hat from the store.* *Tom bought a new cowboy hat from the western store.*	Review blends with your child. Play "Bingo" with spelling words from Weeks 14–17. *See* Spelling, Week 9, number 2.	Reread some of the books from the past 9 weeks. Add to the caterpillar of books your child has read. *See* Reading, Week 9, Friday. Have your child choose his/her favorite book and write a book report on it. He/she should include characters, setting, problem, solution and his/her favorite part.
Friday Review past, present and future tenses with your child. Write several sentences in the present tense. Include regular, irregular and linking verbs. Have your child rewrite each sentence in the past tense. Have your child complete the following sentences one day each week and circle the verb in each sentence: Yesterday I… Today I… Tomorrow I…	**Art:** Help your child make a blend bulletin board. *See* Spelling, Week 18, number 2.	Review location words with your child. Take or find photos of your child in, on, over, next to, behind and under different objects. Have your child glue one picture per page in a blank book and write a sentence describing where he/she is in each picture. If pictures are not available, have your child cut out magazine pictures and draw him/herself in them.

Learn at Home, Grade 1

Math	**Science**	**Social Studies**
Review Week Review graphing with your child. Make a behavior chart. Using a ruler, draw a 5 x 5 grid of half-inch boxes. Write a behavior goal at the top of the page. Along the bottom of the grid, write the days of the week. Each time the new behavior is practiced, place a sticker on the grid. *See* Math, Week 18, number 1.	**Review Week** Review seeds with your child. Have your child use the **Seed Sequencing Cards** (p. 228) to demonstrate the process of growth. Cut the cards along the solid lines and mix them up. Have your child sort the cards into the different types of plants, then arrange each set in order. Pick one set and have your child write a sentence to describe what is happening in each picture.	**Review Week** Review cardinal directions with your child. Play "Simon Says" and give directions such as *Face north* or *Walk two steps east.* Give your child a point for making a mistake and two points for moving without the words "Simon Says." The lower your child's score, the better. Tell your child that zero is a perfect score.
Game/Physical Activity: Review ordinal numbers with your child. Go on an ordinal number scavenger hunt. *See* Math, Week 18, number 2. Have your child complete **Flags First** (p. 227).	Review leaves with your child. Make several copies of **My Leaf Collection** (p. 229). Have your child complete a copy of the sheet for each leaf collected. Combine all the pages into a book titled *My Leaf Collection.*	Review the world map with your child. Have your child name as many continents as he/she can. Then, have your child point to and name the continents. Have your child complete **Scrambled Continents** (p. 231).
Review addition and subtraction with your child. Use a number line to help your child review addition and subtraction facts to 18. *See* Math, Week 18, numbers 3 and 4. Have your child review the practice activities in Weeks 12–14.	Review the parts of a plant with your child. Have your child draw a plant and label all the parts above and below the ground. Have your child complete **Tree Parts** (p. 230).	With your child, review the countries he/she has studied. Have your child read the pages he/she has collected in his/her *Around the World* folder.
Review place value with your child. Use paper cups and toothpicks to model numbers grouped in tens and ones. *See* Math, Week 18, number 5. Write a number on top of a sheet of paper. Have your child illustrate it using tens and ones. Then, have him/her write a description of what he/she did.	**Art:** Help your child make a mural of animal and plant life. Provide butcher paper and paints. Have your child paint the ground and sky first. Let that dry. Then, have him/her paint the background features of the habitats, such as trees, rocks, plants and mountains. When that is dry, have your child paint the animal life, including each category of animal he/she has studied.	Review any words in other languages your child has learned. Encourage your child to sing some songs from other lands.
Help your child build a sense of what a number means by brainstorming ways to "say" a 2-digit number. For example, *18* can be 16 + 2: 1 ten, 8 ones; the age at which you can vote: 20 – 2, 12 + 6, 100 – 82, etc. *See* Math, Week 18, numbers 6 and 7. The more guided practice you give, the more creative and challenging your child's responses will become.	Let your child complete yesterday's mural and add any labels he/she wants.	Have your child dress in the clothes of his/her favorite country and tell why it is his/her favorite. Have your child design a travel brochure for that country.

TEACHING SUGGESTIONS AND ACTIVITIES

Spelling

▶ 1. **Game:** Have your child color and cut out the parts of the **Spelling Bee** on page 226. Glue the body to the center of a sheet of drawing paper. Read one spelling word at a time to your child. Have your child spell the word aloud. When your child spells a word correctly, he/she may add a body part to the bee. When your child has spelled 14 words correctly, he/she will have a "spelling bee." Repeat this activity to review other words.

▶ 2. **Art:** From brown construction paper, cut out the shape of three tree trunks with branches. Write *r* blends on one trunk, *s* blends on another trunk and *l* blends on the third trunk. From green construction paper, cut several leaf shapes. On each leaf, write a word that begins with a blend. Sort the leaves and glue them on the tree with the correct label.

       l blends: *clown, blue, play, glue, clay, blast, slip, clock*

       r blends: *from, drag, cream, brat, grain, prone, tree, breeze, crab, free*

       s blends: *snack, stay, swim, slam, stick, smile, skin, scamper, stomp*

Reading

▶ 1. Help your child make a flip book to create silly sentences. Divide a long strip of paper into thirds. In the first section, write the word *The*. Cut sheets of paper the same size as the second and third boxes and staple the same number of sheets (four to six) to each box. In the second box, have your child write a noun on each page and in the third box, a verb. Then, have your child flip the pages to create new sentences.

The	noun	verb

Learn at Home, Grade 1

Math

▶ 1. Discuss with your child a behavior he/she would like to develop such as being on time, working neatly, being helpful or paying compliments. Write that behavior on the behavior grid. Write the days of the week at the bottom of the columns. Have your child color in a box of the grid every time the desired behavior is practiced on a given day. Review the graph at the end of the week. Notice if there has been any improvement. Reward your child's improvement with a special activity.

▶ 2. **Physical Activity/Game:** Plan a scavenger hunt using ordinal numbers in the clues. Arrange a trail of clues ahead of time. Hide a treat for the final clue. Here are some ideas for clues:

   a. *Read the fifth chapter of your book.* (Place the next clue at the end of the chapter.)

   b. *Do the fourth problem on page ___ in _____. Then, bring the problem to me.* (You will give the next clue.)

   c. *Walk up to the seventh stair. Look under the carpet.*

   d. *Bring me the second pencil from the right on the desk.*
   (Give your child the next clue.)

▶ 3. **Physical Activity/Game:** Using masking tape, make a number line to 9 on the floor. Have your child stand at zero on the number line and toss two bean bags—one toss is an addend, the other toss is the sum. If one landed on 4 and another landed on 5, your child would say the problem 4 + 1 and what it equals (5). Have your child take enough steps to get to the sum, if needed.

▶ 4. The above may be done with a number line to 18. As an alternative, have your child identify the subtrahend, minuend and difference in each problem.

▶ 5. Write some numbers from 0 to 49 on individual index cards. Give your child small drinking cups and toothpicks. Have him/her build a number from an index card using tens and ones. **Example:** 36 would be shown as three cups of ten toothpicks and six single toothpicks.

▶ 6. Write a number on the board. Ask your child to name it as many ways as possible in a minute. He/she may use addition or subtraction problems or place value (1 ten, 6 ones).

▶ 7. Help your child select any ten numbers. Write each number in large numerals in the middle of a 12" x 18" sheet of paper. On each page, your child should write ten different ways of saying the center number. Your child may decorate the page by coloring a design on it. When the ten pages are finished, your child should make a cover from a colored sheet of paper. Staple or use brads to hold the pages of the book together.

Review of Sentences

Underline the subject of the sentence in red. **Circle** the predicate in blue.

1. Most eagles are big and strong.

2. Eagles live all over the world except Antarctica.

3. These birds hunt during the day.

4. Eagles eat other animals.

5. Fish, mammals and other birds make good meals.

Write each **statement** and **question** correctly.

1. is the bald eagle really bald

_____

_____

2. its head feathers are white

_____

_____

3. it looks bald from far away

_____

_____

4. are these birds strong

_____

_____

Extensions

Read the clues. Look at the pictures. **Write** the spelling words on the lines.

If you can spell **take**, then you can spell

_____

_____

If you can spell **gave**, then you can spell

_____

_____

If you can spell **may**, then you can spell

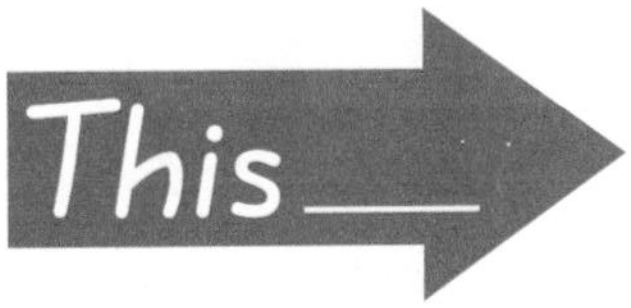

_____

_____

This _____

If you can spell **nail**, then you can spell

_____

_____

Read each sentence. **Write** the missing spelling words in the boxes.

1. That bird has a very big ___.

2. It is not nice to be ___ to anyone.

3. Pete plays on the baseball ___.

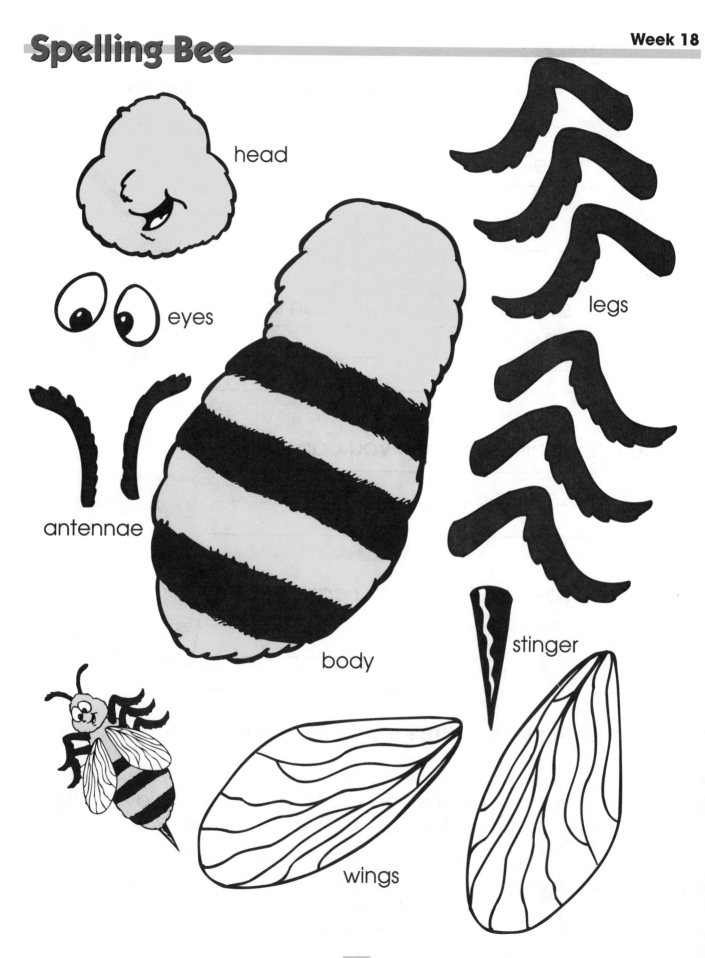

head

eyes

antennae

body

legs

stinger

wings

Learn at Home, Grade 1

Flags First

Color the **ninth** flag red.
Write **O** on the **second** flag.
Color the **eighth** flag blue.
Write **D** on the **fourth** flag.
Color the **sixth** flag yellow.
Write **G** on the **first** flag.
Color the **tenth** flag purple.
Write **O** on the **third** flag.
Color the **seventh** flag green.
Color the **fifth** flag orange.
What word did you spell? _____

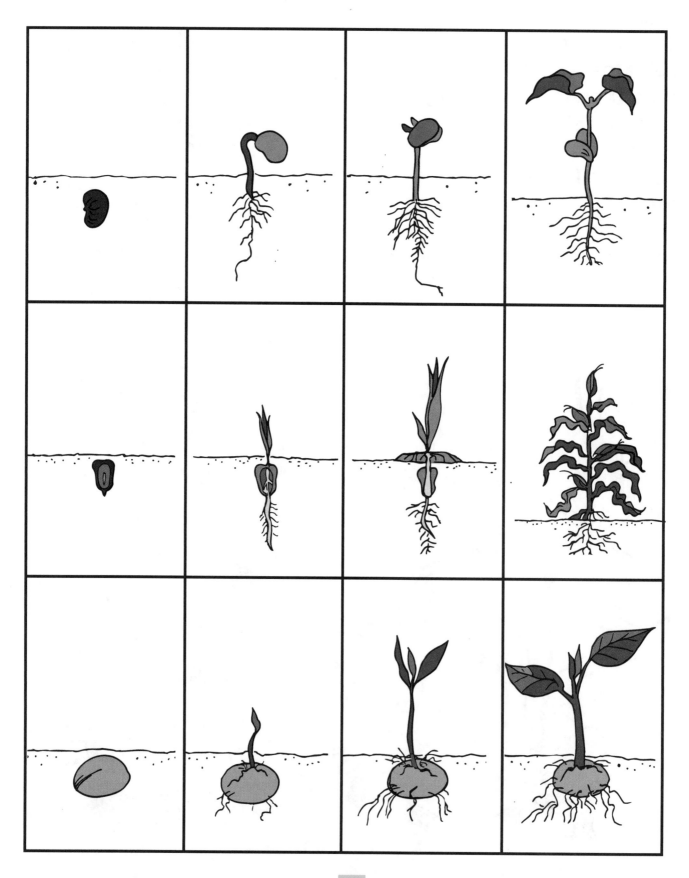

228

Learn at Home, Grade 1

My Leaf Collection

Glue a leaf on this page. **Fill** in the blanks.

Tree _____

Location _____

Date _____

Tree Parts

Trees have three main parts: the trunk, the roots and the leaves. Each part has a special job. Each part helps the tree. **Cut out** the name of each part. **Cut out** the job of each part. **Glue** them on the picture.

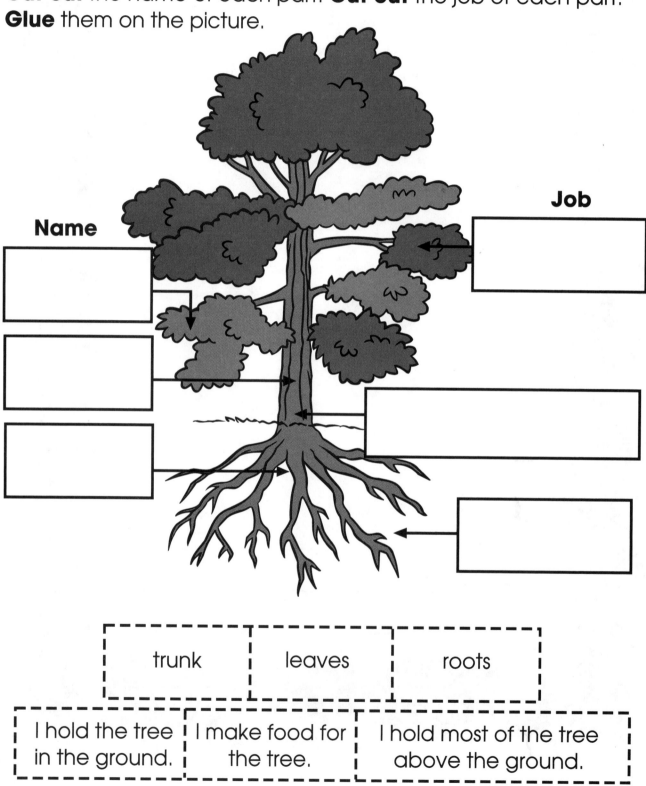

Name

Job

trunk | leaves | roots

I hold the tree in the ground. | I make food for the tree. | I hold most of the tree above the ground.

Learn at Home, Grade 1

Scrambled Continents

Unscramble the words below to spell the continents correctly.
Remember to **cross out** the letters you use. Put in **capital letters**
where they are needed. Use the word box to help you.

Africa   Australia   North America   Antarctica
Asia   Europe   South America

1. rtonh miecara _____ _____

2. cfiara _____

3. eropeu _____

4. uhots ecaamir_____ _____

5. saia _____

6. tnrtaiacac_____

7. asurilaat _____

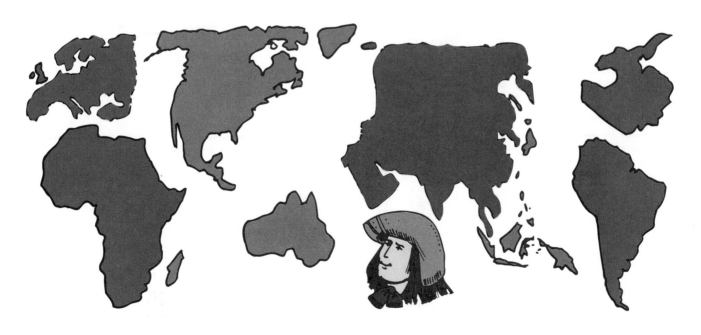

	Language Skills	Spelling	Reading
Monday	Read a variety of rhyming poetry to your child. Discuss the meaning and language of each poem. Discuss rhyming patterns such as the ABAB or ABBA pattern. Read a story written in rhyme like Ludwig Bemelman's *Madeline.* Pause before a predictable rhyming word and have your child supply it. Maintain lists of rhyming words on chart paper for reference when your child writes poems.	Pretest your child on these words: red black yellow brown blue white green pink purple orange Have your child match colors with the words.	Teach your child how to add *ing* to verbs when they have a helping verb. **Examples:** I play I am playing You play You are playing He plays He is playing Have your child apply the verbs *sleep, write* and *jump* to the following subjects and helping verbs: I am We are You are They are
Tuesday	Read a variety of poetry that does not include rhyming words. Point out to your child the use of alliteration (words beginning with the same sounds).	Have your child write the spelling words in sentences. **Art:** Mix paints in the colors on this week's spelling list. Let your child mix the colors and paint a picture.	Read *The Napping House* by Audrey Wood. Have your child list the words in the story with *ing* endings. Have your child rewrite each phrase containing an *ing* ending into a sentence with a helping verb. **Example:** *the dreaming child* becomes *The child is dreaming.*
Wednesday	Write a word to serve as a topic for a poem. Have your child give words or phrases that come to mind. Write your child's words under the topic word. Then, have your child use the words and phrases he/she has brainstormed to write and illustrate a poem.	Have your child spell each word aloud while clapping a rhythm. Have your child complete **Naturally Colorful Canvas** (p. 236).	Write ten sentences, omitting the verb. After each sentence, write the base or root form of the missing verb in parentheses. Have your child write the correct form of the verb in the blank. **Example:** The cat was _____. (sleep) *The cat was sleeping.*
Thursday	Help your child write an acrostic poem. Write a word vertically down the left side of a sheet of paper. Have your child brainstorm words beginning with each letter and write them down next to the letter. Have your child pick the words that best describe the original word. Have your child then write the poem using his/her chosen words.	Using a crayon the color of the word, have your child make block letters that spell each word. Have your child color a pattern inside the letters. **Example:** blue	Teach your child that good writers use a variety of language to make stories more interesting. *Snoozing, dozing, sleeping, slumbering* and *napping* are colorful words that mean approximately the same thing. Brainstorm with your child other groups of synonyms. Have your child write a variation on *The Napping House,* such as *The Working Farm,* including the brainstormed words.
Friday	Shape poems are written in a shape or form that describes the subject. Give your child an outline of a shape and place it under a blank sheet of typing paper. Have your child write the words of the poem in the shape of the object outline.	Give your child the final spelling test.	Have your child write five adjectives that describe *The Napping House,* five adjectives that describe the characters and five adjectives that tell how your child feels about the book.

Learn at Home, Grade 1

Math	**Science**	**Social Studies**
2-Digit Subtraction, No Regrouping Repeat some place value and 2-digit addition activities to determine if your child is ready to move on to subtraction. If your child is ready, introduce 2-digit subtraction with manipulatives and no writing. *See* Math, Week 19, number 1.	**Seasons** Have your child name and describe the seasons. Read *Frederick* by Leo Lionni and discuss the characteristics of each season.	**Taking Care of Animals** With your child, research and adopt an appropriate classroom pet. Have your child write a story about the pet. *See* Social Studies, Week 19, numbers 1 and 2.
Present subtraction problems in written form with and without manipulatives. **Example:** 3 tens 6 ones − 1 ten 4 ones Allow your child to use manipulatives, if needed. *See* Math, Week 19, number 2.	Discuss the current season with your child. What types of activities are appropriate for the season? What are the animals doing? What is happening to the plants? What kind of clothes are appropriate at this time of year? Have your child complete **The Four Seasons** (p. 237).	**Field Trip:** Arrange for a visit to a vet's office or to an animal shelter. Before the trip, have your child compose possible questions to ask. Take a camera. When the pictures are developed, glue them on a large sheet of paper. Have your child tell about each picture. Write a sentence under each one that tells about what your child saw and learned on the visit.
Present 2-digit subtraction problems using a chart like the one shown here. Do not present problems that require regrouping. Provide examples until your child is working problems confidently. On a sheet of lined or grid paper, write several subtraction problems (on tens/ones charts) for your child to do independently. Your child may choose not to use manipulatives. Tens | Ones 4 | 7 − 1 | 2	Looking at a calendar, discuss the attributes of each season as on Tuesday. *See* Science, Week 19, number 1. Cut out a circle from paper and divide it into fourths. Have your child put a season name in each section and illustrate it.	Discuss how pets rely on humans for care and the responsibility one takes with pet ownership. Read together how to care for the pet. Make a schedule of care, including when to feed, wash and exercise the pet, change its bedding and so on. *See* Social Studies, Week 19, number 3. Have your child write a thank you letter to the people he/she'd spoke with at the vet's office or animal shelter.
For guided practice, write 2-digit subtraction problems for your child to solve using manipulatives and a place-value board. *See* Math, Week 19, number 3.	Read poetry about the seasons to your child. Discuss the descriptive words and images. Read *Caps, Hats, Socks and Mittens* by Louise Borden and discuss it with your child.	Help your child make an animal dictionary. *See* Social Studies, Week 19, number 4.
Have your child build any 2-digit number with cubes. Direct your child to remove a stack of ten cubes and state the total out loud. Have your child remove additional stacks and continue counting backward by tens. Repeat, starting with a different 2-digit number. Have your child compare his/her answers to the Hundred Chart. Have your child color patterns, such as *93, 83, 73, 63, 53, 43, 33, 23* and *13* on the **Hundred Chart** (p. 31).	Help your child write poetry about the seasons or one season. *See* Science, Week 19, numbers 2 and 3 for possible frameworks.	Display several pictures of animals. Have your child decide which animals are pets. Have your child tell one thing about each animal, such as what makes it a good pet, its habits, what it eats and who has it as a pet.

◁▬▬ **TEACHING SUGGESTIONS AND ACTIVITIES** ▬▶

Math (2-Digit Subtraction, No Regrouping)

Your child is ready for 2-digit subtraction after he/she has had a great deal of hands-on practice building 2-digit numbers, understands their structure and has applied this understanding when solving 2-digit addition problems. If you feel your child is not ready for this concept, return to Week 17. Otherwise, introduce 2-digit subtraction using a place-value board and some familiar manipulatives.

▶ 1. As an introduction, have your child take away cubes without regrouping or writing. For example, have your child build the number 36 with Unifix cubes. Tell your child to take away four cubes and count the number of cubes left (32). Return the cubes. Repeat with other numbers fewer than six until your child is quick and confident. Then, have your child take away ten cubes, then twenty cubes, each time counting the cubes left. Finally, have your child take away thirteen cubes and count the remaining cubes.

$$\begin{array}{r} 36 \\ -\ 12 \\ \hline 24 \end{array}$$

▶ 2. Write *3 tens and 6 ones* on the chalkboard. Have your child build the number. Under it, write *–1 ten and 4 ones.* Draw a line under the numbers. Have your child subtract in the ones column first and write how many ones will be left. Then, have him/her subtract in the tens column. Write problems patterned like this on a sheet of paper for your child to work on independently.

▶ 3. Write the number *36* on the chalkboard. Have your child build the number on the place-value board. Under the number on the chalkboard, write *–12*. Discuss what 12 means (1 ten and 2 ones). Have your child take away the 2 ones first and then a bundle of tens from the 3 tens. Emphasize that ones are taken away before tens. Next, have your child count how many ones and bundles of ten are left. Write the answer to the problem. Repeat this activity several times, replacing 12 with another number each time.

Science (Seasons)

BACKGROUND
Seasonal changes are caused by the changing position of the Earth around the Sun. It takes the Earth a year to go around the Sun. The Earth is tilted as it travels, which causes the the Sun's rays to strike the Earth at different angles during its journey. The changes in the amount and concentration of sunlight on Earth gives us our seasons.

Fall: This season is characterized by a drop in temperature and shortening of daylight hours. Because of these two changes, many leaves change color and drop and animals prepare for winter.

Winter: Freezing temperatures occur over much of the United States. The number of daylight hours shortens and reaches its peak on the first day of winter. Most plants are inactive. Animals have different habits.

Spring: Temperatures are warmer. The number of daylight hours begins to increase. Buds appear on trees and shrubs, spring flowers bloom and grass begins to turn green.

Summer: Temperatures are at their warmest. Vegetation is at its peak. Birds and animals are busy raising their young. Daylight hours reach a maximum on the first day of summer.

▶ 1. Obtain a yearly calendar with photographs that represent the seasons. Have your child recite the months and sort the months by seasons. Look at the photos by season. Discuss activities that are popular during each season, clothes that are worn and what happens to plants and animals in each season.

Learn at Home, Grade 1

▶ 2. Have your child copy the following sentence starters and complete them for the current season.

In_____, the animals are _____.
In_____, I like to _____.
In_____, I wear _____.
In_____, the birds_____.
In_____, plants are _____.
In_____, the ground is _____.

▶ 3. Have your child follow the pattern of the book *Caps, Hats, Socks and Mittens* to write a new poem. Have him/her complete this sentence starter for each season: *Winter is* _____.

Social Studies (Taking Care of Animals)

BACKGROUND
Children of all ages love animals. However, there is more to having a pet than just loving it. Different kinds of animals have different needs. In order to provide appropriate care, an animal caretaker must be very knowledgeable about the animal, its habits and living requirements. This unit will teach your child about caring for domesticated animals in the home and on the farm, as well as build an awareness of the needs of zoo animals and animals in the wild.

Preparation: Collect pictures of all kinds of animals. Read one of the following books to your child as a prelude to the unit: *Puss in Boots*, retold and illustrated by Lorinda Bryan Cauley or *Two Dog Biscuits* by Beverly Cleary.

▶ 1. Have your child draw his/her new pet on a sheet of 9" x 12" paper.

▶ 2. Discuss names for the new pet and choose the best one. Write the pet's name on your child's picture. Have your child write a story about the new pet's arrival. Have your child write at least one story a week about the pet—its growth and learning, a funny thing it did, a trip to the vet, etc. Keep all of the stories. At the end of the unit, staple the stories in order between a front and back cover.

▶ 3. Discuss the needs of your pet. If you do not have a pet, discuss a friend's or relative's pet. Pets have some of the same needs and emotions that humans have—they eat, drink, get sick, feel loyalty or attachment, need to stay clean and get rid of waste. But there are many things pets depend on humans for. Pets need humans to open cans of food for them, brush or clean their fur (except cats), keep their areas clean and give them medicine. Discuss the care pets may require (feeding, grooming, check-ups, shots, exercising, nail clipping, flea powder, etc.). Then, specifically discuss the care of your new pet and your child's responsibilities. Make a chart listing what your child must do every day and what must be done weekly. Your child should check off duties as they are performed.

▶ 4. Help your child make an animal dictionary. Cut a front and back cover to 6" x 9". Cut thirteen sheets of writing paper the same size. Staple them inside the front and back covers. Have your child decorate the front cover with animal stickers, write *Animal Dictionary* on the front cover and label each page with a letter of the alphabet. Have your child write the names of animals and words related to animals on each dictionary page. Encourage your child to add to the dictionary throughout the unit.

Naturally Colorful Canvas

Use the code to **color** the picture.

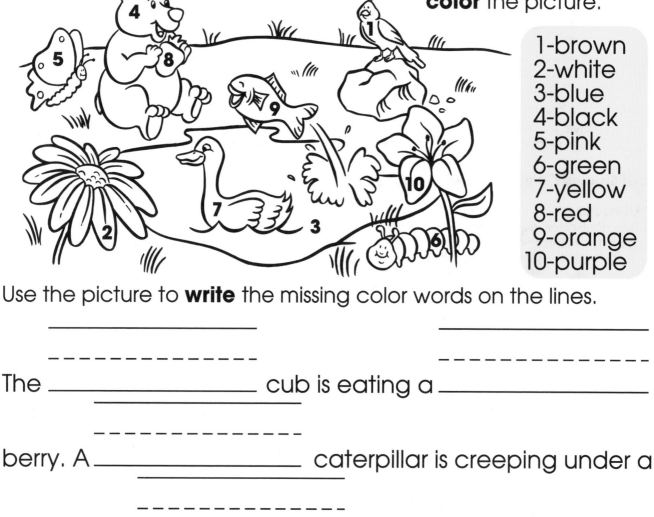

1-brown
2-white
3-blue
4-black
5-pink
6-green
7-yellow
8-red
9-orange
10-purple

Use the picture to **write** the missing color words on the lines.

_____   _____

The _____ cub is eating a _____

berry. A _____ caterpillar is creeping under a

flower. One _____ duck and one

_____ fish are swimming in the

_____ pond. A little _____

bird is resting on a rock. A _____ butterfly will

land on the _____ flower.

Learn at Home, Grade 1

The Four Seasons

Cut out and **glue** the season words in the correct boxes below.

Color the clothes for:

Fall — blue   **Winter** — red   **Spring** — green   **Summer** — yellow

| Spring | Summer | Fall | Winter |

	Language Skills	Spelling	Reading
Monday	**Poetry** As you read poetry with your child, discuss the mood and feelings created by the words of the poem. **Music:** Have your child close his/her eyes while you play different pieces of music. Ask your child to express in words how the music makes him/her feel. Write down your child's words.	Pretest your child on these words: one six two seven three eight four nine five ten Have your child match the numerals with the words.	**Possessives** Introduce the 's used to show possession. Help your child understand the difference between plural *s* and possessive *s*. Choose objects that belong to family members. Have your child write a phrase using a possessive for each object to show which objects belong to which person. Read *Mike Mulligan and His Steam Shovel* by Virginia Burton Lee.
Tuesday	Have your child write a poem about a strong feeling. **Example:** *My cat moved out.* *I felt sad as I watched the car drive away.* *I pictured him at his new home* *Playing in the woods.* *I waved though I couldn't see him.* *Curled in a blanket on the back seat,* *I know he mewed just a little for me.*	Have your child write the spelling words in sentences.	Discuss the main idea (message) of *Mike Mulligan and His Steam Shovel*. See page 8 for a further exploration of **Main Idea.** With your child, discuss the main idea of the story. Then, have your child draw a picture of Mike Mulligan and his steam shovel.
Wednesday	Read some poems of more than one verse. Look for rhyming patterns: ABBA, ABAB, etc. Have your child write a verse about a favorite toy and illustrate it.	Have your child spell each word aloud while jumping rope. Have your child complete **Now, on the Count of . . .** (p. 242).	Have your child look in books for possessives. Have your child list each pair of words that shows ownership. **Examples:** *Mike's friend, day's end, Phil's truck,* etc.
Thursday	A descriptive poem often includes the perspective of several of the senses. *See* Language Skills, Week 20 for activities to help your child develop descriptive language about the senses.	Have your child write four story problems using the number words from the spelling list. Then, have him/her underline the spelling words.	Write ten sentences for your child to rewrite using 's. **Example:** This book belongs to Jane. *This is Jane's book.*
Friday	Have your child describe a recent experience using language about all five senses. **Example:** <u>Niagara Falls</u> *The roaring water sends droplets* *Splashing on my face and hands.* *I taste the icy water,* *And smell the fishy breeze.* *I watch the double rainbow arch across* *The magnificent water.*	Give your child the final spelling test.	Have your child pick two characters in *Mike Mulligan and His Steam Shovel* and write two sentences for each, telling what he/she likes or dislikes about the character.

Learn at Home, Grade 1

Math	Science	Social Studies
Money Allow your child exploratory time with several coins. Observe how your child "plays" with the coins to determine his/her knowledge of coin identification and values. Examine the coins together using a magnifying glass. Teach the value of a penny. *See* Math Week 20, number 1.	With your child, read and discuss library books that describe what animals do in the winter. See Science, Week 20, numbers 1 and 2. Have your child complete **Animals in Winter** (p. 243).	**Farm Animals** Sing "Old MacDonald Had a Farm." After singing, have your child list farm animals on chart paper. Read farm animal poems and have your child add farm animal words to the animal dictionary. *See* Social Studies, Week 20, number 1.
Review yesterday's work with pennies. Introduce nickels and dimes. *See* Math, Week 20, numbers 2 and 3.	Help your child plan and paint a mural of the seasons. *See* Science, Week 20, number 3a.	Have your child compare animals on the farm to pets in a home. Discuss their care and the purpose for having each animal. Have your child describe the difference between raising dairy cows and cattle for beef. Talk about taking farm animals to the market. *See* Social Studies, Week 20, number 2.
Introduce and practice counting change with pennies and nickels. *See* Math, Week 20, numbers 4 and 5.	Have your child continue working on his/her mural of the seasons. *See* Science, Week 20, number 3b.	**Field Trip:** Visit the meat and dairy sections of a supermarket. Make a list of the items in each department and determine which animal each food comes from. Buy lunch food that comes primarily from farm animals.
Teach counting with pennies and dimes. *See* Math, Week 20, numbers 6 and 7.	Have your child complete his/her mural of the seasons. *See* Science, Week 20, number 3c.	**Field Trip:** Visit a farm. Notice what kind of farm it is. What animals are raised? How do the farmers care for the animals? How many animals are there? Does farm machinery make the work easier? What pets did you see around the farm? What crops are grown? After returning from the farm, have your child build a farm with blocks and plastic animals and label each animal.
Use a number line to teach counting with pennies, nickels and dimes. *See* Math, Week 20, number 8. **Game:** Give a hint about what coin you are holding. For example, *My coin has an eagle on one side* or *Its value is equal to 15 minus 5.*	Choose from the following activities, depending on the season and your child's interests: 1. Make paper snowflakes. 2. Grow a garden. 3. Make leaf rubbings.	Have your child read and write poems about farm animals. *See* Social Studies, Week 20, number 3. Have your child write a thank you letter to the people he/she spoke with at the farm.

TEACHING SUGGESTIONS AND ACTIVITIES

Language Skills (Poetry)

1. **Hearing:** Have your child listen to an unfamiliar sound and write words that describe the sound or express how the sound makes him/her feel.

   Sight: Have your child look at a sunrise, sunset or cloud formation and write words that describe the sight or express how the sight makes him/her feel.

   Taste: Have your child taste something unfamiliar and write words that describe the taste or express how the taste makes him/her feel.

   Smell: Have your child smell something unfamiliar and write words that describe the smell or express how the smell affected him/her.

   Touch: Blindfold your child. Have him/her walk barefoot in wet mud or on finger paint and write words that express what it felt like.

Math (Money)

BACKGROUND

By this time in your child's experiences, he/she is at least aware of money and has seen money exchanged at the store on shopping trips or has an allowance. Your child may know the value of a penny, nickel and dime but probably needs experience applying it in given situations.

1. Tape a penny to a wall chart. Ask your child to name the penny. Say *This is one penny* as you write *1 penny* on the chart. Under the penny, write *1 cent* and explain that a penny is worth 1 cent. Also show the symbol for cent (¢). Have your child lay out some pennies in a row, count them and tell how many pennies there are and the total value. Draw circles in a row to represent each coin as your child arranges the pennies. Write 1¢ inside of each circle. When your child says the four pennies in the row are worth four cents, write = 4¢ after your row of circles. Repeat with other quantities.

2. Add a nickel to the chart described above and include the word and its value. Without using money, ask your child to count by fives. Then, have your child lay out rows of nickels and follow the same procedure as with the pennies.

3. Without money, ask your child to count by tens. Then, have your child lay out rows of dimes and follow the same procedure as with the pennies. Add a dime to the money chart.

4. Have your child lay out one nickel and one penny and show him/her how to count (add up) their value. Point to the nickel and say, *Five cents.* Point to the penny and say, *One more cent equals six cents. Five cents plus one cent equals six cents.* Have your child point to and count the nickel and penny. Repeat this activity with one nickel and two, three or more pennies. Then, add more nickels.

5. **Center:** Write a different amount (1–15¢) on each of several index cards. Put several nickels and pennies in a box with the cards. Instruct your child to make the amount written on each card as many ways as possible using only nickels and pennies.

6. Have your child lay out one dime and one penny. Show him/her how to count their value. *See* number 4 above.

7. **Center:** Make a center with dimes and pennies like the one for nickels. *See* number 5. Create cards with different amounts of money from 1–30¢. Tell your child he/she is to make the amount written on each card as many different ways as possible using only pennies and dimes.

Learn at Home, Grade 1

8. Create a number line from 0–20 on a 4" x 20" strip of paper. Draw a rabbit and put it on zero. Make the rabbit "jump" three times: first to 10, then to 15 and finally to 16. Ask your child how far the rabbit jumped the first time (10), the second (5) and the last (1). Write *10 + 5 + 1* and ask, *On what number did the rabbit land?* (16). Write = 16. Put down a dime, a nickel and a penny. Have your child say what each coin is worth. Write 10 + 5 + 1 as your child names the value of each coin. Then, have him/her count: 10, 15, 16 (cents) as you point to each coin. Repeat with other combinations of three coins.

Science (Seasons)

1. **Spelling:** Use the following words in your spelling list: *Fall, Winter, Summer, Spring* and descriptive words taken from poetry.

2. Discuss how some animals migrate, hibernate or stay active. Explain that the coats of some animals thicken and that some animals store food. Have your child make a list of animals that do each.

3. Mural—3 day project:
   a. **Day one:** Divide a large sheet of butcher paper into four equal sections. Label each section with the name of a season. With a pencil, help your child draw a line representing the ground and the trunk and branches of a tree in each section. Have your child paint each of the tree trunks and the ground as it would look in each season.

   b. **Day two:** Put several colors of tempera paints in muffin tins or paper cups. Cut an old sponge into squares about the size of marshmallows. On a separate sheet of paper, teach your child how to sponge-paint. Have your child dip one side of the sponge into paint and dab it two or three times on the paper. Have your child use a different sponge for each color. Tell your child to dab versus dragging the sponge. Using this sponge-painting technique, have your child paint the leaves and plants in each season on the mural.

   c. **Day three:** Using a paintbrush, have your child add details, such as animals and people, to complete the mural.

Social Studies (Farm Animals)

1. Read the poem "'Quack!' Said the Billy Goat" in *An Arkful of Animals,* selected by William Cole. Discuss the silliness of the poem. Reread the poem with your child using appropriate voices.

2. Ask your child what he/she had for dinner last night, breakfast this morning and lunch today. Talk about which foods came from farm animals. Refer to the two-column chart started yesterday. Write which food products each animal gives (pork, beef, milk, eggs, poultry, etc.) in a third column on the chart. Do some farm animals give no food? Your child may add these words to the animal dictionary.

3. **Poetry:** Write a poem starter. Have your child finish it. Ideas could include:

   A horse on the farm eats lots of hay . . .   The rooster crows, "Cock-a-doodle-doo" . . .
   The turkey walks with a wobble . . .   "Oink, oink," says the pig . . .

Now, on the Count of...

one two three
four five six seven
eight nine ten

Trace each number and **write** its number word next to it.

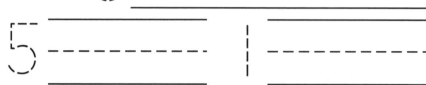

3 _____

7 _____

8 _____

2 _____

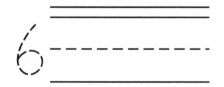

10 _____

5 _____

1 _____

6 _____

9 _____

4 _____

Solve the problems. **Write** the answers on the lines. Then, **write** the answers using the correct number words in the puzzle.

Across

1. 3 + 2 = _____
2. 4 + 2 = _____
3. 2 + 1 = _____
4. 1 + 0 = _____
5. 5 + 3 = _____
7. 2 + 7 = _____

Down

1. 2 + 2 = _____
2. 4 + 3 = _____
3. 0 + 2 = _____
6. 4 + 6 = _____

242

Learn at Home, Grade 1

Animals in Winter

Cut out each animal. **Glue** it in its place. **Write** the animal's name.

| rabbit | bird | bear | squirrel |

This animal hibernates in the winter.

_____

- -

_____

This animal stays active in the winter.

_____

- -

_____

This animal migrates in the winter.

_____

- -

_____

This animal stores food for the winter.

_____

- -

_____

Language Skills	Spelling	Reading
Monday From a variety of anthologies, choose poems that will be interesting to your child. Read a poem aloud while pointing to each word. Then, have your child read the poem with you. Discuss the content of the poem, and read it many times until your child is reading it without your help. Record yourself reading the poems or buy commercial cassettes. Keep poetry tapes and copies of the poems in a listening center for your child to practice independently.	**Digraphs** Pretest your child on these words: chin chop check cheek children chain child chase Call attention to the digraphs found at the beginning of each word. *See* Spelling, Week 21.	**Comparative Language** Introduce comparative language by asking your child to compare your size with his/hers. Fold a sheet of paper in half lengthwise. Label one half *Big* and the other *Little*. Have your child find pairs of objects in the room and draw each under the appropriate column. Discuss the inexactness of the terms *big* and *little*. Read *The Story of Ferdinand* by Munro Leaf.
Tuesday Discuss *onomatopoeia*—words that imitate the sounds of objects with which they are associated, such as *buzz* and *bang*. Brainstorm a list of words and sounds (*splish, splash, squish, moo, cluck, baa, etc.*). Have your child copy his/her favorite word or sound on the bottom of a sheet of paper and draw an image that the word evokes.	Have your child write the spelling words in sentences.	Provide three different sizes of an object, such as bottles. Have your child order them and name each one. Lead your child to include *bigger* and *biggest* or *smaller* and *smallest* in the description. *See* Reading, Week 21, number 1.
Wednesday Show your child a picture of a busy or chaotic scene. Have your child think of sound words that he/she associates with the picture. Write the words on a chart labeled *Onomatopoeia*.	Have your child spell each word aloud while tapping his/her chin with his/her fingertips. Have your child complete **Cheer Up!** (p. 248).	Teach your child to compare attributes of sound (loud, louder, loudest), texture (soft, softer, softest) and appearance (bright, brighter, brightest). Fold paper in thirds and label each column *big, bigger, biggest*. Have your child draw the same object in each column in graduated sizes. *See* Reading, Week 21, number 2.
Thursday Read nursery rhymes with your child. Write any onomatopoeic words that you and your child find or create a list of onomatopoeia that the rhymes inspire. **Examples:** Twee tweedle dee. Hickory, dickory, dock.	Have your child use dried beans or cereal to spell out each spelling word.	Have your child look through *The Story of Ferdinand* to find the descriptive words. Then, have him/her write sentences using the descriptive words in a comparative form. **Example:** Ferdinand is *quieter* than the other bulls.
Friday **Music:** Teach your child several verses of "Hush Little Baby." Have your child make up silly verses to add to the song.	Give your child the final spelling test.	Have your child create a mural of *The Story of Ferdinand* and label the main events.

244

Learn at Home, Grade 1

Math	Science	Social Studies
Set up a "store" with objects your child may "purchase" to practice counting values. Leave the original sales price on objects whenever possible. Keep values below 50¢ to begin with.	**Weather** Ask your child to describe the current weather. Keep a record of your child's daily observations about the weather in a journal, on a graph or chart or on the calendar itself. *See* Science, Week 21, numbers 1 and 2.	**Zoo Animals** **Field Trip:** Arrange a visit to a zoo. Discuss the purpose of a zoo. For each animal your child sees, have him/her write the animal's name and the location of its natural home. Have your child observe how the animals are cared for. Then, have your child play a game with animal crackers. *See* Social Studies, Week 21, number 1.
Choose one 25¢ object from the store. Have your child show several ways to make 25¢. Introduce the quarter, its name and value. Have your child show its value using only pennies, then nickels, and then using pennies, nickels and dimes. *See* Math, Week 21, number 1.	Challenge your child to think about how his/her senses are used in talking about the weather. Ask your child to describe how he/she can see the weather (snow, blue sky), as well as hear, taste, feel and smell the weather. *See* Science, Week 21, numbers 3.	Using the list of zoo animals your child compiled, have him/her find each animal's natural home on a world map. With your child, discuss the pros and cons of keeping animals in a zoo.
Have your child count on from a quarter. Help your child count the value of a quarter and pennies, a quarter and a nickel and a quarter and a dime. Your child may refer to the **Hundred Chart** (p. 31), if necessary. For a challenge, teach the value of two, three and four quarters and introduce the half-dollar coin. *See* Math, Week 21, numbers 2 and 3.	**Art:** Have your child paint a picture of his/her house on a windy, rainy, sunny or snowy day.	Give some examples of animal riddles. Then, have your child write his/her own riddles about zoo animals. *See* Social Studies, Week 21, number 2.
Use story problems to practice counting money. **Examples:** *You have three nickels and four pennies. How much money do you have?* or *Ice cream costs 25¢. You have four dimes. Do you have enough money to buy ice cream?* Then, have your child make up story problems using money.	**Math:** Have your child keep a tally of the number of sunny days and rainy days in a month. At the end of the month, have your child make a graph comparing the numbers. Challenge your child to think of other ways to graph the weather.	Copy a large black and white map of the world. Have your child paint oceans blue and land green or brown. Have your child write and draw the names of animals on cards and pin them onto the map where they are found in the wild.
Set out three to five coins at a time for your child to count. Continue assessing and giving practice until your child counts coins (including quarters, dimes, nickels and pennies) with confidence. Help your child write several story problems using money. Save them for the review week. Add objects as needed to the store begun on Monday, keeping the values below 99¢.	**Music:** Teach your child weather songs. Some suggestions include "The Eensy, Weensey Spider" and "It's Raining, It's Pouring" from *Piggyback Songs* and *More Piggyback Songs* compiled by Jean Warren.	Have your child complete the following pages about each of the continents: **Asia: The Largest Continent** (p. 249). **Africa: A Land of Deserts** (p. 250). **North America: A Land of Variety** (p. 251).

TEACHING SUGGESTIONS AND ACTIVITIES

Spelling (Digraphs)

BACKGROUND
A digraph consists of two consonants that make a single sound. In the digraph *ch*, neither the sound of the *c* nor *h* can be heard—a new sound is created by the combination. Other digraphs include *sh, th, ph, wh, gn, kn* and *wr*. When reading two-syllable words, digraphs and blends are never split into separate syllables.

Reading (Comparative Language)

▶ 1. Write sentences on the board that use comparative language to describe the different sizes of bottles. Circle the *er* and *est* endings. Explain to your child that the *est* ending is used when comparing more than two objects. Other objects to compare include spoons, cups and books.

▶ 2. Write the words *soft, softer* and *softest*. Have your child circle the endings. Write the words *big, bigger* and *biggest*. Call attention to the double *g*. Write *large, larger* and *largest* and note that the *e* was dropped before adding the endings. Knowing that endings may change on root words may help your child identify words in the future. Other words to explore include *late, kind, small, fat, deep* and *tame*.

Math (Money)

▶ 1. Fold a 9" x 12" sheet of paper into six parts. Have your child write 25¢ in the corner of each box. Next, instruct him/her to place coins equaling twenty-five cents in one of the boxes. Your child should draw around each coin with a pencil and write the value of each coin inside its outline. Have your child do the same in the other five boxes, making each a different arrangement of twenty-five cents.

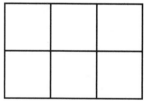

▶ 2. Put quarters, dimes, nickels and pennies in a box. Have your child reach into the box and select a quarter and a penny. Ask how much the two coins are worth. Do the same with a quarter and a nickel and a quarter and a dime. Choose two to five coins at random to count.

▶ 3. Have your child make fifty cents in different ways, using the change in the box. Repeat numbers 1 and 2 above, using fifty cents. Show your child a fifty-cent piece (half dollar) and explain that alone it is equal to fifty cents.

Science (Weather)

BACKGROUND
Weather can influence our activities and mood. People like to talk about the weather and guess the coming weather. During this unit, discuss the weather on a daily basis and build your child's vocabulary and understanding of weather concepts.

Learn at Home, Grade 1

1. **Weather Calendar:** Make a calendar out of wood. Get a piece of wood about ¹/₂-inch thick, 21" across and about 19" high. Paint it a pastel color with an enamel paint. When the paint is dry, draw or paint a grid of seven even columns and seven rows as shown to the right. Write the names of the days in the narrow row. Screw in two eye hooks on the top row where the name of the month will hang. Screw an eye hook in each square and an eye hook in the top right-hand corner of the calendar. That is where a picture of the current weather will hang. You can use this calendar all year.

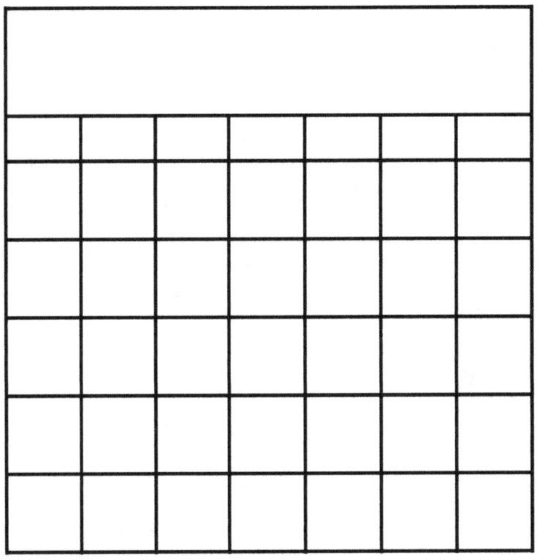

   Using tagboard, make a calendar header about 8" long and 3" tall. Write the name of the month on it, punch two holes in it and hang it up on the two hooks. Cut at least fifty 2" squares. Write the numbers 1–31 on the squares. On the extra squares, have your child draw symbols representing different kinds of weather, or purchase calendar headers and day markers from your local school supply store.

2. Write *Weather Words* at the top of a chart. Brainstorm with your child words that describe the weather, such as *cold, windy, sunny, cloudy* and *rainy*. Keep the chart as a reference for describing the daily weather at calendar time. Use some of the words in your child's spelling list.

3. **Writing:** Have your child complete each sentence below to describe the weather.

   I can see _____ .
   I can hear _____ .
   I can smell _____ .
   I can feel _____ .
   I can taste _____ .

Social Studies (Zoo Animals)

1. Give your child a box of animal crackers. Have him/her sort and count each type of animal. Have your child draw a picture of zoo cages and exhibits. Instruct your child to glue animal crackers in each cage or exhibit.

2. Based on the animals you saw in the zoo and the information you read there, make up several animal riddles. Read the riddles, one clue at a time, for your child to solve.

   Examples:

   I live in North America.
   I was hunted with bows and arrows.
   I have horns on my head.
   I'm an American _____ (bison).

   I live in the desert of Saudi Arabia.
   I can easily carry heavy loads across sand.
   I can carry my food supply on my back.
   I am a one-humped _____ (camel).

   Have your child write several riddles. Provide easy-to-read animal books for your child's reference.

Cheer Up!

Say the name of each picture. **Write** the spelling word that rhymes with it. Read the sentences. Use the spelling words to complete the puzzle.

chop   chin   cheek   check   chain   children   child   chase

Read the sentences. Use the spelling words to complete the puzzle.

Across
3. They will use a ___ to pull the car.
5. Many ___ like to go to the circus.
6. Write a ___ mark in the correct box.

Down
1. The baby spilled food on his ___.
2. Only one ___ is on the slide.
4. They like to run and ___ each other.
6. Dad will ___ the stump into logs.
7. The kitten licked the girl's ___.

248

Asia: The Largest Continent

Asia is the world's largest continent. It stretches for thousands of miles. More than one-half of all the people in the world live in Asia. Asia contains Russia which is the largest country in the world. The country with the most people living in it, China, is also located in Asia. Asia has the world's highest mountains. These mountains are in a country called India. These mountains are so high that the snow never melts. Have you ever seen a panda or an elephant? These animals live in Asia along with many other animals.

Color the map of Asia yellow.
Color the oceans blue.

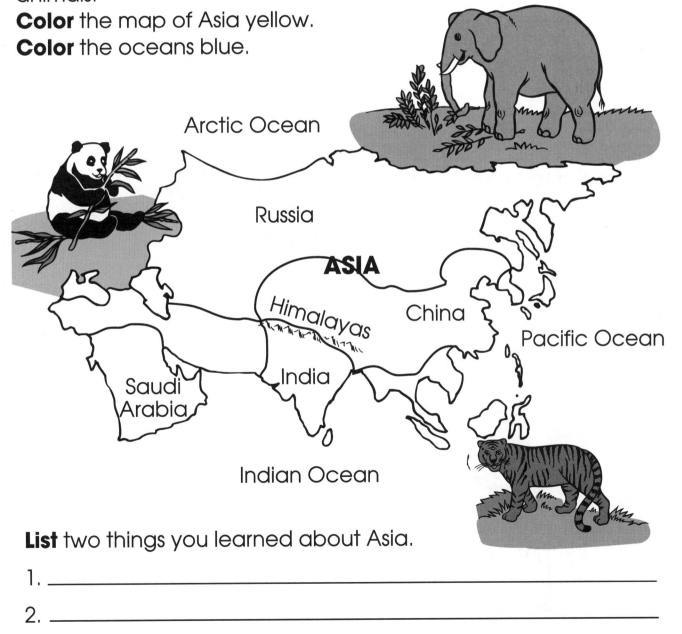

List two things you learned about Asia.

1. _____

2. _____

249

Africa: A Land of Deserts

Africa is the second largest continent in the world. Almost all of northern Africa is a hot, dry desert. It is the largest desert in the world. This desert is called the Sahara, and it is a hot, dry area of sand, rocks and mountains. The longest river in the world, the Nile River, flows through the Sahara Desert. Plants grow along this river. Camels seem to like the desert. They have very long eyelashes to keep blowing sand out of their eyes and can store enough water to walk a long time in the desert without drinking. Many big animals live in the forests of central Africa, such as gorillas, chimpanzees and monkeys. Lions, zebras, giraffes and antelopes live in the grasslands. This central part of Africa is hot, but plants and trees grow well here because there are heavy rains that water them.

1. **Color** the Sahara Desert brown.
2. **Color** the oceans and the Nile River blue.
3. **Color** the rest of Africa orange.

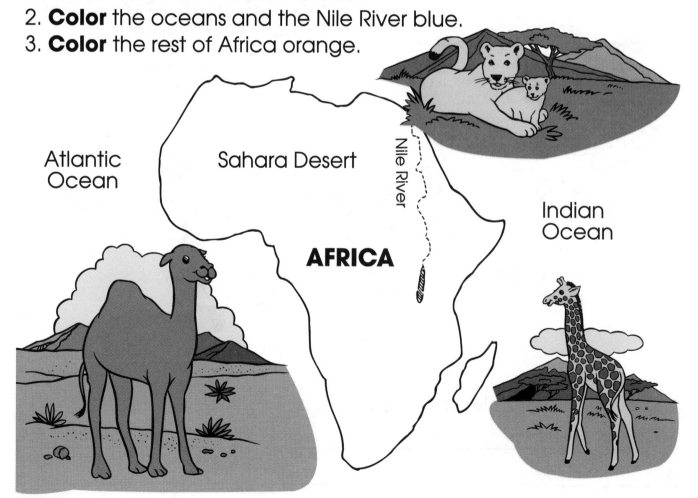

Atlantic Ocean

Sahara Desert

Nile River

Indian Ocean

AFRICA

Learn at Home, Grade 1

North America: A Land of Variety

North America is the third largest continent in the world. It has cold parts and hot parts. Rivers, mountains, lakes, plains, deserts and canyons make up the land. Canada is the largest country in North America. Its northern half is very cold since it reaches almost to the top of the world. Polar bears, seals, moose and whales can be found in Canada. The United States is the country in the middle of North America. It contains a big river called the Mississippi, which divides the east from the west. Deer, turkeys and some wolves live on both sides of this river. South of the United States is a country called Mexico. Mexico has volcanoes and jungles. A special animal called a jaguar hunts in Mexico. The weather can be hot and dry in parts and wet in other areas of Mexico.

1. **Color** the map of North America green.
2. **Color** the oceans and the Mississippi River blue.

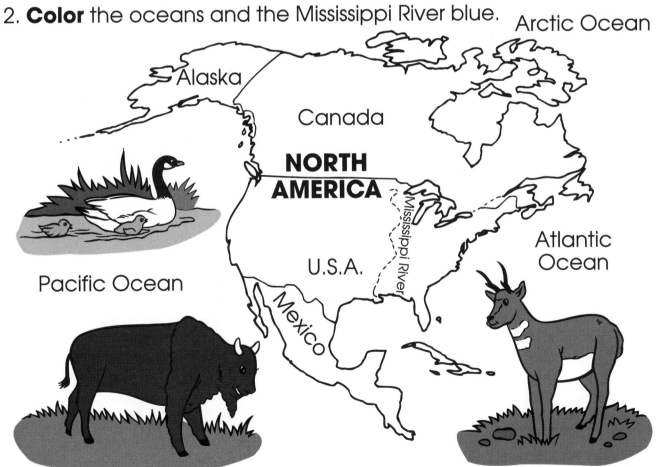

251

	Language Skills	Spelling	Reading

Monday	Choose a piece of your child's writing and have him/her read it aloud to you. Discuss your child's use of punctuation. Teach any lessons necessary about run-on sentences or joining two short sentences. Make sure your child uses question marks when appropriate. Have your child copy the edited sentences on a final copy or publish them in a book with illustrations.	Pretest your child on these words:
		    shake shape
		    sheep shop
		    shell shut
		    ship she
		Teach your child the *sh* digraph.
			Read *We're Different, We're the Same* by Bobbi Jane Kates. Have your child look through the book for words with *er* and *est* endings. Talk about how people are the same and different using comparative language. Then, have your child write sentences and illustrate them.

Tuesday	Choose a piece of your child's writing and discuss his/her use of capital letters. Look for capitals at the beginning of sentences and in proper nouns. Reteach any lessons necessary. Have your child copy the edited sentences on a final copy or publish them in a book with illustrations.	Have your child write the spelling words in sentences.	Have your child list three ways people are the same and three ways people are different. *See* page 13 for a further exploration of **Critical Thinking**. Make a copy of **Everyone Is Welcome** (p. 257) and have your child complete it.

Wednesday	Write a story that includes many contractions and possessives. Have your child read your story and circle all the contractions and possessives. Then, have your child tell what two words make up each contraction and to what object each possessive is referring.	Have your child spell each word aloud while shuffling his/her feet across the floor. Have your child complete **Shuttling Around** (p. 256).	Fold a piece of paper in thirds. Open and fold it in half the other way. The paper will look like this:
			Write a comparative sentence in each box for your child to illustrate.
			Examples:
			   Maria made a big snowman.
			   Forrest made a bigger snowman.
			   Larissa made the biggest snowman.

Thursday	For a challenge, have your child rewrite the story from Wednesday's lesson using no apostrophes and contractions.
	Example:
	  Rick didn't ride Fran's bike to school.
	  Rick did not ride the bike that belongs to Fran to school.
		Have your child write each spelling word in a way which communicates its meaning. For example, have him/her write *shake* in shaky handwriting.	*See* Reading, Week 22, number 1, for a writing activity using comparative language. *See* page 13 for a further exploration of **Drawing Conclusions.** Have your child complete **Reflect on the Riddles** (p. 258).

Friday	Write a sentence without punctuation and have your child tell you what needs to be changed and why. Then, have your child copy the corrected sentence onto lined paper.	Give your child the final spelling test.	Have your child choose eight to fifteen characters from a variety of familiar books. After each character's name, have your child write two or three adjectives that describe the character.

252

Learn at Home, Grade 1

Math	**Science**	**Social Studies**
Linear Measurement Introduce measurement to your child. Collect a variety of familiar objects for your child to measure. Provide Unifix cubes, bottle caps, shoe lengths and other same-sized objects for your child to use as measuring tools. *See* Math, Week 22, number 1. Read *Jim and the Beanstalk* by Raymond Briggs with your child. Discuss with your child how measurement is used in his/her life.	Have available weather maps and weather predictions from a newspaper. Ahead of time, record a weather report from either the radio or TV. Discuss the reports with your child and look at the current weather situation. *See* Science, Week 22, number 1.	Have your child complete the following pages about each of the continents: **South America: Home to Many Plants and Animals** (p. 260). **Antarctica: The Frozen Continent** (p. 261).
Have your child compare the lengths of different objects, estimating which objects might be about the same length. *See* Math, Week 22, number 2. Have your child complete **A String Activity** (p. 259).	Continue yesterday's lesson. *See* Science, Week 22, numbers 2 and 3.	Have your child complete the following pages about each of the continents: **Europe: A Land of Many Countries** (p. 262). **Australia: The Smallest Continent** (p. 263). Have your child compile the completed continent pages between two construction paper covers and give the book a title.
Give your child more practice measuring familiar objects with non-standard units. *See* Math, Week 22, numbers 3 and 4. **Note:** Monitor your child's accuracy in measuring. Objects used for measuring should be placed end to end without gaps and "hug" the side of the item being measured.	Have your child report on the day's weather as if he/she were a weather reporter on a TV station. *See* Science, Week 22, numbers 4 and 5.	Make a word search of wild animals, listing the animals for your child to find in the puzzle. Have your child circle the names of animals found in North America in red; those found in Australia, green; those found in Africa, yellow; and so on.
Assess whether your child needs more time with non-standard units before introducing standard units (centimeters and inches). Introduce centimeters and inches. Use 1-inch blocks and 1-cm blocks to compare to the ruler. If you do not have access to blocks, carefully cut squares out of construction paper. *See* Math, Week 22, number 5. Read *How Big Is a Foot?* by Rolf Myller and discuss the need for standard units of measure.	Teach your child to read an outdoor thermometer. Place it outside (out of direct sunlight) and have your child read it at the same time every day, recording the temperature on a graph. *See* Science, Week 22, number 6.	**Writing:** Have your child write (or dictate) a story about a wild animal.
Teach your child how to use a ruler to measure. Begin with measuring straight lines. If your child is not aligning the ruler correctly, have him/her use the centimeter and inch blocks from yesterday. After your child measures with the blocks, have him/her set the ruler beside the blocks to compare the number. *See* Math, Week 22, numbers 6 and 7. Have your child use the ruler to measure his/her body parts and record the number of inches.	Read *The Cloud Book* by Tomie de Paola. Discuss the characteristics of different clouds. **Art:** Provide your child with 9" x 12" blue paper and cotton balls. Have your child use the cotton balls to form one kind of cloud and glue them onto the top of the paper. Then, have your child use crayons to draw in an outdoor scene that fits the type of clouds.	**Physical Activity:** Say the name of a wild animal. Have your child take the role of that animal and move and make noises as that animal would.

TEACHING SUGGESTIONS AND ACTIVITIES

Reading (Comparative Language)

▶ 1. **Writing Activity:** Use three identical drinking glasses. Fill the first glass with water ¹/₂ inch from the top. Fill the second glass a little fuller. Fill the third glass to the brim. Have your child write three sentences describing how full each glass is. Encourage your child's creativity in expressing fullness.

Math (Linear Measurement)

▶ 1. Fill a box with familiar objects your child can measure. Suggestions for objects include a straw, a crayon, a pencil and strips of colored paper. Use the objects to complete the following.

    a. Fold a piece of paper in half. Write *Longer* at the top of one side and *Shorter* at the top of the other side. Have your child take two objects out of the box, compare their lengths and place the objects on the correct sides of the paper. Have your child return the objects and repeat the activity.

    b. Have your child measure the objects using toothpicks, Unifix cubes or square crackers. Show your child how to place the end of a toothpick even with the end of an object and how to place the next toothpick end to end. Have your child record the length. Allow your child to measure the same items using a different non-standard tool, such as a paper clip.

▶ 2. Cut a piece of string the length of your child's hand span. Have your child use that length to find another object in the room that is the same length. Then, have your child make a statement each time he/she compares the string, such as *The chair is wider than the string* or *My pencil is shorter than the string.*

▶ 3. Using a black marker on newspaper or large butcher paper, trace around your child's body. When your child stands up, he/she may use a variety of non-standard units to measure the length of his/her arms, legs, head, torso, etc.

▶ 4. Have your child measure a variety of objects in the room using different units. Your child may discover that it is easier to measure something longer with a larger unit.

▶ 5. Give your child a ruler with inches and centimeters. Use 1-inch blocks and 1-cm blocks to line up next to the ruler. Have your child count blocks and discover that the number he/she counts matches the written number. Ask your child to point to one inch, four inches, twelve inches, one foot and a variety of centimeters. As you say each increment, write the measurement on paper for your child.

▶ 6. Draw lines measuring three inches, five inches and eight inches. Give your child a ruler to measure them. Tell your child to draw lines of different increments and to label them.

▶ 7. Have your child use centimeters and inches to measure some of the same objects measured with nonstandard units.

Learn at Home, Grade 1

Science (Weather)

▶ 1. Tell your child a person who studies the weather is called a *meteorologist*. Discuss the newspaper's weather forecast. Explain the maps used in the newspaper. Listen to and/or look at the weather report on the radio or TV. Decide if yesterday's weather predictions were accurate. Compare the reports from different sources. Discuss why the reports might be different.

▶ 2. Teach your child about (and show, if possible) some of the instruments a meteorologist uses in studying the weather (thermometer, wind vane, rain gauge and barometer).

▶ 3. Make a chart like the one to the right. At the top of the left-hand column, write *Forecast*. At the top of the right-hand column, write *Weather*. Have your child cut out the weather forecast from the paper every day and glue it in the left-hand column. Then, have your child observe the actual weather the next day and determine whether the forecast was correct. If it was correct, have your child put a star next to the forecast. If the forecast was not correct, have your child describe the actual weather in the right-hand column. As an alternative, have your child summarize the weather report from the radio or TV reports in the left column.

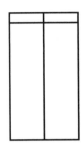

▶ 4. Obtain a piece of cardboard about two feet square. Cut out the center to make a television screen. Have your child paint the frame. Give your child buttons to glue on for control knobs. Have your child hold this up when giving his/her weather report.

▶ 5. **Creative Drama:** Your child's weather report may be accurate, adapted from a forecast, or made up. You may give your child a form like the one below to follow.

Parent: And now here is _____ with today's weather.
Your child: Today is _____ (date).
The weather is _____.
It is _____ degrees outside and _____.
The sky is _____ now and it is expected to _____.
Today would be a good day to _____.

▶ 6. Make a graph as shown below. Label the bottom with dates and the side with temperatures. Help your child record the daily temperature by filling in the spaces above the day's date up to the level of the day's temperature. Have your child use a red crayon to match the mercury in the thermometer. Alternatively, have your child record the temperature at three different times of the day and compare the temperature difference throughout the day. For each temperature recorded, your child should write a word describing the temperature or what type of clothing should be worn.

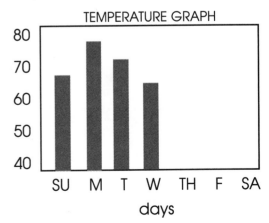

TEMPERATURE GRAPH

Shuttling Around

Write the missing spelling words on the line.

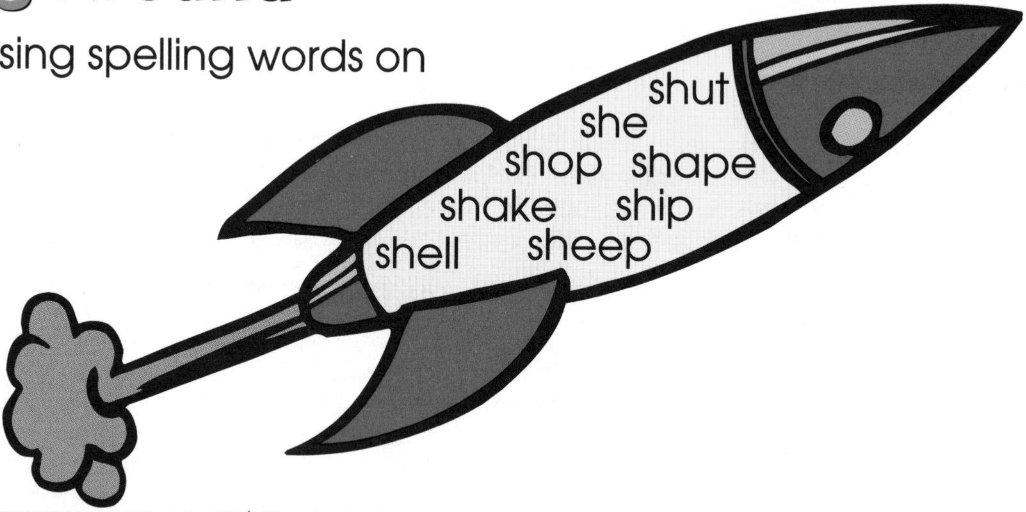

shut
she
shop shape
shake ship
shell sheep

_____

- - - - - - - - - - - - - - - -

1. A flock of _____ graze on the hillside.

_____

- - - - - - - - - - - - - - - -

2. The _____ will sail from the dock very soon.

_____

- - - - - - - - - - - - -

3. We must keep the gate _____ to keep the dog in.

_____

- - - - - - - - - - - - - - -

4. Please _____ the bottle of salad dressing.

_____

- - - - - - - - - - - - - - - -

5. A square is a _____ that has four equal sides.

_____

- - - - - - - - - - - - - - -

6. Does she like to _____ at the mall?

_____

- - - - - - - - - - - - - - - -

8. The clam always stays inside its _____ .

Learn at Home, Grade 1

Everyone Is Welcome

Cut out the pictures of the people at the bottom of the page. Read the clues carefully. **Glue** the people where they belong at the table.

1. Robert already has his hamburger.

2. Kioko will pass the plate of hamburgers to the others at the table.

3. Mike asks Teresa to please pass the pitcher of lemonade so that he may fill his glass.

4. Pablo likes sitting between his friends Kioko and Teresa.

5. Sue likes hot dogs better than hamburgers.

cut

Kioko | Pablo | Sue | Robert | Teresa | Mike

Reflect on the Riddles

Read each riddle. **Find** the answer in the box and **write** it on the line.

| bodies | eyes | people | hair | mouth | nose | skin |

1. There are two of me. We can blink. We can see. We can wink. We can weep. What are we? _____

2. There is one of me. I can sing. I can speak. I can eat. I can even blow a big bubble. I can eat ice cream, too. What am I?

   _____

3. There is one of me. If something tickles me, I will sneeze. I like to sniff flowers. I like the smell of hot dogs, also. What am I?

   _____

4. We need to bend and stretch. We need rest. We need to work and we need to play. We are all different. What are we?

   _____

5. I can be almost any color. I can be long or short. I can be curled and I can be staight. What am I?

   _____

6. I cover a lot. I keep muscles, bones and blood inside your body. I let you know if it is hot or cold outside. I tell you if something is wet or dry. What am I? _____

7. We all have feelings. We all have bodies. We all like to do many of the same things. But, we also are all very different. Who are we? _____

A String Activity

Cut a piece of string as long as your pencil. Use the string to **measure** things. **List** the things you measure below.

Longer	Same	Shorter

Learn at Home, Grade 1

South America: Home to Many Plants and Animals

South America, the fourth largest continent, is south of, or below, North America. It stretches almost to the bottom of the world. The longest mountain chain, the Andes, runs down the western side of South America. The largest tropical rainforest is there, too. This hot, wet forest has so many kinds of trees, plants and animals that many are not named yet. Have you ever heard of the Amazon River? It is located in South America and carries the most water of any river in the world. It is located in an area of alligators, birds and fish.

1. **Color** the map of South America red.
2. **Color** the oceans and the Amazon River blue.

Pacific Ocean

Amazon River

Andes Mtns.

SOUTH AMERICA

Atlantic Ocean

List two things you learned about South America.

1. _____

2. _____

Learn at Home, Grade 1

Antarctica: The Frozen Continent

Antarctica, the fifth largest continent, is the most southern continent. It is covered with ice from one to two miles thick. Antarctica is so cold in the winter that only scientists and exploration groups live there. The summers are more like the winters in the United States. No animals live on the ice, but many live along the edge of the ice by the sea. Penguins, seals and whales are some of the animals that live there.

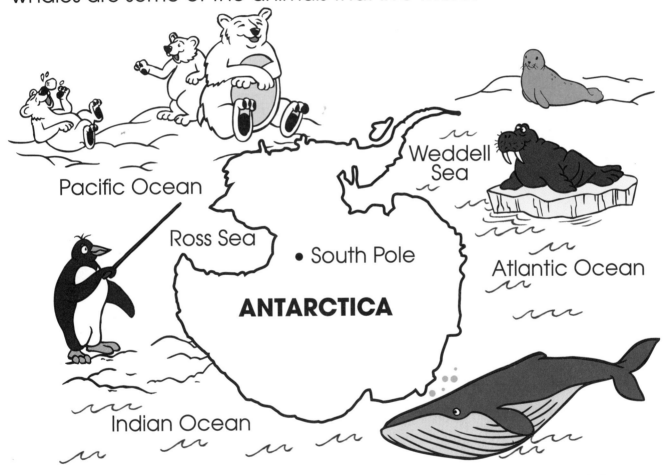

1. **Color** the map of Antarctica gray. 2. **Color** the oceans blue.

Use words from the story above to fill in the blanks.

1. Antarctica is covered with_____ .

2. Antarctica is called the_____ continent.

3. _____ _____ and_____
live in the water near Antarctica.

Europe: A Land of Many Countries

Europe is the second smallest continent in the world. It is between Asia and the Atlantic Ocean. Europe is divided from Asia by the Ural Mountains. The Mediterranean Sea is south of Europe. There are many mountain chains in Europe. One is named the Alps. The weather in northern Europe can be very cold in the winter. It can be very hot in the summer in southern Europe. But in most of Europe, the weather is not too hot or too cold. Many countries make up the continent of Europe. Have you heard of England, Spain or France? These are three countries in Europe. Large wild animals do not live in Europe anymore because there are so many people. Only one animal runs free in northern Europe. Look at the picture on this page. Can you name this animal?

1. **Color** the map of Europe green.
2. **Color** the ocean and the seas blue.

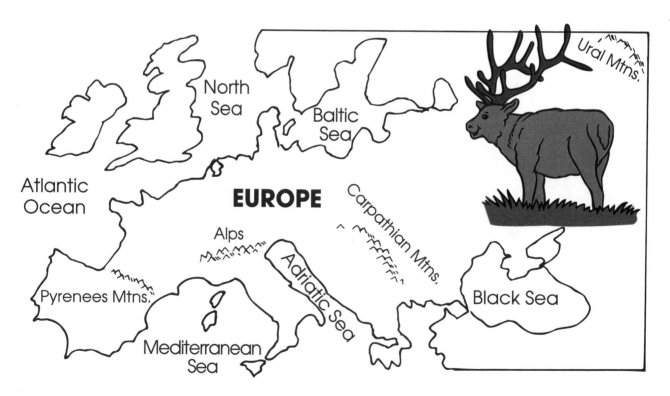

I would like to visit Europe because _____

_____

Learn at Home, Grade 1

Australia: The Smallest Continent

Australia is the smallest continent in the world. It is an island in the South Pacific. Much of Australia is desert, so there are not many people who live there. Since Australia is so far from the other continents, its animals look very different. One of these animals, the kangaroo, is found nowhere else except in a zoo. It jumps long distances and carries its babies in a pouch. Another special Australian animal is the koala bear. What do you think the koala bear eats?

1. **Color** the map of Australia purple.
2. **Color** the oceans blue.

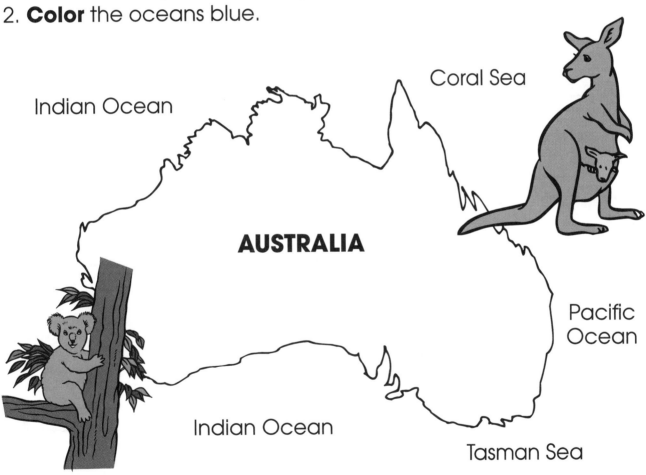

Indian Ocean

Coral Sea

AUSTRALIA

Pacific Ocean

Indian Ocean

Tasman Sea

List two things you learned about Australia.

1. _____

2. _____

	Language Skills	**Spelling**	**Reading**
Monday	Teach location words, such as *up, in, over, under* and so on. Have your child brainstorm some of his/her activities of the day and include where the activities were performed. **Examples:** I brushed my teeth *in the bathroom*. I read a book *on my bed*. I ate breakfast *at the table*. Have your child sequence his/her activities using *first, next* and *last*.	Pretest your child on these spelling words: those there that this them the then they Teach your child the *th* digraph.	**Antonyms** Introduce antonyms to your child. Write a list of words in a column. Write another column containing words that are opposite in meaning to the words in the first list. Have your child match the antonyms.
Tuesday	Fold a paper into thirds. Have your child choose three events from yesterday's list and draw them in sequential order on the divided paper. Have your child write *first, next* and *last* in the appropriate boxes.	Have your child write the spelling words in sentences.	For antonym practice, write a sentence on the chalkboard and underline the word you would like your child to change. Have your child write a sentence that gives the opposite meaning. **Example:** *Tom threw the ball with his <u>left</u> hand.*
Wednesday	Fold a sheet of drawing paper into fourths. Open the paper, and in each box write a preposition that indicates location *(under, over, up, in, on, next to, through, etc.)*. Have your child draw him/herself in each position. **Example**: <u>on</u> *the swing set*	Have your child spell each word aloud while thumping the table with his/her knuckles. Have your child complete **Thundering, Thumping Clouds** (p. 270).	Read *Amazing Grace* by Mary Hoffman. With your child, brainstorm the important events in *Amazing Grace*. Write the events on individual index cards and scramble the cards. Then, have your child read each card and put the events back in order.
Thursday	Read *Charlie's Cloak* by Tomie de Paolo Have your child complete **Where Is That Sheep?** (p. 268).	Have your child use a stamp pad to create thumbprints. He/she should stamp his/her thumbprints in the shape of the letters of each spelling word.	Have your child search through *Amazing Grace* for words and their opposites and make a list of antonym pairs. Then, have your child find descriptive words in the book and think of an opposite that is not in the book.
Friday	**Physical Activity:** Have your child perform actions you direct, such as the following: *Step to the left; Put a hand on the clock; Sit under the table;* and *Put your pencil in your desk*. Instruct your child to name the words that indicate location or direction. Have your child complete **Family Portraits** (p. 269).	Give your child the final spelling test.	Have your child make a list of new words from the book. Your child may make flash cards and review the words independently. Then, have your child write sentences using each of the words on the flash cards.

Math	Science	Social Studies
Time Have your child look for clocks around the house and compare them to each other. Discuss when we use clocks and why they are important to us. Help your child make a learning clock with movable hands using details he/she has observed on other clocks. To attach the hands, push a paper fastener (brad) through the hands and the clock face, then fold the ends back.	Conduct a cloud experiment with your child. Discuss how clouds are formed. *See* Science, Week 23, number 1.	**Social Skills** Discuss the need for rules and laws. Read the story to your child and discuss. *See* Social Studies, Week 23, number 1.
Have your child practice telling time to the hour. *See* Math, Week 23, numbers 1 and 2. Then, read *The Grouchy Ladybug* by Eric Carle. Have your child record the times from the book and what the ladybug was doing.	Conduct a 2-day experiment with your child to observe the effects of warm sun on water. *See* Science, Week 23, number 2.	Read the rules provided for a variety of situations. Discuss the need for such rules. *See* Social Studies, Week 23, number 2.
Teach your child time to the half hour. *See* Math, Week 23, number 3. Have your child complete **Who "Nose" These Times?** (p. 271).	Complete yesterday's lesson.	Ask your child to tell rules he/she must follow at home, school, the library, a park and other places. Teach your child to state rules positively (*Be on time* rather than *Do not be late*). Discuss how your child's rules compare to a friend's rules. Then, look at and compare rules for various places. Why are some different and others the same?
Move the hands on the clock through the hours of the day discussing what your child would be doing at each hour. Demonstrate that there are 12 hours on a clock and 24 hours in a day. Have your child look at the (real) clock frequently throughout the day. State the time and give your child's schedule, such as *We'll be done with school in one hour.* Have your child draw pictures showing activities for each hour of the day between 8:00 A.M. and 8:00 P.M., including a clock face in each picture.	Discuss the destructive kinds of weather most typical in your region. Discuss a plan of action in case severe weather occurs. Make and hang up a chart, *What to Do in Case of a _____.* Check out a video from the library showing different types of weather.	On a sheet of 12" x 18" paper folded into fourths, have your child draw four pictures, each illustrating a home rule. With a black marker, write the illustrated rule in each section. Hang the poster up in your home.
Move the learning clock's hands to a time on the hour or half past the hour. Have your child write down the time. Vary the activity, asking your child to move the hands on the clock to show a given time.	Choose a weather activity. *See* Science, Week 23, numbers 3–5.	Write a rule song to the tune of "The Wheels on the Bus Go 'Round and 'Round." **Example:** The children in this house say, *please, please, please, . . .*

TEACHING SUGGESTIONS AND ACTIVITIES

Math (Time)

BACKGROUND
Telling time is a very difficult skill. You should build your child's awareness of time by mentioning the time aloud frequently as you go about your day. With the availability of digital clocks, your child may read the time but not know its meaning. Another tool for keeping time is the calendar. It keeps track of time over a greater span of time than does the clock. To help your child gain a sense of time, maintain a consistent daily schedule and refer to it often so your child becomes familiar with a routine and understands what an hour feels like.

▶ 1. Teach the jobs of the two hands and introduce the term *o'clock*. Place the minute hand at twelve and move the hour hand to various hours. Have your child practice naming the hours. Explain to your child that when writing the time, the hour is followed by a colon (:) and two zeros which explain there are no minutes, thus 5:00 is read as *five o'clock*.

▶ 2. Set the clock on the hour (three o'clock). Have your child write the time on a sheet of paper.

▶ 3. Point to the twelve on the clock and ask your child what number is exactly halfway around (6). Set the clock hands at four o'clock and ask your child to tell what time it is. Now, move the minute hand to the six and explain it has moved halfway around the clock. Therefore, it is now *half past four* or *four thirty*. Write 4:30 as you say it. Explain that when the minute hand is on the six, it is always half past the hour. Call out half-hour times or write them on the board to give your child practice setting the clock at different half-hour times.

Science (Weather)

▶ 1. Conduct the following experiment with your child to show how clouds work.

  a. Fill a jar ⅓ of the way with very warm water and tape black paper to one side of the jar.

  b. While your child is prepared to quickly cover the jar, light a match and drop it into the jar.

  c. Let your child immediately cover the jar with a bag of ice.

  d. Watch for a cloud to form inside the jar. The black paper makes it easier to see.

  Talk about what happened and how it relates to clouds. (Clouds are made up of drops of water. The water evaporated and then condensed on smoke particles that hung in the air. This happens in the sky where the air is cool.)

▶ 2. Have your child fill two glasses halfway with water. Then, have your child cover one glass with plastic wrap, place a rubber band around it and set both glasses in a warm spot. Have your child check for changes twice a day for 2 days. Your child should record observations by drawing the water line each time on a record sheet. Make a copy similar to the one below for your child to mark. After two days, discuss what happened and where the water is.

First Check   Second Check   Third Check   Fourth Check

Learn at Home, Grade 1

▶ 3. Produce "rain" by boiling water in an uncovered pan. When the water is boiling, have your child observe the evaporating water. Hold an ice cube tray about 5 inches above the steam until drops of water form on the bottom of the tray, grow heavy and fall like rain. Have your child draw a diagram of the water evaporating and condensing.

▶ 4. Discuss with your child when it is all right to be outside in the rain and when it can be dangerous.

▶ 5. Make a wind indicator:

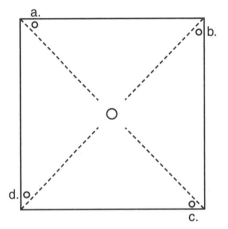

a. Give your child a copy of the square at right. Have him/her decorate the back side using crayons or markers and cut out the square on the solid line.

b. Have your child cut on the dotted lines.

c. Punch a hole at each corner and show your child how to fold corners a, b, c and d into the center and put a brad through the holes and the center circle.

d. Have your child wrap the prongs of the brad around the top of a pencil and secure it with tape.

e. Your child may take the wind indicator outside to check the wind's direction. The pinwheel will spin best when the wind is blowing directly into the front of the pinwheel.

Social Studies (Social Skills)

BACKGROUND

You will need to analyze your own philosophy of appropriate behavior and the need for rules. Think about the rules in your life and why they are necessary. Choose a few essential and fair rules for your classroom and enforce them consistently. Discuss with your child why these rules are important. Think about the social skills that will best equip your child for a diverse and changing world. The best method for teaching these social skills is to model the appropriate behavior. Children will watch what you do rather than listen to what you say. Make an effort to speak to your child in a respectful manner as you would like him/her to speak to you and others. Your child will likely be interacting with a variety of people in his/her life—from the neighbor to people with vastly different cultures and upbringing. Think now about how you would like him/her to act and teach those social skills.

▶ 1. Discuss why rules and laws are necessary and what the world would be like without them. Read the following to your child: *Mr. Jones was late for his doctor appointment. He sped down a one-way street the wrong way. When he got to the doctor's office, the parking lot was full. He parked behind two other cars, blocking them in. He locked his car and went in for his appointment.* Discuss what laws he broke and what might have happened as a result. Have your child rewrite (or dictate) a story in which Mr. Jones goes to the doctor without breaking the law.

▶ 2. Present the rules below (and some of your own) one at a time to your child. Have your child analyze whether it is a good rule and where the rule would apply.
Boys must wear sport coats. Girls must wear skirts.
Parking allowed with a permit.
Put all trash in the container next to the picnic shed.
Only three books may be checked out at one time.
Do not chew gum or eat candy.

Learn at Home, Grade 1   **267**

Where Is That Sheep?

Read the sentences below. **Color** the pictures. **Cut out** and **glue** each sheep where it belongs.

The sheep is on the table.	The sheep is under the loom.
The sheep is in the berry bush.	The sheep is beside the cloth.
The sheep is on Charlie's hat.	The sheep is between the pieces of Charlie's cloak.

cut

268

Learn at Home, Grade 1

Family Portraits

Families may be big or small. No matter how many people are in a family, each person is important to the others.

Cut out the pictures at the bottom of the page. **Read** the clues. **Glue** the pictures of the members of this family in the frame where they belong.

- Grandfather is in the middle.
- The girl is on the right end.
- The boy is on the left end.
- Mother is between Grandmother and the boy.
- Father is beside the girl.

 cut -

Thundering, Thumping Clouds

Circle the spelling words in the puzzle.

Look up and down.

those there this the them then they that

t	t	d	t	t	t	t	h	e
h	h	o	h	h	h	e	t	h
e	e	e	y	i	e	o	s	h	e
m	y	e	s	r	s	d	e	s
t	h	a	t	e	e	t	n	o

Read each sentence. **Write** the missing spelling words in the boxes.

1. Is ___ your coat on ___ last hook?

2. Are ___ coming to pick you up after school?

3. Do ___ books over there belong to you?

4. We will have a picnic, ___ we will go on a hike.

5. ___ are two slices of pizza left for ___ .

6. Please take ___ apple to your teacher.

Learn at Home, Grade 1

Who "Nose" These Times?

Write the time under each clock.

Example:

4:00   4:30

Language Skills	Spelling	Reading
Monday **Friendly Letter** Teach your child the correct form of a friendly letter. Point out the date, greeting, body and ending. Write a letter to your child that requires an answer. Have your child write a response that includes all the parts.	Pretest your child on these spelling words: which whip whale why where when what wheel Teach your child the *wh* digraph.	**Antonyms** Have your child work to create a center activity for practicing antonyms. *See Reading, Week 24, numbers 1–3.* Copy **Garden Scene Patterns** (p. 278) on heavy paper such as tagboard.
Tuesday After reading a nursery rhyme, have your child write a friendly letter to one of the characters. The letter may include words from the nursery rhyme and ask questions about the character's life or actions. Your child may draw a picture of him/herself with the character in the setting of the nursery rhyme. Have your child complete a copy of **A Friendly Letter** (p. 276).	Have your child write the spelling words in sentences.	Read *Alexander and the Terrible, Horrible, No-Good, Very Bad Day* by Judith Viorst. Discuss Alexander's problem and how he solved it. Have your child relate similar experiences.
Wednesday Have your child write a friendly letter to a relative or friend who lives far away.	Have your child spell each word aloud while clapping the consonants and tapping the vowels. Have your child complete **Whistle a Tune** (p. 277).	Help your child write about a day when everything went well for Alexander. Encourage your child to use some of the same language but fill in opposites. **Example:** *It was a wonderful, terrific, fantastic, very good day.*
Thursday Read a story aloud to your child. Discuss the characters in it and list any questions your child has about the story. Have your child use **A Friendly Letter** to write to one of the characters and ask the questions. (Write back to your child as if you were the character and answer your child's questions.)	Have your child write each spelling word on an index card with a black marker. Using a crayon, have your child then write the word shadowing the black letters. He/she should use a different color to trace the letters again. Have your child continue tracing the letters in this manner, creating a rainbow of colors shadowing the black letters.	**Game:** Have your child make twenty pairs of cards that show pictures of antonyms. **Examples:** right/left (hand), on/off (switch), up/down (arrow), night/day, etc. Have your child mix up the cards and play "Concentration."
Friday **Field Trip:** Call the post office and ask if you may have a tour of the mail room. Observe how incoming mail is handled and sorted. Look for charts of postal rates and zip code maps. Count the number of employees who work at the post office. Upon your return, have your child address, stamp and send a thank you letter to a relative or friend.	Give your child the final spelling test.	Have your child look through books for three words for which there are antonyms. Have him/her copy the sentence in which each word appears and underline the word. Tell your child to rewrite each sentence, substituting an antonym for the underlined word.

Math	**Science**	**Social Studies**
Calendar Make a calendar for the current month or use the calendar made in Science, Week 21, number 1. *See* Math, Week 24, number 1. Have your child complete **Desk Calendar** (p. 279)	**Solar System** Ask your child to name everything he/she knows about the Sun. Write his/her ideas down, whether they are accurate or not. Then, have your child ask questions about the Sun or name things he/she would like to know about the Sun. Write these down next to what your child knows.	Help your child create an original game. It may be a board game or one requiring physical activity. Have your child write the rules for the game and give it a unique name.
Provide your child with practice telling time to the hour and half hour. Brainstorm a list of words related to time. Discuss the number of hours in a day, days in a week and months in a year. Explain that hours are made up of minutes and that minutes are made up of seconds. Have your child complete **It's About Time** (p. 280).	Review the facts and questions gathered yesterday. Find resources at the library or at a planetarium that will answer your child's questions, and help your child write the answers to his/her questions as he/she finds them. Have your child draw a picture of the Sun and make its rays by writing some of the facts he/she learned.	Discuss the difference between rules and laws. Generally, rules are for a small group or organization. Rules help us get along and make the environment more pleasant. Laws are usually made by a government and may require a vote. Laws help keep us safe. With your child, brainstorm a list of rules and laws. Have your child sort the list into two categories—rules and laws.
Comparing: Discuss attributes, such as size, mass, volume, color and number, that can be used when comparing things. Compare your child to a brother, sister, parent or friend, using physical attributes and age. Have your child sort buttons into categories, such as yellow, two holes, larger than a dime, smooth and striped. Have your child label the categories. Then, have your child think of new categories and sort again.	Discuss what makes Earth different from the other planets. *See* Science, Week 24, number 1. Discuss what Earth would be like without the Sun.	**Poetry/Art:** Read "Rules" by Karla Kuskin in *The Random House Book of Poetry for Children,* selected by Jack Prelutsky. Discuss the ridiculous rules. Have your child create some silly "do not" rules for his/her bedroom and illustrate each rule.
Have your child compare objects according to their mass. Encourage him/her to use vocabulary, such as *heavier, lighter, less* and *more.* Have him/her sort objects, such as stones into categories (*light, medium* and *heavy*). Have your child use the **Brainy Balancing Activity Cards** (p. 281). *See* Math, Week 24, number 2.	Demonstrate the movement of the Moon around the Earth. Place a large ball on the ground to represent the Sun. Act out the part of the Earth by walking slowly around the Sun as you spin. Have your child act out the part of the Moon that quickly runs around the Earth, each time around representing approximately one month. *See* Science, Week 24, number 2.	Have your child participate in some role playing with you and/or another child. *See* Social Studies, Week 24, numbers 1 and 2.
Teach your child the concept of *greater than* (>) and *less than* (<). To help your child remember the < and > symbols, explain the open end always faces the larger number. Play a game to develop comparative language: *I am thinking of a number that is greater than 4 and less than 6. What is it?* *See* Math, Week 24, number 3. Write two numbers on the board with a circle between them. Have your child fill in the circle with the correct symbol. Repeat.	Discuss facts about the Moon: the first Moon walk, what makes the Moon "shine," life and weather on the Moon, etc. *See* Science, Week 24, numbers 3 and 4.	Discuss getting along with other people. Read *Making Friends* by Fred Rogers. As you read the book, talk about the qualities people need for getting along well with others, and have your child make a list of them. Add others that you and/or your child think are important for getting along with others.

TEACHING SUGGESTIONS AND ACTIVITIES

Reading (Antonyms)

Have your child use the **Garden Scene Patterns** on page 278 for both activities.

▶ 1. **Flower Activity**:

   a. Have your child trace and cut out the leaf and stem patterns ten times on green paper.

   b. Have your child trace and cut out the flower pattern on different colors of paper ten times.

   c. Use a marker to write pairs of antonyms—one word on a leaf and the other word on a flower. Glue a leaf on each stem.

   d. Have your child match the flower with the antonym to the correct leaf and stem.

▶ 2. **Butterfly Activity:**

   a. Have your child trace and cut out the wing pattern eight times on colored paper.

   b. Have your child trace and cut out the body eight times on different colors of paper.

   c. Use a marker to write pairs of antonyms—one word on each wing.

   d. Have your child match the antonyms on each butterfly wing and place them on a body.

▶ 3. To make a bulletin board, glue the completed flowers at least 2" apart along the base of butcher paper. Then, have your child glue the butterflies above the flowers.

Math (Calendar and Comparing)

BACKGROUND (Calendar)
Maintain a calendar in the classroom to teach many skills. Open each day with 5 minutes of calendar work. Have your child state the date, count how many days until an event, read the days and months, make patterns with the dates, add or subtract calendar numbers and so on.

▶ 1. Make a calendar for the month on an 18" x 24" sheet of paper. Cut out 28–31 squares for the dates. (Use different colors if you wish to make patterns.) Write the dates on each square. Write the name of the month at the top of the calendar. Have your child tack up the date each day of the month and say the full date. **Example:** Monday, March 4th, 1999.

BACKGROUND (Comparing)
Comparing is an essential problem-solving skill. Your child must have hands-on experience comparing objects before being asked to do so visually or mentally.

▶ 2. **Center:** Make a balance scale. Place two 2-foot-long strings on a table in the shape of an X. Tape the intersection to the bottom of a small margarine tub. Bring the ends of the strings together and tie. Prepare two tubs in this manner and balance the margarine tubs on either end of a hanger. Hang the hanger from the ceiling over a table and low enough for your child to reach the tubs. Make a copy of **Brainy Balancing Activity Cards** (p. 281). Let your child choose an activity card and answer the question using the balance scale and the named objects.

▶ 3. Play a comparing game with a deck of cards. Take out the face cards and share the deck. At the same time, have your child turn over the top card. The person who has the card with the greater value takes both cards. Repeat. If both players turn over the same card, each turns over one more card. The greater number takes all four. The game is over when one player has all the cards. **Variation:** Each player turns over two cards at once and adds the sum of their cards. They then compare sums to determine the winner of each round.

274

Learn at Home, Grade 1

Science (Solar System)

BACKGROUND
Our solar system consists of nine planets rotating around the Sun, their moons, asteroids, meteoroids and comets. The sun provides the heat and light that the Earth needs to support life. Earth is the only planet in our solar system that we know has life. Our solar system is part of the Milky Way galaxy. We can see the Milky Way on a clear dark night away from city lights.

▶ 1. Make two signs. Write Sun on one and Earth on the other. Pin Sun on you and Earth on your child. Have your child walk around you one time. Explain to your child that the Sun stands still and Earth and other planets go around the Sun. Each planet has its own path, called an orbit, so the planets will not crash into each other. It takes the Earth 1 year to orbit around the Sun. As the Earth moves around the Sun, it is spinning. Each turn of the Earth equals 1 day.

▶ 2. Discuss the movement of the Moon. It takes the Earth 1 year to travel around the Sun. Show your child twelve months on a calendar. It takes the Moon a little less than a month to travel around the Earth (28 days).

▶ 3. Explain that the Moon has no light of its own. It gets its light from the Sun. The Moon is actually a sphere, but at different times of the month it appears to be a sliver or half-Moon shape. Observe the phases of the Moon shown below. Ask your child: *Which phase is the Moon in tonight?*

▶ 4. Fold a sheet of paper into fourths. Have your child observe the Moon for four nights and draw what it looks like each time. Have your child label the boxes with the date of the observation. Have your child look at the Moon about every third day so there will be a visible change.

Social Studies (Social Skills)

Creative Dramatics: Set up some role-playing situations. Read the following or some of your own situations for your child to role-play:

▶ 1. Eight o'clock was the latest Alex was allowed to stay out on a week night. He was playing kickball in Louie's yard and the score was tied. He knew he should leave for home, but he did not want to spoil the game before the tie was broken. Alex got home 20 minutes after eight o'clock. What excuse did Alex give? What did Alex's mother say?

▶ 2. When Helen goes to the store for her mother, she has to cross a busy street. There is a traffic light to help her. One day the light seemed to stay green forever. Helen looked both ways. No cars were coming, so she crossed the street. When she got to the other side, a policeman stopped Helen and told her that she had broken a law and that he should give her a ticket. What do you think Helen and the policeman said to one another?

A Friendly Letter

_____

- - - - - - - - - - - - - -

_____
date

Dear _____ ,

- - - - - - - - - - - - - -

_____

- - - - - - - - - - - - - -

_____

- - - - - - - - - - - - - -

_____

- - - - - - - - - - - - - -

_____

- - - - - - - - - - - - - -

_____

- - - - - - - - - - - - - -

Your friend,

- - - - - - - - - - - - - -

_____

Whistle a Tune ♪ ♫ ♪ ♫

Read each sentence. **Write** the missing spelling words.

which	whip	whale	why	where	when	what	wheel

1. _____ are we going this afternoon?

2. _____ red dress will Wendy buy?

3. A huge _____ swam near the shore.

4. _____ are they going to the basketball game?

5. The shopping cart has a broken _____.

6. _____ will we see at the zoo?

7. Leon sat down when his trainer snapped the _____.

8. _____ is Mother Duck taking her ducklings to the pond?

Garden Scene Patterns

Learn at Home, Grade 1

Desk Calendar

Sunday	Monday	Tuesday	Wednesday	Thursday	Friday	Saturday

It's About Time

There are many ways we measure time. A year is made of 365 days. A week has 7 days. A day has 24 hours. An hour has 60 minutes. A minute has 60 seconds. A second goes very quickly.

day   year   minute   week   hour

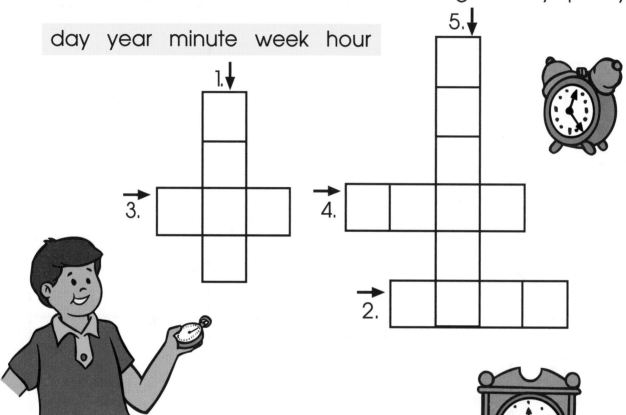

Write the words in the blanks.

1. ↓ 365 days make a y__ __ __.

2. → 7 days make a w __ __ __.

3. → 24 hours make a d __ __.

4. → 60 minutes make an h __ __ __.

5. ↓ 60 seconds make a m __ __ __ __ __.

Learn at Home, Grade 1

Brainy Balancing Activity Cards

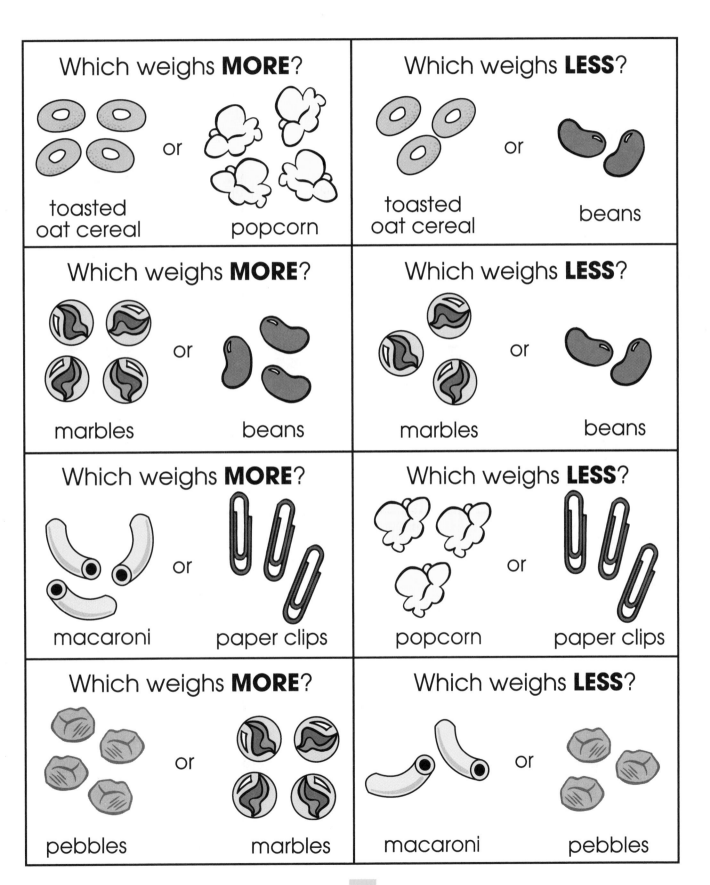

Which weighs **MORE**?

toasted oat cereal   or   popcorn

Which weighs **LESS**?

toasted oat cereal   or   beans

Which weighs **MORE**?

marbles   or   beans

Which weighs **LESS**?

marbles   or   beans

Which weighs **MORE**?

macaroni   or   paper clips

Which weighs **LESS**?

popcorn   or   paper clips

Which weighs **MORE**?

pebbles   or   marbles

Which weighs **LESS**?

macaroni   or   pebbles

Language Skills	Spelling	Reading
Monday **Spoken Language** Through role-playing, teach your child appropriate ways to respond orally in a variety of situations. *See* Language Skills, Week 25, number 1. At all times, model speaking clearly and in complete sentences to encourage your child to use appropriate spoken language.	Pretest your child on these spelling words: rich wash peach wish teach dish fish brush Review digraphs and teach the *sh* and *ch* digraph at the ends of the spelling words.	**Synonyms** Read a sentence from a familiar book. Then, reread the sentence, substituting a silly word for one of the words in the sentence. Your child should catch your "mistake." Reread the sentence again, replacing the word with a new word but keeping the meaning of the original sentence. Ask your child if that word is okay. Write the original word and the synonym on paper. Repeat with other sentences.
Tuesday **Creative Dramatics:** Role-play proper and improper manners in a variety of settings: playing at the park, answering the telephone, shopping at a store, eating in a restaurant or waiting in a line.	Have your child write the spelling words in sentences.	Make a list of synonyms. Do not write them in pairs. Have your child rewrite the list by pairing up the synonyms. *See* Reading, Week 25, number 1. Read *Blueberries for Sal* by Robert McCloskey. Ask comprehension questions after reading.
Wednesday Have a conversation with your child in which he/she asks and answers questions in complete sentences. Encourage your child to sit still, give his/her complete attention and demonstrate active listening. Possible topics include an upcoming family vacation, what your child did at a friend's house or a book you have just read.	Have your child imagine a very large paper is on the floor and his/her feet are a pencil. Have him/her "walk out" the spelling of each word. Have your child complete **Catch a Fish** (p. 286).	Have your child identify the story elements in *Blueberries for Sal*. See page 9 for a further exploration of **Story Elements**. Ask your child how old Sal might be. Ask your child to explain his/her guess. Have your child complete **Similar Meanings** (p. 287).
Thursday Memorize a story to tell your child. Have your child recall the story events while you write them on individual pages. Retell the story. Have your child refer to the written events to see if they are accurate and make any changes necessary. Then, have your child draw a picture of the events on each page. Have your child put the events in order and retell the story by referring to the pictures and speaking in complete sentences.	Have your child write acrostic poems using all the spelling words.	**Art:** Have your child write pairs of synonyms in a creative way. **Example:** *Good Great* Provide a list of synonyms from which he/she may select words.
Friday Have your child select a story he/she would like to tell. Ask your child to tell you the events of the story in order. List them on the chalkboard. Then, have your child tell the story into a tape recorder so he/she can hear him/herself.	Give your child the final spelling test.	Have your child find and copy a sentence from *Blueberries for Sal* that tells: ...where the characters are. ...why the bears were eating blueberries. ...why Sal's mother was picking blueberries. ...why Mother Bear backed away from Sal. ...why Mother backed away from Little Bear. ...how many blueberries they picked.

Learn at Home, Grade 1

Math	**Science**	**Social Studies**
Place Value—Hundreds Place Build numbers to 99 to determine if your child is ready to move on to the hundreds place. When your child has 99 on the place-value board, add one more and ask your child what to do. You may need to tell your child that 10 tens need regrouping. Show your child how to bundle ten groups of ten together with a rubber band or by placing them in a plastic bag or large margarine tub. Call this unit *one hundred*.	**Poetry:** Read "Night and Day," "The Moon" and "The Sun Travels" from Robert Louis Stevenson's *A Child's Garden of Verses*. Read one verse of "Night and Day" at a time and write it on a large sheet of paper. Have your child illustrate each verse.	Go over the list of personal qualities for getting along with others you and your child compiled on Friday. Ask your child to define or give an example of sharing, cooperation, helping, including, giving, taking, kindness, consideration and understanding. Discuss specific experiences your child has had that illustrate each one. *See* Social Studies, Week 25, number 1.
Provide your child with practice grouping tens into one hundred. Use a different manipulative each time or make it a game so your child doesn't tire of the activity. Write each number as your child builds it, connecting the concrete manipulative activity with the symbolic number. *See* Math, Week 25, numbers 1 and 2.	Study a picture of the solar system. Help your child become familiar with the names of the planets. Work together to develop a mnemonic sentence to help your child remember the names of the planets in order. Have your child complete **Far Out!** (p. 288).	Have your child write a poem about getting along. *See* Social Studies, Week 25, number 2.
Have your child build numbers over one hundred. Have your child say the place values of the number, such as *one hundred, two tens and five ones*. Write the digits and have your child read the number you wrote *(125)*. *See* Math, Week 25, numbers 3 and 4. Write a list of numbers over 100 and have your child build and say each one.	Help your child to create a model of the planets using balloons. Hang a wire across the room. Obtain one large yellow balloon and several different colored small balloons. Obtain books to help add specific characteristics of each planet. *See* Science, Week 25, numbers 1 and 2.	Read *The Giving Tree* by Shel Silverstein. Discuss which character showed the qualities of a good friend—the boy or the tree. Discuss why the other character was not a good friend. In what ways does your child think he/she can act like the tree? Is acting like the tree always the best way to act? Have your child explain his/her answer.
Working together with your child, count 100 manipulatives and place them in a resealable plastic bag. Repeat several times. Keep completed bags so your child has several hundreds in reserve. Have your child roll three dice to determine what number to build in each place (hundreds, tens and ones). After building the 3-digit number, have your child record the number on lined paper and read it aloud.	Have your child continue working on the model of the solar system begun yesterday.	Discuss situations in which getting along goes beyond how to treat a friend. Discuss how your child should treat his/her future co-workers, service people and clients. Discuss the mission of the United Nations in the world. Share articles from the newspaper that illustrate the need for understanding and cooperation in the world. Have your child make a poster showing how others should be treated.
Find 3-digit numbers in books and around the house. Have your child read each number and state it in terms of place value (356, 3 hundreds, 5 tens and 6 ones). *See* Math, Week 25, number 5.	**Music:** Teach the song "Catch a Falling Star" from a recording and/or sheet music. There are also CD's, tapes and sheet music available. Discuss the difference between stars and meteors. Have your child complete **A Falling Star** (p. 289).	Explain to your child that many disagreements are caused by misunderstandings. Help him/her to see that choosing the correct words and tone of voice to express what you mean can make the difference between a positive and negative interaction. *See* Social Studies, Week 25, number 3. Have your child relate a time when he/she was misunderstood or when he/she misunderstood someone else.

283

Learn at Home, Grade 1

TEACHING SUGGESTIONS AND ACTIVITIES

Language Skills (Spoken Language)

▶ 1. Teach your child polite language for situations such as greeting someone, saying good-bye to someone, stepping on someone's toes, asking for something or receiving a gift. Act out several situations with your child.

Sample dialogues:	**Greeting**	**Asking a favor**
	Hello.	Please hand me a pencil.
	(Hello.)	(Here is a pencil.)
	How are you?	Thank you.
	(Fine, thank you.)	(You're welcome.)
	Introduction	**Giving/Receiving**
	I'd like you to meet John.	Happy birthday.
	(Hello. Welcome.)	(Thank you.)
	Please show John around.	You may open your gift.
	(Okay, I'd be happy to.)	(Thank you. It is just what I wanted.)

Reading (Synonyms)

▶ 1. Write pairs of synonyms on individual index cards—one word per card. Have your child match the words that have similar meanings. For added interest, write the words on colorful shapes.

Math (Place Value–Hundreds Place)

BACKGROUND
This lesson will build upon earlier place-value lessons. If your child is not ready to move ahead, review the past lessons in place value with him/her (Weeks 15–16).

hundreds	tens	ones

▶ 1. Give your child the place-value board and manipulatives. Have your child roll one die to determine how many manipulatives to add each time. Have your child keep rolling and adding manipulatives until he/she reaches 99.

▶ 2. Let your child discover how to move from 99 to 100. The ten bundles can be placed in a margarine container and slid over to the left of the tens place. You should have a sheet of 18" x 6" paper ready to add to the place-value board for the hundreds place. Before offering it, see if your child thinks about needing a hundreds place.

▶ 3. On individual index cards, write numbers greater than 100. Hold up one number card at a time. Have your child make the number using manipulatives.

Learn at Home, Grade 1

4. Write the number *102* on the chalkboard. Have your child build it on the place-value board. Continue adding up to 109. Ask your child to add one more and describe what he/she is doing (bundling the ones into a ten). Have your child write the number after it is built. At this point, move on to adding if you feel your child is ready.

5. **Game:** Give your child one die. Have him/her roll it and write the number. Have your child roll it again and write that number to the right of the first one. Have your child roll again and write the third number next to the second one. Have your child read the 3-digit number aloud.

Science (Solar System)

1. Blow up a large yellow balloon to represent the Sun. Write *Sun* on it with a marker and tie a string to it. Hang the Sun on the left end of the wire. Refer to a picture of the solar system as you blow up other balloons in proportion to the size of the planets, but much smaller than the Sun. Write the planet's name on each balloon. Help your child draw the outlines of the continents on the Earth balloon. Put on the specific markings of the other planets: the red spot on Jupiter, Mercury's craters, etc. Hang the completed planets in order from the Sun on the wire.

2. Explain how each planet travels around the Sun in its own path and stays in the same order. (**Exception:** Pluto and Neptune, the farthest planets from the Sun, cross paths for a short time.) Tell your child that Mercury takes only 88 days to go around the Sun, but Earth takes 365 days. Ask your child to explain why he/she thinks that happens.

Social Studies (Social Skills)

1. On sentence strips, write sentence starters, such as *Sharing is . . .* and *Cooperation is. . . .* Have your child finish (write or dictate) each one. Hang up the sentences around the room.

2. Help your child write a short poem about one of the qualities discussed on the previous two days.
    Example: *It is nice to share.*
    It shows you care.
    It makes the world a better place.
    It makes a better human race.

3. Sometimes language or tone gets in the way of communicating exactly what we mean. When someone says something that is unclear to you, it is best to ask for clarification immediately. A good practice is to repeat back to someone what you think he/she just said. That is the best way to avoid miscommunication. Sometimes people from other cultures use different words.
    Meaning may change with tone of voice:
    I caught you (as in tag). *I caught you* (doing something sneaky).
    Please hold it. Please, hold it!
    Meaning may change because of punctuation:
    "The teacher," said Bill, "is going to stand on his head."
    The teacher said, "Bill is going to stand on his head."

Catch a Fish

Write a spelling word to complete each sentence.

wash

teach

peach

brush

rich

wish

fish

dish

1. Don't forget to _____ your hands before lunch.

2. Father dropped the_____into the paint.

3. I have a pet_____.

4. My favorite fruit is a _____.

5. A _____ man bought the big house on the hill.

6. I made a _____ upon a star.

7. Can you _____ me to play that game?

8. My brother dropped a _____ and broke it.

Learn at Home, Grade 1

Similar Meanings

Read the words in the box. **Write** two words under each picture.

rock start road begin street stone
shut sad talk unhappy speak closed

_____

_____

_____

_____

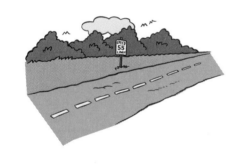

_____

_____

_____

_____

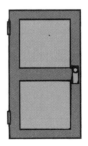

_____

_____

_____

_____

Learn at Home, Grade 1

Far Out!

Imagine that you are traveling from the Sun to outer space. **Write** Sun first. Then, **write** the names of the planets in order.

_____   _____
1. _____   6. _____

_____   _____
2. _____   7. _____

_____   _____
3. _____   8. _____

_____   _____
4. _____   9. _____

_____   _____
5. _____   10. _____

A Falling Star

Have you ever seen a falling star? Falling stars are not really stars. They are small pieces of rock. As falling stars fall, they get hot and burn. They look big because they give off so much light. That is why they are so bright in the night sky. Did you know that meteor is another name for a falling star?

Circle the correct answer.

A falling star is really a star.

Yes   No

Falling stars are pieces of rock.

Yes   No

Falling stars burn as they fall.

Yes   No

Unscramble the answer.
Another name for a falling star is _____ .

e r m o t e
2 6 1 5 3 4

Draw two yellow falling stars in the picture.

	Language Skills	**Spelling**	**Reading**
Monday	**Other Forms of Expression** Teach your child to pantomime familiar actions for you to guess. Suggestions include eating dinner, swinging a bat, riding a bike and swimming. Reverse roles—you pantomime an action that your child guesses.	Pretest your child on these spelling words: bath bang teeth rang path hang math sang Teach your child the *ang* ending and the unvoiced *th* digraph. *See* Spelling, Week 26.	Write some poems on lined paper. Read the poems with your child. Have your child underline rhyming words in the same color crayon. Note patterns such as ABAB rhymes. Read *Jesse Bear, What Will You Wear?* by Nancy White Carlstrom. Have your child fill in the rhyming words on the second reading.
Tuesday	**Creative Movement:** Play different musical selections. Have your child move to them and imagine the type of setting in which he/she is moving. **Music/Art:** Provide a variety of paints and different selections of music. Have your child paint on large paper the way the music makes him/her feel.	Have your child write the spelling words in sentences.	Discuss the character of Jesse Bear. List all the things from the book that Jesse Bear "wears" throughout the day. Have your child write a sentence for each part of the day, describing what he/she will "wear."
Wednesday	Provide materials such as an old sock and sewing notions for your child to make a puppet of his/her favorite storybook character or make stick puppets using tongue depressors and paper. Have your child use his/her new puppet to put on a show.	Have your child spell each word aloud as he/she marches around the room. Have your child complete **A Long Path** (p. 294).	Have your child select an animal or object for the title of a descriptive poem. Have your child write describing words (adjectives) or phrases on each line of the poem, then add words to make sense. **Example:** <u>Elephant</u> With its huge ears And enormous body, This giant animal Is afraid of nothing. Did someone say *mouse*?
Thursday	**Creative Dramatics:** Have your child dress up like a famous person or character and speak words that that person might say.	Have your child use finger paints to write each spelling word on a large poster.	Brainstorm a list of words that could be used to replace the word *said* in your child's writing. Look in books for ideas. Have your child invent a dialogue between an animal and its mother. Encourage him/her to use words other than *said* in the animals' conversation.
Friday	**Reader's Theater:** Read passages from a book as dialogue. Have your child read one part while you read another.	Give your child the final spelling test.	Have your child fold a sheet of drawing paper into thirds. In the first box, have your child draw something that happened in the beginning of the story *Jesse Bear, What Will You Wear?* In the other two boxes, have your child illustrate something that happened in the middle and at the end of the story.

Learn at Home, Grade 1

Math	Science	Social Studies
3-Digit Addition and Subtraction, No Regrouping Introduce 3-digit addition using manipulatives and a place-value board. Use the bags of 100 manipulatives you created last week to make building easier. *See* Math, Week 26, number 1. Provide your child with four 3-digit addition equations to solve independently.	**The Milky Way Galaxy** Teach your child that our solar system is part of a larger group called a galaxy. There are billions of stars in the galaxy and some, like our Sun, may have planets circling them. There are also billions of galaxies in the universe. *See* Science, Week 26, number 1.	**Manners** Read poems about manners with your child. Discuss and list both good and bad manners. Read "Manners" and "Table Manners" in *The Random House Book of Poetry for Children* by Jack Prelutsky, as well as "Politely" in *When We Were Very Young* by A. A. Milne.
Teach your child to find the missing addend with 3-digit addition problems. *See* Math, Week 26, number 2. Give your child four equations with missing addends to solve. Encourage him/her to use manipulatives if needed.	Look at star charts with your child and help him/her identify constellations. Observe the shapes that the constellations appear to form, such as animal shapes.	Teach appropriate manners at the dinner table and at a restaurant through role-playing. *See* Social Studies, Week 26, number 1.
Use the numbers in yesterday's problems to introduce 3-digit subtraction. If your child recognizes the relationship, compliment him/her. Show your child that subtraction is another way to find missing addends. *See* Math, Week 26, number 3.	Make constellations using a coffee can, flashlight and cardboard. *See* Science, Week 26, number 2.	Teach manners appropriate at the movies, in the library and on the phone. Go to these places and have your child practice using good manners.
Have your child work independently to solve six 3-digit subtraction and six 3-digit addition equations. Caution him/her to watch for the plus and minus signs.	**Music:** Sing "Twinkle, Twinkle, Little Star" with your child. Help your child write a response from the star. Then, sing "Twinkle, Twinkle, Little Star" and let your child sing his/her response. Have your child complete **Twinkling Starlights** (p. 295).	Teach the appropriate way to introduce someone and what to say when being introduced.
Introduce mental math to your child. Tell your child to picture a number in his/her head. (Encourage your child to picture the number in place-value form.) Then, tell your child to add or take away some tens or ones and state the new number. **Examples:** *Picture 52. Take away 5 tens. What is left?* or *Picture 239. Add 3 tens. What is the number?* **Note:** Be sure to avoid equations that require regrouping. Practice mental math daily.	Explain that stars are always in the sky. Ask your child to explain why he/she thinks stars cannot be seen during the day. Discuss the many sizes and colors of stars. Explain that our Sun is medium-sized and that stars appear small because they are very far away. Have your child observe stars to see the different colors.	Through role-playing, teach your child how to react to someone who does something rude. *See* Social Studies, Week 26, number 2.

TEACHING SUGGESTIONS AND ACTIVITIES

Spelling (Unvoiced *th* Digraph)

BACKGROUND
The *th* digraph makes two sounds—voiced and unvoiced. The voiced *th*, as in week 23, is heard at the beginning of words such as *there* and *then*. Have your child notice the vibration of the *th* sound against his/her front teeth. The unvoiced *th* is heard at the beginning of words, such as *thin* and *thistle*. Have your child notice the vibration of his/her voice box and his/her breath moving between his/her tongue and teeth as he/she makes the unvoiced *th* sound.

Math (3-Digit Addition and Subtraction, No Regrouping)

BACKGROUND
If you feel your child is not ready for this concept, work more with place-value and 2-digit addition (Week 17) or 2-digit subtraction (Week 19). Activities similar to this week's lessons were taught in Weeks 17 and 19. You may want to look at those lessons and their activity sheets. This lesson may wait until second grade or be combined with Week 35.

▶ 1. Write a 3-digit number on the chalkboard. Have your child build it on his/her place-value board. Write another number below the first one. (Make sure when the two are added that no regrouping is necessary.) Draw a line under the two numbers and write a plus sign to the left of the second number. Make an arrow pointing down over the ones column. Remind your child that he/she should begin addition problems in the ones column. Ask your child how many ones there are altogether in the two numbers and write his/her response under the line in the ones column. Do the same for the tens column and the hundreds column. Repeat this activity several times.

▶ 2. Say a 3-digit number *(three hundred two)*. Have your child build it on a place-value board and write it and put a plus sign to the left. Write 457 below the line. Ask how many more ones are needed to have seven ones altogether (5). Ask how many more tens are needed to have five tens all together (5). Ask how many more hundreds are needed to have four hundreds all together (1). Have your child read the new addend and make it on his/her place-value board. Have your child read the problem and the answer aloud: *Three hundred two plus one hundred fifty-five equals four hundred fifty-seven.* Repeat this activity with other numbers.

▶ 3. Use the same numbers as in activity 4 above. Write 624 on the chalkboard. Tell your child to build *624* on the place-value board. Write – 213 under it. Ask your child how many the problem says to take away. Have your child remove them from his/her place-value board. Ask how many are left. When the entire answer is written, ask your child to read the answer. Repeat with other numbers. Compare the equations.

Science (The Milky Way Galaxy)

BACKGROUND
Our solar system is part of the Milky Way Galaxy. Our Sun is one of billions of stars that make up the galaxy. The Milky Way Galaxy is spiral-shaped and consists of billions of stars. Because we are part of the galaxy, we do not see its spiral-shape. On a clear, dark night, we can see the galaxy. Since we see it from the side, it looks like a stripe of concentrated stars stretching across the sky.

Stars do not move but they appear to move because of the spinning of the Earth. Stars that are in one part of the sky early in the evening appear in another part of the sky later in the same evening. At different times of the year, you will see different stars in the sky.

Learn at Home, Grade 1

1. Explain to your child that thousands of years ago people made up stories about the stars and imagined that groups of stars formed the shapes of people and animals. These star shapes are called *constellations*. Duplicate a star chart for your child. Have your child connect stars to form pictures. Your child may name his/her own constellations and then look for them in the night sky.

2. Help your child make a coffee can constellation:

    a. Use a can opener to remove the bottom of an empty coffee can. Trace the lamp end of a flashlight and cut a hole in the plastic lid of the can. The hole should be just large enough for the end of the flashlight to fit snugly.

    b. Trace the coffee can to make a circle on a piece of thin cardboard. Cut it out. Poke holes in the cardboard with a pin to form a real or invented constellation.

    c. Paint the inside of the can and plastic lid black.

    d. Put the plastic lid on one end of the can with the flashlight head inside the can. Tape the cardboard circle over the other end.

    e. Turn out the lights. Pull the shades. Turn on the flashlight and point it toward an empty wall to see the constellation.

    f. Replace the cardboard circle with others to display a variety of constellations.

Social Studies (Manners)

BACKGROUND
A unit on social skills would not be complete without teaching about manners. Having good manners involves being polite and courteous. Manners are learned through teaching, by example and by practice.

Creative Dramatics
1. Following are some role-playing situations for your child. Add some of your own.

    a. The doorbell rings. You answer it. There is a woman you do not know there to talk to your mother.

    b. At the movie theater, there is a long line to buy tickets. You see a friend at the front of the line who invites you to cut in.

    c. The waiter brought your hamburger but forgot your french fries. Tell him about it and also tell him you would like mustard and ketchup.

    d. You are having dinner at a friend's house. They are serving something that you do not like at all.

    e. You and your parent see your friend's mother at the grocery store. Introduce her to your mother or father.

2. Try these role-playing situations to learn how to act when someone is rude.

    a. Someone interrupted you when you were telling a story.

    b. Someone took too many potatoes and none were left when they were passed to you.

    c. Someone pushed you when you were waiting to buy an ice-cream cone.

    d. Two people came late to the movie and stood in the aisle talking while looking for a seat.

A Long Path

Write the spelling words in alphabetical order. The first one has been done for you.

| bath | bang | teeth | rang | path | hang | math | sang |

1. **bang**   2. _____   3. _____   4. _____

5. _____   6. _____   7. _____   8. _____

Complete in the sentences below.

1. The hammer struck the nail with a loud _____ .

2. At 7:00, Casie's alarm _____ .

3. Joseph likes to help_____ the laundry on the clothesline.

4. My brother _____ in the choir.

5. Renee's favorite subject in school is _____ .

6. Ron lost his first two baby_____ .

7. My friends like to go hiking on a _____ through the forest.

8. Sara takes a _____ on Saturday night.

294

Learn at Home, Grade 1

Twinkling Starlights

Stars change as they get older. They start out big and then shrink. As they shrink, they change color. **Color** the stars the correct color.

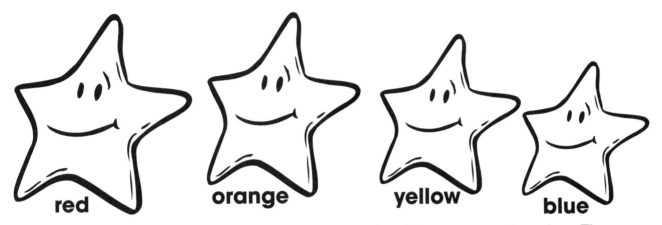

red   orange   yellow   blue

Look at the stars below. **Color** each star the correct color. Then, **draw** a circle around the youngest stars and a box around the oldest ones.

	Language Skills	**Spelling**	**Reading**
Monday	**Review Week** Review poetic language with your child. On both sides of a cutout of a familiar shape, have your child brainstorm words that are related to the shape. Repeat using other shapes. Staple the completed cutouts to a long piece of ribbon and hang them on the wall. Play a rhyming domino game. *See* Language Skills, Week 27, number 1.	**Review Week** Review color words with your child. Write words on index cards and have your child place the cards on objects of the given color. Point to colors around the room and have your child spell the color on the chalkboard.	**Review Week** Review verbs with your child. Write a different sentence on each of 20 index cards. Draw a blank line in place of the verb in each sentence. On 20 smaller cards, write the missing verbs. Instruct your child to match the small cards to the sentence card where the verb makes sense. Then, have your child write each sentence on lined paper.
Tuesday	Review contractions and possessives with your child. Write ten sentences containing contractions and possessives. Have your child circle the contractions with a red pencil and the possessives with a blue pencil. Then, have your child tell you what two words make up each contraction and what objects belongs to each possessive.	Review number words with your child. Give your child number word cards to arrange in order. Then, tell your child a number. He/she should find two number word cards whose combined value adds up to the number given. Ask your child to find another combination of numbers that adds up to the same sum. Repeat with other numbers.	Review possessives with your child. Have your child think of all the people he/she knows who have pets. Have your child draw a picture of each pet and label whose pet it is with a sentence that includes *'s*. **Example:** *This is Helena's parrot.*
Wednesday	Review location words with your child. Have your child follow directions such as these: *Put this button before the thimble.* *Put this paper under the door.* *Tape this coin to the bottom of the lamp.* *Sit next to the plant with the pink flower.* Ask your child to identify the location word in each sentence.	Review digraphs with your child. Write words on index cards and cut the digraph off each. Mix up the cards and have your child match the parts to spell the words. Have your child complete **Digraphs** (p. 300).	Review comparative language with your child. Have your child fold a sheet of 12" x 18" paper in fourths in one direction, turn and fold it in fourths the other way so that when it is opened, the paper has sixteen boxes. Have your child write an adjective in the first box of each row. In the second box, have your child draw a picture fitting the description. He/she should write the word with *er* in the third box and *est* in the fourth box and illustrate them.
Thursday	Review writing a friendly letter with your child. Write a letter to your child containing directions. Ask your child to read and follow the directions exactly. *See* Language Skills, Week 27, number 2 for a sample letter.	Review ending sounds and digraphs with your child. Give your child a word that rhymes with a spelling word. Ask your child to identify the spelling word. Then, play rhyming bingo.	Review antonyms and synonyms with your child. Have your child complete **Same or Opposite?** (p. 301).
Friday	Review oral or spoken language. Have your child create a news program including personal and family news. Also, have your child look in the newspaper for news articles that could be added to the news program. Have your child broadcast the news from a television set made from a refrigerator box.	Give a review spelling test using riddles. Pick and choose spelling words to use. **Example:** *I am both a color and a fruit. What am I?*	Have your child list books he/she has read in the past 9 weeks. Have your child write the titles of books he/she has read on the circles and add them to the "reading caterpillar" begun in Week 9. Then, have your child choose a favorite book and write a book report on it.

Learn at Home, Grade 1

Math	**Science**	**Social Studies**
Review Week Review money and coin values with your child. Prepare "piggy banks" for family members and friends. Count and compare the money in each. *See* Math, Week 27, numbers 1 and 2.	**Review Week** Review seasons with your child. Fold a sheet of paper into fourths. Write a season in each. Have your child draw a picture for each season. | Winter	Summer
---	---
Spring	Fall		**Review Week** Review animals with your child. Make three headings: *Pets, Farm Animals* and *Zoo Animals*. Give your child a variety of animal pictures to sort under the correct headings.
Review measurement with your child. Have your child measure objects around the room using his/her hands as a non-standard unit. Have your child compare his/her hands to your hands. Use your hands and then your child's hands to measure the same distance (across the table). Discuss why the measurements come out differently.	Review weather with your child. Explain how a rainbow forms in the sunshine after a rain. Conduct an experiment in front of a window on a sunny day to see how a rainbow forms. *See* Science, Week 27, numbers 1 and 2.	Have your child write (or dictate) an acrostic poem about an animal and draw a picture to go with it. **Example:** This cat is orange and black. I like the way it sounds. Growling, growling, growling, Every muscle's twitching, Ready to pounce on its next meal.
Review time with your child. Have your child set the hands on the learning clock to a named hour or half hour. Then, set the clock on the hour or half hour while your child writes the time. Switch roles and have your child give you times to show. Deliberately make a mistake or two for your child to correct. Have your child complete **Sock Clocks** (p. 302).	Review the solar system with your child. Have your child make a diorama of the Earth, the Sun, Moon and stars. *See* Science, Week 27, number 3.	On small cards, write the names of the animals for which you have pictures. Have your child match the animal pictures with the names.
Review the calendar with your child. Have your child read today's date from a calendar. Look for upcoming events and discuss how long in days, weeks or months it is until those events. Have your child complete **Hmm, What Month Is It?** (p. 303).	Review the stars with your child. On a clear night, have a barbecue outside and watch the "movement" of the stars. Have your child find a familiar constellation before dinner. After dinner, have your child find the same one. Have books available for your child to use as references.	Review social skills with your child. Read examples of manners, rules and laws. Have your child tell whether each is a law, a rule or good manners. Then, he/she may tell in what situation the behavior should be practiced. *See* Social Studies, Week 27, number 1.
Review comparing and place value with your child. Have him/her compare 2-digit numbers using the greater than (>) and less than (<) signs. *See* Math, Week 27, numbers 3 and 4.	Help your child make Moon phase cookies. Using a sugar cookie recipe, make several round cookies and bake them. Your child may frost each cookie with chocolate and white (or yellow) icing, showing different phases of the Moon. Store the decorated cookies in the freezer and let your child eat each cookie when the Moon is in that phase.	Copy the provided story about a boy who is not using his social skills. *See* Social Studies, Week 27, number 2. Read the story with your child. Discuss the boy's behavior. Have your child copy the story and make changes so the boy is polite and obeys the rules of the game.

Learn at Home, Grade 1

TEACHING SUGGESTIONS AND ACTIVITIES

Language Skills

▶ 1. **Game/Center:** Play a game of rhyming dominoes. Divide several index cards in half by drawing a black line down the middle of the card. Write a word on half of a card and a rhyming word on another card half. Repeat until all cards have two words written on them.

   Directions for play: Have your child select one card, place it on the playing surface and look for a card with a word that rhymes with either word of the original card. Have your child place the rhyming word next to its match on the playing surface. Continue matching the unmatched ends of the cards in play until all the cards are used.

▶ 2. Review the format and parts of a friendly letter. Give your child the following to complete:

> Date
>
> Dear _____,
>
> In this letter, please circle the date. Then, underline the greeting. Next, make a red box around the body of the letter. And finally, cross out the closing with a blue X.
>
> Sincerely,
>
> _____

Math

▶ 1. Draw one outline of a piggy bank for each member of your child's family and some friends. Label the banks. Place some change (not to exceed 50¢) "in" each bank. Make a two-column chart on lined paper. Have your child write each name in the left column and the amount of money in the right column. Compose several questions for your child to answer about the chart data, such as *Who has the most money?* or *Who has three coins that total 40¢?* (See information at right.)

▶ 2. **Game:** Make a grid with ten 1" squares across and ten 1" squares down. Have your child fill each square with a single coin value (1¢, 5¢, 10¢, 25¢ or 50¢). On index cards, write values such as *34¢, 2¢* and *16¢*. Do not make any amount more than 50¢. Have your child select a card and put that amount of real coins on the grid in this manner: a penny must be put on a 1¢ square, a nickel on a 5¢ square, etc. Your child may cover the amount in any way. To "win" the game, your child must fill all the spaces.

SAM   GRACE   JOY

Name	Amount
Sam	17¢
Grace	40¢
Joy	50¢

1. Who has the most money? _____
2. Who has 3 coins that total 40¢?
3. How many coins does Grace have?

Learn at Home, Grade 1

▶ 3. Make a place-value grid with a ones column and a tens column. Write the numbers 21 and 26 on the grid. Ask your child which one is greater and how he/she can tell. Repeat a few times, always having the same number of tens but a different number of ones. Next, keep the ones the same but show a different number of tens. Write 25 and 45 and ask which is greater. Ask your child how he/she can tell.

▶ 4. Make a number line to 100 for the floor. Have your child throw a beanbag onto a number. Ask your child to put a beanbag on a number greater or less than the number landed on. Ask how he/she knows this number is greater than or lesser than the first number. Have your child write a number sentence about it using the > and < signs. Repeat this activity many times.

Science

▶ 1. a. Have your child fill a glass baking dish half full with water.

   b. Next, have your child set a small mirror in the water.

   c. Have your child move the mirror until a rainbow is formed on the wall of the room. The sun reflecting in the water will make the colors. Ask your child to name all the colors he/she sees. Explain that rainbows form when water bends the sunlight.

▶ 2. **Art/Writing:** Have your child paint a rainbow. When the paint dries, ask your child to dictate a sentence about each color of the rainbow. Write each sentence on the arc of its color.

▶ 3. To make a diorama, have your child paint the inside of a box black. After it dries, have your child place star stickers all over the inside of the box. Next, have your child form three balls of white clay—one large, one medium and one small. When the clay hardens, your child should paint the large ball yellow, the medium one blue and the small one white. Have your child place the balls—Sun, Moon and Earth—on the bottom of the box and label them.

Social Studies

▶ 1. Read these examples of rules, laws and manners. Add some of your own.

   A person must be eighteen years old before he/she can vote.
   Do not talk with food in your mouth.
   Walk inside the house.
   Park your car between the yellow lines.
   Sit in your seat once the movie starts and do not talk during the show.
   There is a six-percent sales tax on all merchandise.
   Anyone under the age of sixteen must be home by ten o'clock on weeknights.
   Open the door for someone whose arms are full.
   The president of the United States may hold office only for two terms.
   Empty the trash on Monday and Friday before going to school.

▶ 2. Copy the story below and read it with your child.
   Bobby and his friends were taking turns throwing the ball at a wall. Each boy took one turn and went to the back of the line. When Bobby took his turn, the ball did not go as he wanted it to. Instead of going to the back of the line, Bobby threw the ball again. When he got in line, he stepped on Tony's foot. Tony said, "Ouch." Bobby made a mean face at him. When it was Bobby's turn again, he grabbed the ball from the player who had it last and threw the ball over the wall.

Digraphs

Circle the correct digraph for each picture. **Color** the pictures.

sh ch

wh th

ch sh

wh th

sh ch

ch sh

sh ch

ch sh

wh th

sh ch

ch sh

wh th

Learn at Home, Grade 1

Same or Opposite?

Color the spaces yellow if they have word pairs with **opposite** meanings. **Color** the spaces blue if they have word pairs with the **same** meanings.

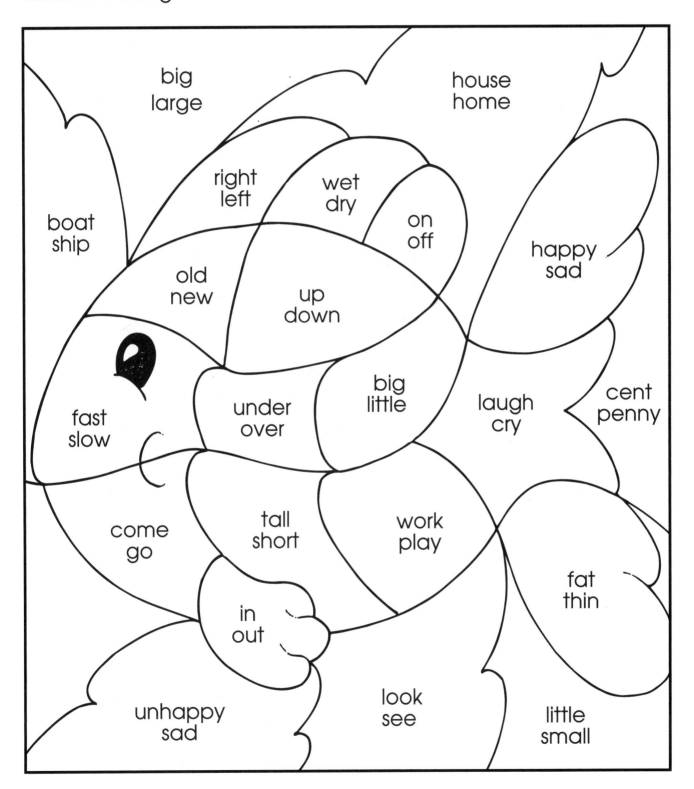

Sock Clocks

Draw the hands on the sock clocks.

1:30

7:00

4:30

10:00

3:30

9:30

4:00

2:30

6:00

302

Learn at Home, Grade 1

Hmm, What Month Is It?

There are 12 months in a year. The first month is January. The last month is December. Some months have 31 days. Some months have 30 days. February is the shortest month with 28 days.

Write 1 to 12 in the boxes to put the months in order. The first one is done for you.

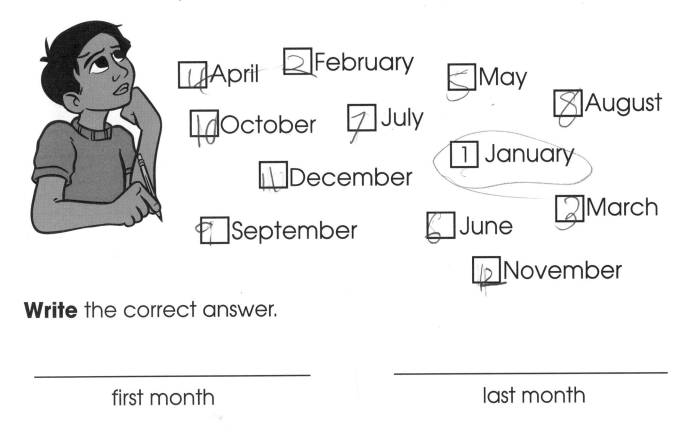

[4] April   [2] February   [5] May   [8] August
[10] October   [7] July   [1] January
[11] December   [3] March
[9] September   [6] June
[12] November

Write the correct answer.

_____   _____
first month   last month

Circle the correct answer.

Some months have 30 days.   (Yes)   No

Some months have 31 days.   (Yes)   No

February is the longest month.   Yes   (No)

February has 28 days.   (Yes)   No

	Language Skills	**Spelling**	**Reading**

Monday	**Writing Ideas**
	Copy and enlarge a comic strip and remove the words. Glue the comic onto a strip of drawing paper and cut it into sections. Have your child dictate new dialogue for the comic strip.
	Hint: Choose a comic strip that your child has not already read but one in which he/she knows the characters well.
		R–Controlled Vowels
		Pretest your child on these spelling words:
		    car arm
		    park scarf
		    march star
		    barn cart
		Teach your child *r*-controlled vowels.
			Homophones
			Write *for* and *four* on the chalkboard. Read each one to your child and explain the difference. Have your child use each word in a sentence. Explain that homophones sound the same but have different meanings and different spellings. Teach the following homophones: *I-eye, new-knew, to-two, bear-bare, dear-deer, so-sew, there-their-they're, be-bee* and *pear-pair.*

Tuesday	Have your child write and illustrate an original cartoon.	Have your child write the spelling words in sentences.	Ask your child to recall a positive experience with snow. If your child has no experience with snow, ask your child to describe what he/she thinks it might be like. Read *The Snowy Day* by Ezra Jack Keats. Ask your child to compare Peter's experiences with his/her own. **Art:** Make paper snowflakes. Have your child write details from the story on the snowflakes. Display your child's completed snowflakes.
Wednesday	Show your child an interesting picture from a book or magazine. Discuss what is happening in the picture, then encourage your child to write about it.	Have your child spell each word aloud while writing large letters in the air. Have your child complete **On Your Mark** (p. 309).	In the book *The Snowy Day*, help your child find homophones for each of the following words: *new, write, hi, maid, son, haul* and *knew.* Then, have your child copy the sentence containing each homophone. *See* Reading, Week 28, number 1.
Thursday	Write a three-sentence story, one sentence per index card. Mix up the cards and have your child place the cards in the correct order. Have your child reread the sentences in order to confirm that they make sense. Then, have your child write three sentences to make his/her own three sentence story. Have your child complete **Sentence Sequence** (p. 308).	Have your child cut out a large star shape from yellow construction paper. On both sides of the star, have your child write *Words that contain ar.* Encourage him/her to include words other than his/her spelling words.	Read *Peter's Chair* by Ezra Jack Keats. Use a Venn diagram to compare this story to *The Snowy Day. See* page 11 for a further exploration of **Comparing and Contrasting.**
Friday	With your child, brainstorm possible writing topics. The easiest stories to write are those from your child's own experience. Have your child think of recent events and activities that could be described in a story. Also, your child may enjoy writing about people and pets. Have your child write a story of his/her choice.	Give your child the final spelling test.	Ask your child to describe important events from *The Snowy Day* or *Peter's Chair.* Write each event on an index card. Have your child read the cards and arrange the events in sequential order to make a time line.

Math	Science	Social Studies
Column Addition Use flash cards to assess your child's mastery of addition facts to 18. Have your child add three single-digit numbers using dot cards. *See* Math, Week 28, numbers 1 and 2.	**Magnets** Demonstrate that a magnet appears to "stick" to certain objects, such as a filing cabinet or refrigerator. Gather several household objects. Have your child sort the objects into groups of things he/she thinks will "stick" to the magnet and those that he/she thinks will not. Record your child's predictions. Have your child touch the magnet to each object and determine the accuracy of his/her predictions.	**Early Americans** Explain to your child that there were many Native American tribes living in this country before the Europeans arrived 500 years ago. Read about the tribes in the various regions of the U.S. (There are many books available at the library.) Discuss the Native American way of life. Have your child complete **Native American Tribes** (p. 311).
Provide several equations for your child to practice with the help of the dot cards. Periodically replace dot cards with number cards until your child is solving problems without the aid of the dot cards. *See* Math, Week 28, number 3.	Work with your child to find magnetic objects around the house using **Sticky Hunt** (p. 310). Before beginning the activity, have your child read the warning at the bottom of the activity sheet.	Read about Native American homes with your child. Discuss how the climate and local materials influenced home construction. Have your child complete **Native American Homes** (p. 312).
Write several equations in vertical form. Teach your child to group numbers in a way to make addition easier. **Example**: When adding 4 + 7 + 6 =, have your child start with 4 + 6 to make 10, then add the 7. Your child may circle numbers lightly to keep track of which numbers have already been added or write the first sum next to the numbers. Have your child solve several column-addition problems independently.	Set up a "fish pond." Fill a plastic tub or glass baking dish with paper clips, nails, candy, a wire, pieces of paper, a rubber band, a tack, staples, a staple in paper and other small objects. Tie one end of a string onto a stick and the other end onto a magnet to make a fishing pole. Have your child "fish" for the magnetic objects.	Discuss the types and uses of Native American tools. Have your child complete **Native American Tools** (p. 313). Ask your child to compare Native American tools with the tools we use today.
Use the number line to present column addition to your child. Write a problem vertically. On a number line, have a rabbit, frog or cricket hop the three numbers of the equation. Have your child solve several column-addition problems using the number line.	Allow your child time to explore several shapes of magnets (bar, horseshoe, disk and rectangles). Demonstrate the two poles of the magnets. Let your child discover through experimentation that opposite poles attract and like poles repel. *See* Science, Week 28, numbers 1 and 2.	Teach your child about Christopher Columbus. Read a short biography of Columbus. Teach the rhyme "Columbus sailed the ocean blue in fourteen hundred ninety-two." *See* Social Studies, Week 28, numbers 1 and 2.
Use a place-value board to present column addition. Have your child add the three numbers in the ones place, regrouping into tens as necessary. Write several practice problems on a place-value grid for your child to solve. *See* Math, Week 28, number 4. tens | ones 4 4 + 5	Give your child a compass to determine north. Then, have your child use a magnet to find north. *See* Science, Week 28, number 3.	**Music/Poetry:** Help your child to learn more about Christopher Columbus through songs and poetry. *See* Social Studies, Week 28, numbers 3 and 4.

TEACHING SUGGESTIONS AND ACTIVITIES

Spelling (R-Controlled Vowels)

BACKGROUND
When *r* follows a vowel, the vowel does not make its usual long or short sound. In Week 28, you will teach the *ar* sound as in *car*. In Week 29, you will teach that *er, ir* and *ur* make the same sound as in turn; and, in Week 30, you will teach the *or* sound as in *for*. When reading two-syllable words, the two letters of the *r*–controlled vowels are never split into separate syllables.

Reading (Homophones)

▶ 1. **Game:** Make a game board. Write *Start* in the upper right-hand corner and *Finish* in the lower left-hand corner. Draw stepping stones from start to finish. Draw water and other pond features around the stones. On one to four stepping stones, write phrases such as *Choose another card, Lose a turn,* or *Go ahead two spaces.* Make 10–20 game cards by writing a homophone and a number (1, 2 or 3) on index cards. To play, have your child choose one card and use the homophone in a sentence. If your child uses the homophone correctly, he/she may move forward on the stepping stones the number indicated on the card. If the word is used incorrectly, your child must move back that many spaces.

Math (Column Addition)

BACKGROUND
Column addition is an extension of what your child has already learned. When adding a column, your child will learn to add two numbers, hold their sum in his/her head and add the next number to the sum of the first two.

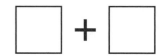

▶ 1. Make a set of nine cards with one to nine dots on each. Also, make a card with a plus sign. Put out two cards with a plus sign in between (seven dots and six dots). Then, ask: *What is seven plus six?* Use the dot cards to review several addition facts to eighteen.

▶ 2. Make another plus sign to go with the cards above. Put out two cards (three dots and four dots) with a plus sign between them. Have your child read the problem and say the answer. Tell your child to remember *seven* as you put down another plus and a six-dot card. Your child then adds 7 + 6 as he/she did in number 1.

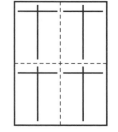

▶ 3. Have your child put three dot cards together with two plus signs, then write the number sentence on the chalkboard (2 + 6 + 7 =   ). Have your child solve the problem aloud—*Two plus six equals eight, and eight plus seven equals fifteen.*

▶ 4. Have your child fold a sheet of paper into fourths and draw a place-value grid in each section. Have him/her label the ones and tens in each column. On the chalkboard, write four-column addition problems with three single digits each. Instruct your child to copy one in each section and to solve each problem.

Learn at Home, Grade 1

Science (Magnets)

BACKGROUND

Magnetism is a force in nature, acting between objects called magnets. Magnetic fields surround every magnet. The Earth itself acts as a large magnet, and a magnetic field surrounds the Earth. We use magnets and magnetism in many ways. Magnets are used on tapes, computer disks, compasses and electrical appliances. We could not use electricity to do all the things it does without magnetism.

▶ 1. Teach the meaning of the word *repel*. Demonstrate to your child that two like poles repel or push apart when placed next to each other. Teach the meaning of the word *attract*. Demonstrate to your child that two unlike poles attract or pull together when they are placed next to each other.

▶ 2. Give your child two bar magnets. Ask your child to find the poles that attract. When your child finds them, tell him/her that one pole is called the *north pole* (write N) and the other is called the *south pole* (write S). Repeat with two different-shaped magnets.

▶ 3. Teach your child to find the north pole of a bar magnet. Tie a string around the center of a bar magnet. Let it hang freely. The north pole of the magnet should swing to the north as indicated by the compass. Write *N* on the north pole of the magnet. Have your child find the north poles of two or three other magnets. Ask your child how the other end of the bar magnet should be marked *(S)* and why. Put up signs indicating *north* and *south* in the room.

Social Studies (Early Americans)

BACKGROUND

This unit includes a short review of our nation's early history encompassing Native Americans, Columbus, the Mayflower, Pilgrims, the first Thanksgiving and colonial Americans.

▶ 1. Read a biography of Christopher Columbus and look at a current world map with your child. Explain that Columbus would not have had a map like this. As you read Columbus' biography, trace his routes on the map. What part of the world was Columbus hoping to find a route to? Why? Discuss how Columbus' discovery influenced our country. (It opened up exploration of the New World.)

▶ 2. Read *Columbus* by Ingri and Edgar d'Aulaire.

▶ 3. **Music:** "He Knew the Earth Was Round - O" was written in 1893. It has many versions. One source is in *The Holiday Song Book*, edited by Robert Quackenbush.

▶ 4. **Poetry:** Read "Christopher Columbus" in *A Book of Americans* by Rosemary and Stephen Vincent (or another poem about Columbus). Discuss the poem's words and story. Make a copy of the poem for your child. Have your child write (or dictate) a verse to add to the poem.

Sentence Sequence

Sentences can tell a story. **Write** 1, 2 and 3 in the circles to tell what happened first, second and third. **Write** a sentence to tell about each picture.

1. _____

2. _____

3. _____

On Your Mark

Write the spelling word that ends with each letter.

park barn cart scarf
car march arm star

T
R
N
R

K
F
M
CH

Write a spelling word to complete each sentence.

1. The animals on the farm sleep in the _____ .

2. Father drove the _____ to the _____ .

3. When I am in the band, I would like to _____ in the parade.

4. A black and white horse pulled a red _____ .

5. We searched the night sky for the brightest _____ .

6. Jane wore a red _____ around her neck.

7. Tommy fell and broke his _____ .

What things will a magnet attract? Make lists of the things that a magnet will and will not attract.

Magnets attract:

_____

- - - - - - - - - - - - - - - - -

_____

- - - - - - - - - - - - - - - - -

_____

- - - - - - - - - - - - - - - - -

_____

- - - - - - - - - - - - - - - - -

_____

- - - - - - - - - - - - - - - - -

_____

Magnets do not attract:

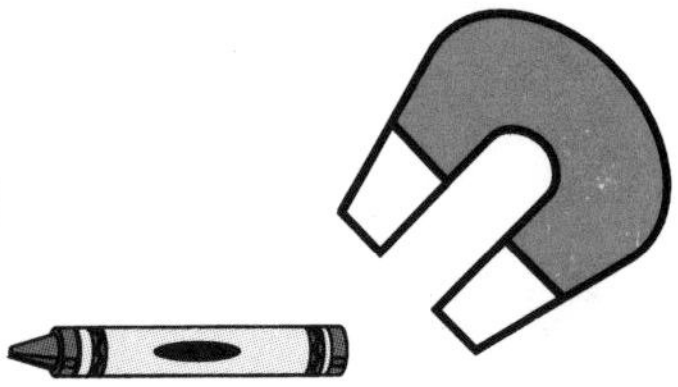

_____

- - - - - - - - - - - - - - - - -

_____

- - - - - - - - - - - - - - - - -

_____

- - - - - - - - - - - - - - - - -

_____

- - - - - - - - - - - - - - - - -

_____

- - - - - - - - - - - - - - - - -

_____

Caution: Do not try your magnet on these things.

TV	Computer disks
VCR	Cassette tapes
Computer	Video tapes
Radio	Credit cards
Tape recorder	Telephone

Learn at Home, Grade 1

Native American Tribes

1. **Color** the pictures and the different locations on the map.
2. **Cut out** and **glue** each picture on the map.

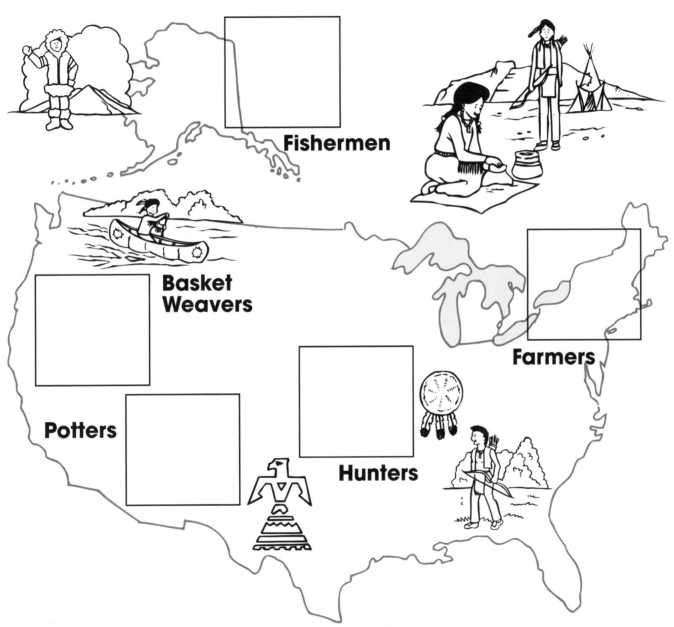

Fishermen

Basket Weavers

Farmers

Potters

Hunters

This is where these Native Americans lived long ago.

1. **Write** teepee in box 1.
2. **Write** adobe in box 2.
3. **Write** wigwam in box 3.
4. **Write** longhouse in box 4.
5. **Draw** a sun on the teepee.
6. **Color** the longhouse brown.
7. **Draw** small windows on the adobe.

1.

2.

3.

4.

Learn at Home, Grade 1

Native American Tools

1. **Draw** a red circle around the corn mortar and the salmon spear.
2. **Draw** a blue triangle around the digging stick and the fishhook.
3. **Draw** a green rectangle around the bow and arrow, the canoe paddle and the hoe.
4. **Draw** a yellow square around the copper knife and the grinding stones.
5. **Color** each picture.

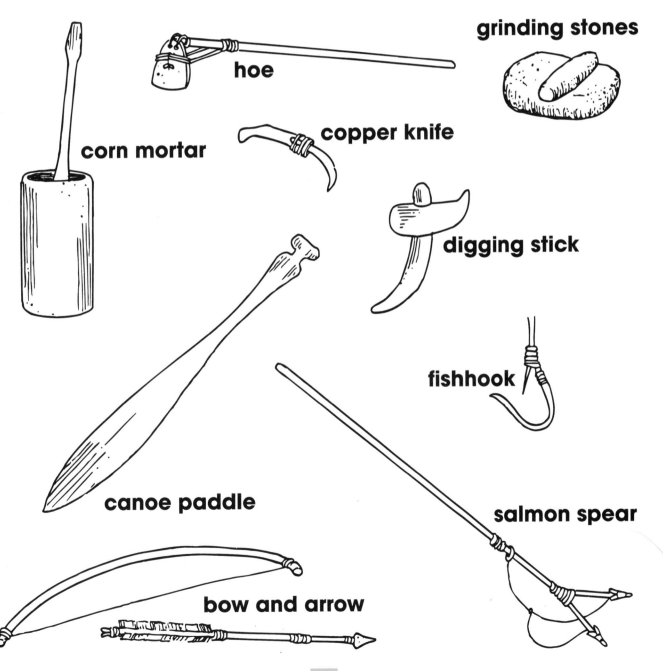

grinding stones

hoe

copper knife

corn mortar

digging stick

fishhook

canoe paddle

salmon spear

bow and arrow

	Language Skills	**Spelling**	**Reading**

Monday	**Sentences**
	Write sentences on the chalkboard, omitting the subject, the verb or the object of the preposition. Have your child fill in a missing word.
	Examples:
	   The big ___ has to stay in its yard.
	   The red ball ___ down the hill.
	   The happy boy is sitting on the ___.
		Pretest your child on these spelling words:
		   curl bird
		   girl fern
		   church dirt
		   her turn
		Teach your child the *er, ir* and *ur* spellings of the *r* sound. *See* Spelling, Week 29, number 1.
			Read from *Just So Stories* by Rudyard Kipling. With your child, discuss the use of language by the author. If possible, rent a video version of one or more of the stories. Have your child compare and contrast the movie production to the written story.

Tuesday	With your child, brainstorm several nouns and verbs. Write one word on each index card. Choose two cards and have your child make up a silly sentence using both words. Then, have your child write the sentences on lined paper. *See* Language Skills, Week 29, number 1.	Have your child write the spelling words in sentences.	Write several example sentences that include two homophones in each:
			   Suzie <u>read</u> a story called Red Rose.
			   Carrie <u>blew</u> out all the <u>blue</u> candles.
			Have your child underline the homophones in each sentence. Then, list several pairs of homophones and help your child create original sentences containing two homophones each. Create a crossword puzzle for your child to solve in which the clues are homophones.

Wednesday	Build a story with your child. Have your child begin an oral story with one sentence. You add the second sentence. Alternate turns until someone brings the story to a close. When the story is completed, record it and play it back.	Have your child spell each word aloud in a "growly" voice. Have your child complete **The Angr-r-ry Dog** (p. 319).	**Art:** Brainstorm several pairs of homophones with your child. Provide paints and a large sheet of butcher paper. Have your child paint a homophone graffiti mural. Encourage him/her to creatively write (and draw) the homophones generated in the brainstorming session.
Thursday	Using the **Flip Book Pattern** (page 318), help your child make a flip book of sentence parts. *See* Language Skills, Week 29, number 2.	Draw three columns on a sheet of paper. Write *er, ir* and *ur* at the top of the columns. Have your child write spelling words and other words that contain those vowel combinations in the correct columns.	Have your child think of an animal that has a characteristic feature (such as a lion's mane or a parrot's bright colors) and write a story about how the animal got that feature. Have your child edit and publish his/her "Just So" story.

Friday	Have your child use the flip book made yesterday to invent silly sentences. Your child chooses a person, place or thing from one sentence and a verb and location phrase from other sentences. A silly sentence might include the following:
	The brown bear ran quickly at my school.
		Give your child the final spelling test.	Help your child build a word pyramid about a given story:
			   In one word, describe the main character.
			   In two words, describe the setting.
			   In three words, state the problem.
			   In four words, describe an event.
			   In five words, describe another event.
			   In six words, state the conclusion or solution.
			   In seven words, tell your opinion.

Learn at Home, Grade 1

Math	Science	Social Studies
Measuring Weight Teach the concept of heavier and lighter by placing an object in each of your child's outstretched hands. Have your child describe the difference between the objects using the words *heavier* and *lighter*. Have your child place a series of objects in order by their relative weight. *See* Math, Week 29, numbers 1–3.	Help your child explore the properties of several magnets. Pose the following questions to your child: *Can you make a paper clip act like a magnet? Can you make a needle act like a magnet?* See Science, Week 29, numbers 1 and 2.	Refer to a map of the United States and help your child find Massachusetts, the location of the Pilgrim settlement. Discuss the Pilgrims' reasons for making the journey. Have your child complete **Mayflower Shipshape** (p. 323).
Teach your child to use a balance scale. *See* Math, Week 29, numbers 4 and 5. Have your child complete **Worth Its Weight Record Sheet** (p. 320).	Explain that all magnets are surrounded by a magnetic field which is made up of invisible lines of force. Help your child see this force by placing a magnet under a paper covered with iron fillings. *See* Science, Week 29, number 3. Have your child complete **Working With Magnets** (p. 322).	Watch a video about the Pilgrims. Have your child write a journal entry as if he/she were aboard the Mayflower. Have him/her include what he/she would be excited about as well as the difficulties of the journey.
Introduce standard units of weight measurement to your child. Place some familiar household objects on the bathroom scale to build your child's sense of 1 pound. *See* Math, Week 29, numbers 6 and 7.	**Art:** Cut steel wool into tiny pieces with an old pair of scissors. Then, help your child create a work of art with the help of a magnet. *See* Science, Week 29, number 4.	Discuss the Pilgrims' struggle leading up to the first Thanksgiving. Ask your child: *How did the Native Americans help the Pilgrims? What kinds of foods did they eat? What do you like to eat at Thanksgiving?* Have your child complete **The First Thanksgiving** (p. 324).
Have your child compare the weight of several pairs of objects. See Math, Week 29, numbers 8–9. Have your child complete **Heavyweight Champ!** (p. 321).	Help your child explore the strength of magnets. Place a magnet on one side of a piece of cardboard and a magnetic object on the other side. Ask: *Will the magnet attract the object through the cardboard? Through what other materials will a magnet attract?* Encourage your child to experiment using a magnet to attract through a variety of materials, including a glass of water.	Talk about what life must have been like for the early settlers. Discuss why people were willing to go through such hardships. *See* Social Studies, Week 29, number 1.
Look for objects that are large but do not weigh much, as well as objects that are small but very heavy. Have your child write a "Heavy and Light" story. Encourage your child to make the story silly and fill it with exaggeration.	**Game:** Draw facial features, cut them out and tape each to a paper clip. Draw a circle (face without features) on a sheet of heavy paper. Place the features randomly on the face. Hold the paper off the table with two hands. Have your child move a magnet under the paper in an attempt to arrange the facial features in appropriate locations on the circle.	Explain to your child that when settlers came to America, they had to build their own homes. Explain that many settlers built homes of logs and other materials they found here. Help your child build a "log cabin" of his/her own. Have your child complete **Homes of Long Ago** (p. 325).

TEACHING SUGGESTIONS AND ACTIVITIES

Language Skills (Sentences)

▶ 1. To write silly sentences, have your child brainstorm several nouns and verbs. Make up sentences using two of the words at a time. **Examples: cat** and **song**—My **cat** sang a beautiful **song; friend** and **run**—My best **friend** can **run** faster than I can. Discuss with your child if each sentence could be real.

▶ 2. **Flip book:** Make several copies of the **Flip Book Pattern** (p. 318). Have your child write a word or phrase in each box as indicated. Your child may add a small picture to illustrate the word or phrase. The three boxes together should be a complete sentence. Cut on the dotted lines. Punch a hole in the upper left corner. Assemble all of the pages together on a ring. **Example:** *The brown bear rode its one-wheeled bike to the store.*

Spelling

▶ 1. Read the spelling list to your child and ask him/her to listen for the vowel sound. Ask your child to repeat the vowel sound. After the pretest, discuss the three spellings (*er, ir* and *ur*) of the same sound.

Math (Measuring Weight)

▶ 1. Put several assorted objects on a table. Give your child time to pick them up and compare the weight of two objects at a time. Ask your child: *Which is heavier?*

▶ 2. Have your child arrange the objects above from the lightest to the heaviest.

▶ 3. Cut out pictures of animals, furniture, people, etc. Have your child compare their weights through discussion. Bring out the relativity of what is being compared. **Example:** A man is lighter when compared to an elephant, but a man is heavier when compared to a rabbit.

▶ 4. If possible, go to an area where a seesaw is available. Invite your child to sit on one end. Talk about what happened when you sat down on the other end and why. Discuss how the seesaw could be made to balance. (Experiment with moving forward and backward or adding weight.)

▶ 5. Explain how to use a balance scale. Use pennies or washers as a measurement unit. Put an object on one side. Have your child place pennies on the opposite side until the scale balances. Count the pennies. Repeat until your child understands how to use the scale.

▶ 6. Show several kinds of scales to your child. Talk about what they are used for and what their units (pounds/ounces) of measurement are.

▶ 7. Share with your child his/her weight during growth using his/her baby book or your pediatrician's records. Weigh your child. Make a line graph with your child to show his/her growth over time. Ask your child to project what he/she will weigh in a year.

Learn at Home, Grade 1

8. **Field Trip:** Arrange a visit to a local meat market, deli, fitness club, doctor's office or bulk food section of a grocery store. Look at scales that measure dry ingredients and meats, then scales that measure people.

9. Collect several boxes of varying sizes and fill each with sand. Leave the largest one empty. Ask your child to predict which box is the heaviest and why. Have your child pick up each box to test its weight. Lead your child to understand that a larger container will weigh more than a smaller container if it contains the same material.

Science (Magnets)

1. Using a bar magnet, have your child rub one end of a needle about 40 strokes in one direction. Your child may then use the magnetized needle to pick up small magnetic objects.

2. Show your child that the needle has been magnetized and that the pointed end is the north pole. Place the magnetized needle on top of a small piece of cork. Use masking tape to hold it in place. Fill a plastic glass with water. Float the cork in the water. The needle should slowly spin until it points north.

3. Spread some iron filings on a sheet of paper. Hold the paper at either end and lift it above the table. Tell your child to place a magnet under it and see what the filings do. Explain that the shape they take shows the invisible lines of force in the magnet's magnetic field. Use several magnets to show that they are of different strengths and different magnetic fields.

4. **Art:** Give your child a sheet of 12" x 18" paper. Have him/her place it over a magnet. Tell your child to sprinkle the steel wool pieces on the paper and watch them move into a pattern. Your child may pick up the paper and move it over the magnet to create different patterns. When he/she has a desired pattern, have him/her carefully set the paper down. Spray the filings with a clear, plastic fixative with the magnet still underneath. Let the steel wool design dry on the paper. Then, lift the paper off the magnet.

Social Studies

1. Talk about how settlers had to procure food. Give your child a sheet of drawing paper folded in half. On the left side, write *Time of Early Settlers* with a black marker. On the right side, write *Today.* Have your child draw pictures illustrating how food gathering has changed.

prepositional phrase (location)	action verb	person, place or thing

prepositional phrase (location)	action verb	person, place or thing

318

Learn at Home, Grade 1

The Angr–r–ry Dog

Sort the spelling words in the columns according to the **r** spellings.

| curl | turn | bird | fern |
| girl | dirt | her | church |

er words

_____
- - - - - - - - - -
_____
_____
- - - - - - - - - -
_____

ir words

_____
- - - - - - - - - -
_____
_____
- - - - - - - - - -
_____
_____
- - - - - - - - - -
_____

ur words

_____
- - - - - - - - - -
_____
_____
- - - - - - - - - -
_____
_____
- - - - - - - - - -

Complete the sentences below with words from the spelling list.

1. The _____'s dress got _____ on it when she fell.

2. The _____ landed on the bell outside the _____.

3. The farmer told Zach to go in the barn and _____ left.

4. The leaves on the _____ plant are large and green.

5. Maria's father asked _____ to dry the dishes.

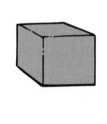

weighs _____ pennies.

weighs _____ pennies.

weighs _____ pennies.

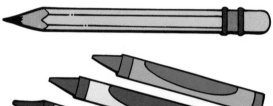

weighs _____ pennies.

weighs _____ pennies.

weighs _____ pennies.

weighs _____ pennies.

weighs _____ pennies.

weighs _____ pennies.

Learn at Home, Grade 1

Heavyweight Champ

Preparation: Set up ten stations around your room. At each station put two to three objects that have obvious differences in weight. Number each station using index cards.

Draw the "champ," or heaviest object, in each station next to the correct station number below.

Working With Magnets

Spread some iron filings on a sheet of paper.
Hold a magnet above the filings.

What happened?_____

_____

_____

_____

_____

_____

Move the magnet around under the paper.

What happened?_____

_____

_____

Testing Magnets

Test several magnets.
Tell how many paper clips each magnet
picked up.

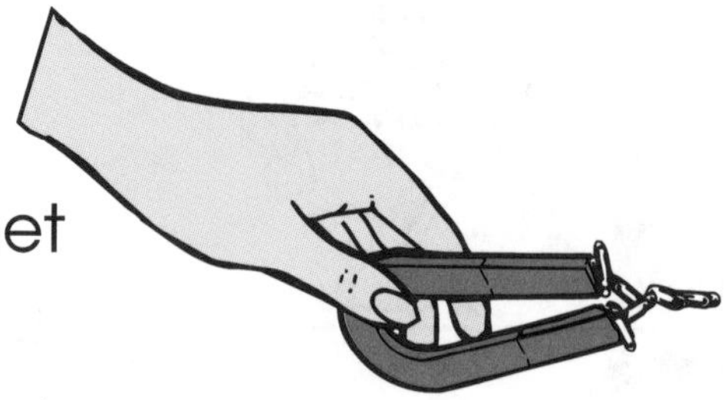

	Number Picked Up	Type of Magnet
Magnet #1	_____	
Magnet #2	_____	
Magnet #3	_____	

Learn at Home, Grade 1

Mayflower Shipshape

1. **Color** the ship and the sails.
2. **Cut out** and **glue** the shapes correctly on the ship below.

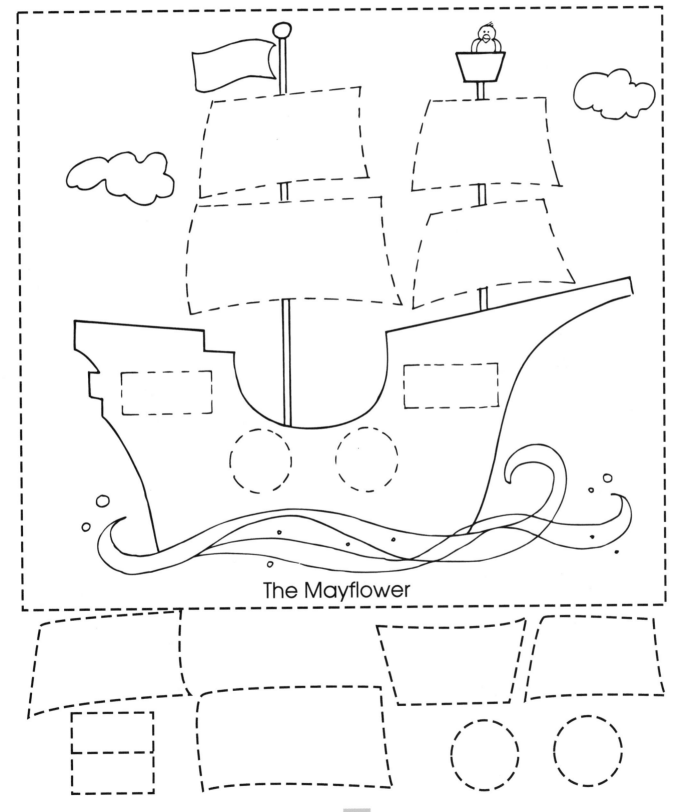

The Mayflower

Help the pilgrims find food for the first Thanksgiving.
1. **Circle** each food from the box hidden in the picture below.
2. Then, **color** the picture.

corn   pumpkin   squash   turkey
onion   beans   berries   fish

324

Learn at Home, Grade 1

Homes of Long Ago

Color and **cut out** the house and **glue** it to a sheet of construction paper. Cover your house with glue. Place pretzels in rows to form logs across the house. Add trees and farmland using crayons.

cut -

Language Skills	Spelling	Reading

Monday

Synonyms and Antonyms
On the chalkboard, write *The little boy was crying*. Under the sentence, write the words *weeping, smiling* and *sitting*. Ask your child to circle the word (synonym) that means about the same thing as the underlined word. Repeat with other sentences and words. *See* Language Skills, Week 30, number 1.

Pretest your child on these spelling words:
for	sport
north	born
pork	stork
thorn	porch

Teach your child the *or* sound.

Prefixes
Introduce the prefix *un* to your child. Give him/her directions, such as *tie your shoes, zip your coat* and *wind this kite string*. Write each verb on the board. Add the prefix *un* to each word. Then, ask your child to read the new words and perform the tasks. Discuss the meaning of *un*. Help your child brainstorm a list of words that begin with the prefix *un*.

Tuesday

Repeat yesterday's activity but do not supply word choices for the synonym. Make the words familiar enough that your child can come up with synonyms on his/her own.

Have your child write the spelling words in sentences.

Introduce the prefix *dis* to your child. Brainstorm with your child words that begin with *dis*. Discuss the meaning of *dis*. Read *Ira Sleeps Over* by Bernard Waber. Have your child retell the story in his/her own words.

Wednesday

Write a list of synonym pairs. Write the words on index cards and mix them up. Play a memory game. For each pair, help your child write a sentence using both words.
Example: *The big elephant took a giant step*.
Repeat this activity until your child understands. Then, have your child write the rest of the pairs in sentences.

Have your child spell each word aloud as he/she writes it on the chalkboard.
Have your child complete **Morning Glory** (p. 330).

Call your child's attention to the use of quotation marks in *Ira Sleeps Over*. Explain how they are used. On a sentence strip, have your child copy a sentence that contains quotation marks. Then, have him/her glue elbow macaroni on the sentence strip in place of the quotation marks. Tell your child to make sure that the commas and periods are in the correct place (within the quotations marks).

Thursday

On the chalkboard, write *It is sunny today*. Ask your child to write a sentence that states the opposite meaning (antonym). Repeat with other sentences. *See* Language Skills, Week 30, number 2.

Give your child an orange. Talk about how it feels, looks, smells and tastes. Have your child paint an orange picture. Then, have him/her write the spelling words on it with a dark marker.

Have your child write about an experience sleeping over at a friend's house. Your child may include a description of something that surprised him/her about the friend. Or, your child may choose to write about a favorite stuffed animal. Ask your child: *Would you take an animal to sleep over at a friend's house?*

Friday

Write a list of antonym pairs. Write the words on index cards and mix them up. Have your child match the pairs. Have your child fold the ends of a long strip of paper to the middle. Have him/her write a pair of antonyms, one on each flap. Your child should then lift the flaps and illustrate the antonym pairs.

Give your child the final spelling test.

Have your child compare Reggie and Ira or Ira and his sister using a **Venn diagram** (p. 331).   **Reggie   Ira**

Both
Fill in the diagram with characteristics and actions that are alike and different as your child dictates them to you.

Math	**Science**	**Social Studies**
Measuring Volume Gather a variety of containers, bowls, measuring cups, caps and bottles. Pour rice, sand or water in a dishpan. Fill a 1-cup measuring cup with rice, sand or water and ask your child to sort the other containers into two groups—those that hold *more* than a cup and those that hold *less* than a cup. Then, let your child explore with the containers to see if he/she sorted correctly.	**Movement and Machines** Focus your child's attention on the objects in motion around him/her. Have your child identify what is causing the objects to move, labeling each motion as a *push* or a *pull. See* Science, Week 30, number 1.	Discuss the three basic needs humans have—food, shelter and clothing. Explain to your child that the Pilgrims had no supermarkets in the new world, so they needed tools, cooking utensils, soaps, candles, material and blankets in order to maintain their basic needs. Pilgrims brought these things with them, made their clothing and shelter and hunted for their food. Discuss how much time it would take just to survive.
Provide the same materials as yesterday. Have your child compare containers by pouring rice, sand or water in and out of them to determine the relative volume. Have your child place the containers in order from the least to the greatest volume. *See* Math, Week 30, number 1.	Have your child place a pencil on the table in front of him/her. Ask your child to make the pencil move. Discuss the force your child applied to the pencil. Challenge your child to think of other ways to move the pencil. Discuss the source of the force each time.	Discuss life in colonial America with your child. Make some colonial crafts. *See* Social Studies, Week 30, numbers 1–4.
Label some standard-sized containers, such as teaspoon, tablespoon, cup, pint, quart, liter and gallon. Let your child make comparisons using the rice, sand or water. Help your child become familiar with the names of these units. Use a recipe to make microwave fudge together. *See* Math, Week 30, number 2. Guide your child as he/she measures the ingredients.	Look at a photo that shows things in motion. Have your child identify what is moving and what made each thing move. Discuss the concept that nothing moves unless something acts upon it with a push or a pull. *See* Science, Week 30, number 2.	Continue working on the crafts from yesterday's lesson.
Estimation/Probability: Help your child build a sense of 1 minute. Have your child estimate, then prove how many times he/she can jump in a minute. Propose other activities to compare to a minute, such as whether or not your child can sing a familiar song in 1 minute. Have your child complete **How Long Does It Take?** (p. 332). Discuss your child's responses. *See* Math, Week 30, number 3.	A force can also change the way something moves. Have your child experiment with toy cars. Push a car toward your child and challenge him/her to change the way the car is moving by either changing its speed or direction. *See* Science, Week 30, number 3.	The settlers continued to improve their lives. They depended on the community to share responsibilities. If one man was good at making shoes, he made shoes for others in the community in exchange for other services. Discuss how a community works together to provide all our needs. Ask your child: *Is there anything our community does not provide that we need to go to another community to obtain?*
Provide a small jar full of objects such as buttons. Have your child estimate and count the number in the jar. Provide other containers with objects for your child to estimate and count. Use large objects in some jars (blocks) and small objects in other jars (paper clips) to increase the difficulty of estimating. Each jar should contain only one type of object (not mixed). Record the estimate and count of each container. *See* Math, Week 30, number 4.	Some objects require more force to move than other objects. Give your child materials to compare the amount of force needed to push a light object and a heavy object. Explore whether something on wheels is easier to move than something not on wheels. *See* Science, Week 30, number 4.	Have your child complete **Colonial Workers** (p. 333).

TEACHING SUGGESTIONS AND ACTIVITIES

Language Skills (Synonyms and Antonyms)

▶ 1. Write sentences on a sheet of paper and underline a word that your child may replace with a synonym. Under each sentence, write two or three words from which your child may choose. Have your child rewrite each sentence using the synonym.

▶ 2. Write sentences on a sheet of paper and have your child rewrite each sentence so that it has the opposite meaning.

Math

BACKGROUND (Measuring Volume)

The activities presented in this unit will help your child develop an understanding of volume as it relates to how much a container holds. Provide your child with a variety of containers and time to explore relative volumes. Volume can be misleading when containers have odd shapes. Although it is not necessary for your child to memorize that 2 cups equal 1 pint, the activities build a sense of the relationships between standard units of volume.

▶ 1. Gather liquid products (milk, bottled water, soda, salad dressing, etc.) and discuss how they are measured. Look at the containers. What are they made of? Why? Read the volume. Does the biggest container have the largest numbers? (Discuss safety if you are looking at toxic liquids.)

▶ 2. **Cooking:** Have your child prepare the recipe below to practice measuring tablespoons.

MICROWAVE FUDGE

3 T powdered sugar   2 T milk
2 T cocoa   2 T butter

Mix the sugar and cocoa in a bowl. Add milk. Mix. Put the mixture in a microwave-safe pan. Add the butter. Microwave the mixture until the butter melts. Stir. Refrigerate 1 hour. Cut the fudge into small pieces.

BACKGROUND (Estimation and Probability)

Estimation and probability require problem-solving skills. One does not just make a wild guess but attempts a reasonable, "educated" one based on information previously learned. Your child will want proof of the actual number in the beginning, so keep numbers low enough for your child to verify the results. Point out improvement in estimation skills so that your child feels pride in making a good estimate.

▶ 3. Pose an estimation question at the beginning of each day. Have your child write his/her estimation. Sometime during the day, have your child find the answer. Below are some ideas for estimation questions.

> *How many blue crayons are in the crayon box?*
> *How many steps long is this room?*
> *How long will it take to complete the math activity sheet?*

▶ 4. Provide experiences to help your child gain confidence in estimating. Group objects, such as pencils, chairs and books, for your child to estimate quantity. When asking for the actual number (be careful not to say "correct" number), ask your child to think about whether his/her estimation was too high, too low or reasonable.

Learn at Home, Grade 1

Science (Movement and Machines)

BACKGROUND

We see motion all around us—children running, cars moving, clouds drifting and bugs crawling. A *force* is needed to make things move. That force can be either a *push* or a *pull*. *Gravity*, for example, is a pulling force. Force can also work to change the speed or direction of a motion. A machine does work or makes work easier. It acts as a force to change the motion of an object. Something must provide the machine with energy to create the force. In these lessons, your child or gravity will provide the energy. There are six types of simple machines. One or more simple machines make up all other machines. Your child will explore the simple machines and identify the type of force used to make them work and what work they accomplish.

▶ 1. Have your child open a jar, kick a ball, lift a book, write his/her name and go down a slide. Ask your child to describe each motion as either a *push* or a *pull*. List your child's responses in two columns.

▶ 2. Have your child draw a picture of him/herself doing something like taking off a sweater, walking the dog or sweeping the floor. Your child should draw arrows indicating the direction of each motion.

▶ 3. Have your child think about times when something was already moving and he/she used force to change its speed or direction. Ideas include riding a bike, walking a dog, throwing or catching a ball and tackling a running friend.

▶ 4. Load a toy truck with three bricks. Have your child push the truck across the room. Take the bricks out and have your child push the truck across the room again. Discuss how he/she pushed differently each time.

Social Studies

▶ 1. Sew a small quilt with your child. Cut at least nine same-sized squares from scraps of material. Teach your child to sew them together forming a large square. Cut a square piece of muslin the same size as the large square. Sew the large squares on three sides, good sides together. Turn the quilt right side out. Put a layer of quilt batting inside and sew the third side closed. Show your child how to sew one fancy stitch in the center of each square through all thicknesses.

▶ 2. Read about and make soap, candles and/or paper.

▶ 3. Discuss how domesticated animals were helpful to settlers. Discuss colonial professions, such as blacksmith, cobbler, miller, lamplighter, town crier, glass blower and barrel maker. Point out the fact that each profession developed because of need. Tell your child that today factories do some of the same work, that some skills still exist but as an art and that some have disappeared due to a lack of need. Make a list for each category.

▶ 4. If possible, visit a nearby museum or historical society to see objects used in colonial America.

Morning Glory

for thorn born pork north sport porch stork

Write the spelling words that rhyme with the pictures below.

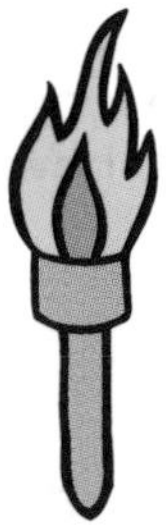

_____ _____

_____ _____

_____ _____

_____ _____

_____

_____

Complete the sentences below with spelling words.

1. Ryan's baby sister was _____ last night.

2. The lion has a _____ in its paw.

3. At night, the family likes to swing on the _____ .

4. My house is on the _____ side of the street.

5. Baseball is Francisco's favorite _____ .

Learn at Home, Grade 1

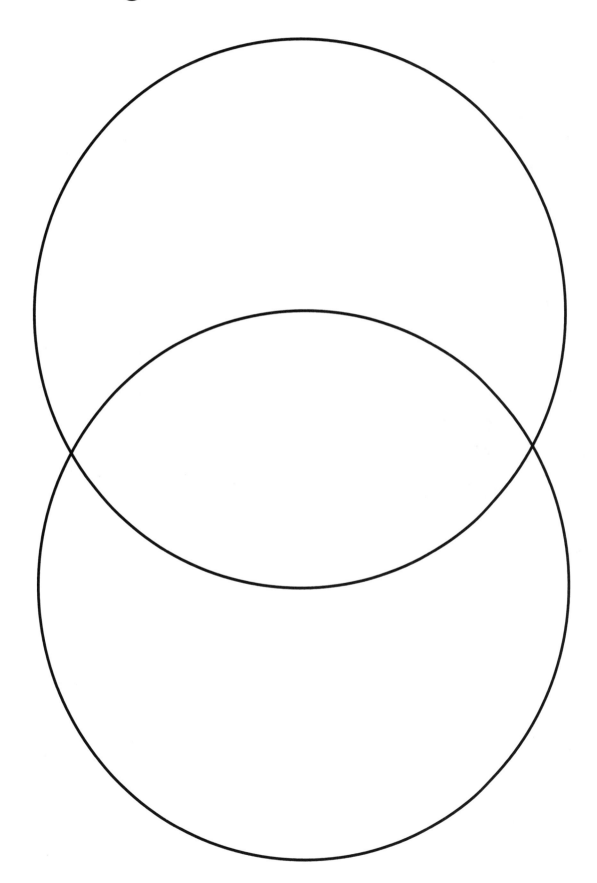

How Long Does It Take?

Look at the activity in each picture. How long do you think each thing will take? **Circle** the best estimate for each.

1 minute   1 hour

1 minute   1 hour

1 minute   1 hour

1 minute   1 hour

1 minute   1 hour

1 minute   1 hour

Learn at Home, Grade 1

Colonial Workers

1. **Draw** shoes in the window for the shoemaker.
2. **Make** some dough for the baker to make bread.
3. **Put** a hammer in the blacksmith's hand.
4. **Draw** a dress on the hanger for the dressmaker.
5. **Draw** a saddle for the saddlemaker.
6. **Make** sacks of flour and sugar for the storekeeper.

Blacksmith

Storekeeper

Dressmaker

Saddlemaker

Shoemaker

Baker

Language Skills	Spelling	Reading

Making a Filmstrip
Help your child make a "filmstrip" about him/herself. *See* Language Skills, Week 31, numbers 1–6.
Day One: Have your child write two sentences to introduce him/herself and draw a picture. (Have your child begin on the third frame. The first two are for the title and credits.)
	Pretest your child on these spelling words:
	  mule good
	  cute moon
	  tune look
	  food foot
	Teach your child the long *u* and double *o* sounds.
		Read *Caps for Sale* by Esphyr Slobodkina with your child. Have your child tell you whether or not he/she thinks the peddler is clever. Then, have your child explain his/her answer.

Day Two: On the fourth frame, have your child write two sentences that tell about his/her family and where he/she lives. Then, have him/her illustrate his/her sentences.	Have your child write the spelling words in sentences.	Point out the ellipses (…) used by the author in *Caps for Sale*. Explain to your child the purpose of an ellipsis. Then, show your child the exclamation points used in the book. Explain the purpose of them as well.
Day Three: Have your child write two sentences on the fifth frame that describe his/her hobbies and other things he/she likes to do. Then, have him/her draw a picture that illustrates each.	Have your child spell each word aloud while tracing the letters in a pan of sand, shaving cream or pudding. Have your child complete **Luke Looks Cool** (p. 338).	Teach your child about the climax of a story. Challenge your child to identify the climax of *Caps for Sale*. Help your child chart the interest (excitement) level of the story. *See* Reading, Week 31, number 1.
Day Four: On the sixth frame, have your child write sentences describing his/her favorite and least favorite foods. Then, have him/her draw a picture to illustrate his/her sentences.	Have your child write each spelling word on an index card. Then, show him/her how to use glue to trace over the letters in each word and sprinkle glitter on them. Have your child sort the cards into three categories—*u, oo* as in *cool* and *oo* as in *look*.	Have your child find and copy words from *Caps for Sale* that contain long vowels spelled with a silent *e* at the end or with double vowels (as in r<u>ai</u>n). Then, have your child find and copy the words that contain only one vowel.
Day Five: Have your child write about an exciting experience on the seventh frame. Have him/her draw a picture of him/herself experiencing it. Then, have your child go back and finish the first two frames. Turn the scroll, frame by frame, while your child reads the story.	Give your child the final spelling test.	Have your child make a diorama of the setting and characters from *Caps for Sale*, using a shoe box. Have him/her paint the setting and make characters out of clay or pipe cleaners and construction paper. Use scraps of material to make clothes and caps. Then, help him/her attach the characters to the inside of the box. Have your child write a summary of the story and glue it on the top of the diorama.

Math	Science	Social Studies
Introduce the terms *chance* and *probability*. *See* Math, Week 31, number 1. Have your child choose one number on a die and estimate how many times that number will show up in six throws. Have him/her try it. There is a good probability that the number will show up once. Then, have him/her try six more throws and see if that number comes up about the same number of times. Repeat this activity several times.	**Simple Machines** Tell your child you need a box filled with newspaper moved across the room. Your child should find the work difficult. Produce a wagon. Ask your child how he/she might use the machine (wheel and axle) to move the heavy box. Discuss how machines can make work easier. *See* Science, Week 31, number 1. Have your child draw and color things that have wheels.	**Citizenship** Introduce the word *independence* and discuss its meaning. Explain why the Declaration of Independence was written—and that on July 4, 1776, the Declaration of Independence officially proclaimed the American Colonies free from British rule. Explain that July 4th is the country's birthday. Discuss with your child what happens on July 4th and enlist your child's help to plan a "red, white and blue" party.
Fractions: Read *Eating Fractions* by Bruce McMillan. Teach your child about fair sharing. Split a cookie in half. Cut a bagel into thirds. Cut an apple into fourths. Have your child analyze whether the foods were split carefully enough to call them equal. If so, teach your child the names of the parts (*halves, thirds* and *fourths*). *See* Math, Week 31, number 2.	Help your child make a toy vehicle. Your child may use an empty milk carton to make a car or truck. Challenge him/her to decide what to use for axles and wheels. Then, allow him/her to decorate the vehicle.	Explain to your child that when our new country needed to establish laws, several representatives from the states worked together to write the Constitution of the United States. They did such a good job that we still follow the laws over 200 years later. Show your child a copy of the Constitution in an encyclopedia. Then, help your child create a "constitution" to be followed at home.
Read *Fraction Action* by Loreen Leedy. Look around for familiar things that come in halves, thirds and fourths. *See* Math, Week 31, number 3. Have your child complete **Equal and Unequal Parts** (p. 339).	Using toy cars, teach your child about inclined planes. Give your child a stack of books, a thin, flat board and a toy car. Challenge your child to make the car move longer and shorter distances by raising and lowering the height of the stack of books. Discuss how the simple machine (ramp) made work easier. The force in this case is provided by gravity. *See* Science, Week 31, number 2.	Recite the "Pledge of Allegiance" with your child. Discuss the meaning and purpose of the Pledge (a pledge of loyalty). Write the Pledge on white paper with red and blue markers and hang it up in the room. Discuss with your child what it means to be a good citizen. Then, help him/her write an original pledge to encourage good citizenship.
Divide a set of objects into fractions. Have your child count out the objects into fair groupings. Ask your child to verbally give the grouping its fraction name and count (*one-third, two-thirds, three-thirds*). *See* Math, Week 31, number 4. Then, read *The Doorbell Rang* by Pat Hutchins and have your child act out the story. Have your child complete **Fraction Food** (p. 340).	Use the same box you used on Monday. Challenge your child to lift the heavy box up to a low shelf or table. Provide your child with a long board. Discuss how the board can make the work easier. *See* Science, Week 31, number 3.	Discuss the symbolism of the American flag. Look at flags from other countries. Discuss your child's family heritage. Have your child draw and color the flag of the U.S. and several other countries, including those of his/her ancestry.
Draw geometric shapes and challenge your child to divide each one into equal parts and name the fractions. Have your child complete **Fraction Review** (p. 341).	Play on the see-saw together to help your child explore one form of a lever. When your child is in the air, ask him/her to suggest ways that he/she might be able to bring you up in the air. If your child doesn't suggest it, try moving forward and back on the plane and adding weight to one side.	Teach your child some patriotic songs and discuss the meaning of the lyrics. Have your child choose one of the songs to make into a book. Write a phrase on each page and have your child illustrate its meaning.

TEACHING SUGGESTIONS AND ACTIVITIES

Language Skills (Making a Filmstrip)

Help your child to make a small "filmstrip projector" to display your child's movie about him/herself:

1. Use a shoe box or other small box. Turn the box on its long side so the bottom faces you. On the side facing you (the former bottom), cut two slits from top to bottom approximately 5 inches apart.

2. Use a sharp tool such as an awl to punch two holes in the top of the box close to the front edge and on the outside of each slit. The hole should be the diameter of a pencil.

3. Purchase white shelf paper and cut a strip of paper the width of the box and approximately 45 inches long. Starting four inches from the left edge, draw lines about every 5 inches to mark the width of each frame.

4. Have your child write and illustrate the frames of the "filmstrip."

5. When the filmstrip is complete, tape one end of the shelf paper to an unsharpened pencil. Line up the bottom corner of the paper with the eraser end of the pencil. The unsharpened end will extend above the paper. Working from the back, put the unsharpened end of the pencil in one of the holes created at the top of the box. Thread the shelf paper out of the box through the slit and then back into the box through the other slit. The filmstrip should face out. Tape the other end of the shelf paper to the other pencil. Working from the back, put the unsharpened end of the second pencil in the opposite hole. Cap the end of each pencil with a pencil-top eraser.

6. The film can be advanced or rewound by turning both pencils.

Reading

1. To create an excitement chart, first list the main events of the story on individual index cards. Then, draw four horizontal lines across the chalkboard and label the lines from bottom to top: *calm, interesting, very interesting* and *exciting.* Evaluate the excitement level of each event from the story. Using scotch tape, place each event (index card) on the appropriate horizontal line, moving sequentially from left to right. When all the cards are placed, connect them with a chalk line. The finished product will look like a line graph. The highest point is the climax.

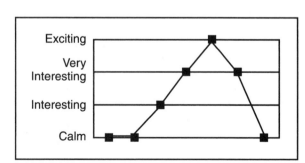

Learn at Home, Grade 1

Math (Estimation and Probability)

▶ 1. **Ask your child:** *What is the probability of a tiger walking through the door? When there isn't a chance, we say the probability is zero.* Ask more questions such as the following:

   What is the chance of snow today?
   What do you think the probability is of no schoolwork?
   What is the chance that we will have ice cream for dessert?

BACKGROUND (Fractions)
Teach fractions through the sharing of food. Start with simple sharing such as thirds and halves, emphasizing that the parts are *equal* (fair). Develop the language of fractions as you speak and write the words and match the symbol. Do not expect the your child to write fractions yet.

▶ 2. Cut construction paper into different shapes. Ask your child to divide each into two parts. Ask your child if the two parts are the same. Teach your child to fold the shape, carefully matching the corners to create two parts that are the same. Repeat this activity with three or four other shapes. Teach the words *equal* and *unequal.*

▶ 3. Tell your child that when one thing is split into two equal parts it is divided in half. Write the fraction $\frac{1}{2}$ as you say it. Ask how a cookie or apple can be shared. When you each have half, state *I have one half.* Repeat with $\frac{1}{3}$ and $\frac{1}{4}$.

▶ 4. Use twelve pieces of cereal, crackers or some other small food. Tell your child he/she is to share the cereal fairly with another person. Ask how he/she will do this. When the food is divided, ask what fraction each part is called. Next, tell your child to share the equal parts with three people, and then four people.

Science (Simple Machines)

▶ 1. Show your child the underside of a toy car, wagon or truck (or look under a real one). Ask your child to identify the part that attaches the wheels to the car. Explain that the long bar is called an *axle.* Give your child two empty spools of thread and a narrow dowel. Have him/her make a wheel and axle. Note that wheels cannot turn if they are attached directly to the car without an axle.

▶ 2. Have your child explore changing the motion of a moving object using the ramp. Have him/her place sand paper, wax paper or cloth on the ramp. How does that affect the motion of the car?

▶ 3. When your child leans a board from a higher level to the floor, the board becomes an inclined plane that may be helpful in lifting heavy objects. Brainstorm with your child other places he/she has seen an inclined plane such as a wheelchair ramp, a conveyor belt and on a moving van.

Luke Looks Cool

Write the three spelling words from the list that are spelled with the vowel **u**.

mule	cute	tune	moon
food	good	look	foot

_____   _____   _____

_____   _____   _____

Write the spelling words that rhyme with the pictures below.

_____   _____

_____   _____

Find the spelling words in the puzzle. **Circle** them and **write** them on the lines below.

```
n y o u m u l e f o o t
d e f o a t h o e f o r
l g o o d r u e u f o m
o b o o m l n a s o r o
o c u t e u o d e o o o
k d o o t f r o n d n n
```

_____   _____

_____   _____

_____   _____

_____   _____

Learn at Home, Grade 1

Equal and Unequal Parts

Cut out each shape below along the solid lines. Then, **fold** the shape on the dotted lines. Do you have equal or unequal parts? Sort the shapes by equal and unequal parts.

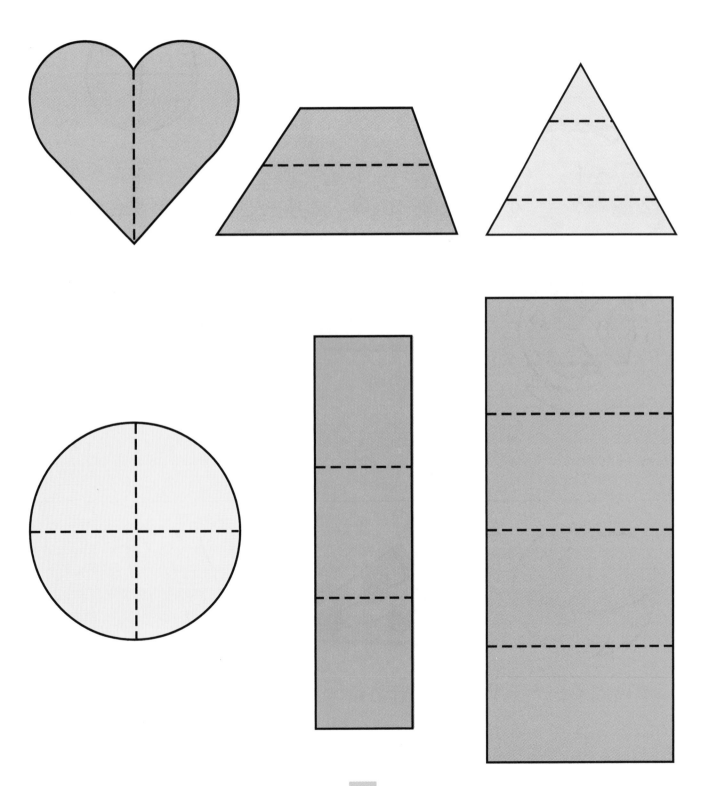

Fraction Food

Count the equal parts. **Circle** the fraction that names one of the parts.

$\dfrac{1}{2}$　$\dfrac{1}{3}$　$\dfrac{1}{4}$

$\dfrac{1}{2}$　$\dfrac{1}{3}$　$\dfrac{1}{4}$

$\dfrac{1}{2}$　$\dfrac{1}{3}$　$\dfrac{1}{4}$

$\dfrac{1}{2}$　$\dfrac{1}{3}$　$\dfrac{1}{4}$

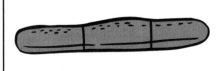

$\dfrac{1}{2}$　$\dfrac{1}{3}$　$\dfrac{1}{4}$

$\dfrac{1}{2}$　$\dfrac{1}{3}$　$\dfrac{1}{4}$

$\dfrac{1}{2}$　$\dfrac{1}{3}$　$\dfrac{1}{4}$

$\dfrac{1}{2}$　$\dfrac{1}{3}$　$\dfrac{1}{4}$

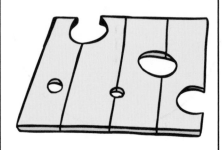

$\dfrac{1}{2}$　$\dfrac{1}{3}$　$\dfrac{1}{4}$

Learn at Home, Grade 1

Fraction Review

How many equal parts?

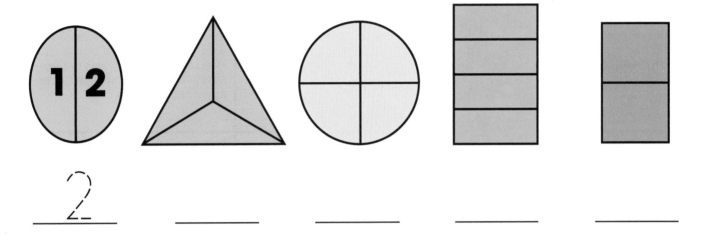

2 _____ _____ _____ _____ _____

Color shapes with 2 equal parts red. **Color** shapes with 3 equal parts blue. **Color** shapes with 4 equal parts green.

	Language Skills	**Spelling**	**Reading**
Monday	Write a sentence on the chalkboard. Underline the nouns. Ask your child to identify the part of speech of the underlined words. Write sentences that are missing nouns. Have your child fill in each blank with as many nouns as he/she can think of that make sense.	Pretest your child on these spelling words: 　　draw　　fawn 　　claw　　jaw 　　yawn　　lawn 　　hawk　　crawl Teach your child the *aw* sound (also spelled *au* as in *laundry*).	**Syllables** Introduce syllables to your child. Tell your child that words are like music in that they have a beat—some have one beat, some have two or more beats. *See* Reading, Week 32, number 1. Read *Don't Wake Mama* and *Five Little Monkeys* by Eileen Christelow. Have your child clap the beat as you read it a second time.
Tuesday	Write a sentence on the chalkboard. Underline the adjectives. Ask your child to identify the part of speech of the underlined words. Write sentences with the adjectives missing. Have your child fill in appropriate adjectives.	Have your child write the spelling words in sentences.	Teach your child to say a word and clap the number of syllables. Have your child look through the book you read together and make a list of the two-syllable words. *See* Reading, Week 32, number 2.
Wednesday	Write a sentence on the chalkboard. Underline the verbs. Ask your child to identify the part of speech of the underlined words. Write sentences with the verbs missing. Have your child fill in appropriate verbs.	Have your child spell each word aloud with a silly voice. Have your child complete **Who Says Caw, Caw?** (p. 346).	Teach your child that long words are made up of syllables. Encourage your child to look for familiar chunks and read words syllable by syllable. Teach some common endings such as *-tion, -ble, -ing, -er* and *-able*. *See* Reading, Week 32, number 3.
Thursday	Write a sentence. Ask your child to circle each noun, mark an *X* on each adjective and underline each verb. *See* Language Skills, Week 32, number 1. When your child approaches an unfamiliar word while reading, encourage him/her to use sentence syntax as one of three cues: what part of speech the word might be, what makes sense and phonics.	Have your child write each spelling word in large letters on an index card. Use a paper punch to punch holes along the lines of the letters for your child. Then, have him/her trace the letters with his/her index finger.	When reading an unfamiliar two-syllable word, help your child determine where to divide the syllables by noting what follows the first vowel. If a single consonant or a blend follows the vowel, the syllable stops after the vowel. **Example:** *na-tion, re-play* and *su-per*. If two consonants follow the vowel, the consonants are split into separate syllables. **Example:** *big-ger* and *sup-per*. Give your child other examples for practice.
Friday	Have your child write a make-believe story about an animal with a problem. Instruct him/her to include action words and descriptive words. Your child should make sure that the problem gets solved through the animal's actions. **Ideas:**　An elephant has no peanuts. 　　　　　A panda is lonely. 　　　　　A squirrel has burrs in its tail.	Give your child the final spelling test.	Have your child look through *Don't Wake Mama* and *Five Little Monkeys* to find words that answer the questions *who, what,* and *where* about the stories. Draw three columns on a sheet of paper. At the top of the columns, have your child write *who, what* and *where*. Have your child write words from the books in the appropriate columns.

Learn at Home, Grade 1

Math	Science	Social Studies
Adding and Subtracting Money Review addition of 2-digit numbers using manipulatives and a place-value board. Teach your child to use the dollar sign and a decimal point when writing money. *See* Math, Week 32, number 1. Make a store for your child by selecting small objects and putting a price tag on each. Keep prices below $ .45. Have your child write the price on each objects using a decimal point and a dollar sign.	Help your child experiment with levers. Challenge him/her to try to dig while holding a shovel close to the scoop. Have your child set a ruler across a pencil that is lying on the table. Have him/her set a ball of clay on one end of the ruler and push on the other end to lift the clay. Then, have your child move the pencil closer to and farther away from the clay to find the position for the greatest lifting power.	**Famous Americans** Teach your child about George Washington by discussing his accomplishments. *See* Social Studies, Week 32, numbers 1 and 2. Draw an outline of a dollar bill. On the bill, have your child write facts he/she has learned about George Washington. Have your child complete **George Washington** (p. 348).
Have your child choose an objects from the store (*see above*) and count dimes and pennies to match the price. Have your child do this for all the store objects. Choose two objects. On a place-value board, have your child add the coins to determine the price for both objects. *See* Math, Week 32, number 2.	Help your child experiment with pulleys. *See* Science, Week 32, numbers 1 and 2.	Teach your child about Abraham Lincoln and discuss his accomplishments. *See* Social Studies, Week 32, numbers 3 and 4. Cut out two pieces of paper in shape of Lincoln's stovepipe hat. Glue or staple the edges of the two pieces together except along the bottom. Have your child write facts about Lincoln on index cards and put them in the hat. Have your child complete **Abraham Lincoln** (p. 349).
Have your child complete **Shopping With Cents** (p. 347). *See* Math, Week 32, number 3.	Help your child gain experience with wedges. Explain that a wedge is a simple machine often used for cutting. A wedge is triangle-shaped and can be found on a knife, axe, screwdriver or it may hold open a door. Have your child look for wedges in the kitchen and among the garden tools. Discuss how a wedge uses force to push two things apart. Explain that it can also hold things together as in the case of a nail or staple.	Teach your child about Harriet Tubman, the escaped slave who helped other slaves escape through the "Underground Railroad."
Tell your child money story problems involving subtraction. Have your child use dimes and pennies to build each problem. *See* Math, Week 32, number 4. **Example:** *I have $ .45 in my pocket. An ice pop costs $ .32. If I buy the icepop, how much will I have left?*	Show your child that a screw is a twisted inclined plane. Have your child run a fingernail through the threads of a screw to see that it is one continuous plane. Demonstrate to your child that a screw may be used to hold together two pieces of wood. Challenge your child to find objects that are held together with screws.	Teach your child about Clara Barton, founder of the American Red Cross, who nursed wounded soldiers during the Civil War. Help your child find out more about the Red Cross. Have your child complete **Clara Barton** (p. 350).
Tell your child addition and subtraction story problems with money. Let your child think through whether to add or subtract the dimes and pennies. *See* Math, Week 32, number 5. Have your child complete several addition and subtraction money problems on paper.	Have your child observe a machine that has moving parts. Help your child identify all the simple machines involved. Ask your child to point out the direction that the parts are moving. Ask your child to identify the source of the force (the *push* or *pull*).	Teach your child about the life and work of Martin Luther King, Jr. *See* Social Studies, Week 32, number 5. Have your child complete **Martin Luther King, Jr.** (p. 351).

TEACHING SUGGESTIONS AND ACTIVITIES

Language Skills

▶ 1. Write several sentences for your child to copy. Leave a blank in place of the nouns, adjectives and/or verbs. Provide a word bank of choices. Have your child copy each sentence and fill in the missing words where they belong.

Reading

▶ 1. **Music/Physical Activity:** Play different pieces of music. Have your child keep time by clapping or walking.

▶ 2. On a chart, label two columns *One Syllable* and *Two Syllables.* Have your child listen as you say some one- and two-syllable words. Tell your child to repeat each word and clap the number of syllables in it. Under your child's direction, list words in the appropriate column of the chart.

▶ 3. Write some double consonant words, such as *little, biggest, dinner, hammer, buzzer, butter* and *dresser.* Read each word to your child. Ask your child to name the number of syllables. Divide a word into syllables by drawing a line between the double consonants. **Example:** lit|tle . Have your child divide the rest of the words in the same manner.

Math (Adding and Subtracting Money)

▶ 1. Write these amounts on the chalkboard: 3¢, 10¢, 19¢ and 36¢. Tell your child that, until now, this is how he/she has written coin amounts. It is correct, but when adding or subtracting cents, it is written differently. Next to each amount you wrote on the chalkboard, write a dollar sign and a decimal point ($.). Explain that the number of cents are always to the right of the decimal ($ .03, $ .10, $ .19, $ .36). Write several different amounts with a cent sign. Have your child write each using the dollar sign and decimal point.

▶ 2. Have your child use dimes and pennies to build 2-digit numbers. Ask your child to show thirty-seven cents. Guide your child into recognizing that dimes are equal to ten pennies (tens) and pennies are ones.

▶ 3. Explain that adding cents is no different than adding 2-digit numbers. Write a problem like the one to the right. Say the problem as it is written: *Thirty-four cents plus forty-one cents equals seventy-five cents.* Say: *Four ones plus one one equals five ones: Three tens plus four tens equal seven tens: The answer is seventy-five cents.* Have your child work some money addition problems. Allow your child to use manipulatives if necessary.

$$\begin{array}{r} \$\ .34 \\ +\ .41 \\ \hline \$\ .75 \end{array}$$

▶ 4. Create subtraction problems using money for your child to solve. Have your child build seventy-six cents. Ask your child to remove thirty-four cents and tell how much is left. Write the problem on the chalkboard.

▶ 5. Teach your child to make change. Hold up a pencil with a twelve-cent price tag. Give your child fifteen cents to pay for it. Show your child how to make change by saying the cost (twelve cents) and handing one penny and saying *thirteen,* handing another penny and saying *fourteen* and handing a third penny and saying *fifteen.* Repeat this activity several times using classroom objects. No object should be sold for more than forty-nine cents.

Learn at Home, Grade 1

Science

▶ 1. Obtain a pulley and some rope from a hardware store. Let your child explore the movement of a pulley and how it helps make lifting easier. Let your child observe the work of pulleys on a flagpole, on curtains and on construction machinery.

▶ 2. Hang a pulley from a hook in the wall. Have your child fill a small sandbox bucket with sand or rocks and tie one end of a rope to the bucket's handle. Then, have your child thread the rope through the pulley and take hold of the other end of the string. Your child may lift the bucket by the handle then pull the rope to lift the bucket. Ask if it was easier to lift the load with the pulley than by hand. Discuss why.

Social Studies (Famous Americans)

▶ 1. Here are some facts about George Washington to get you started:

He was a great military leader.
He was the first president of the U.S.
He helped to write the Constitution.
He is on the one dollar bill and the quarter.
The national capital, Washington D.C., was named after George Washington.
He was the only president that did not live in the White House.

▶ 2. Read *A Picture Book of George Washington* by David A. Adler.

▶ 3. Here are some discussion starters.

Abraham Lincoln worked as a lawyer.
He grew up poor.
Lincoln was the 16th president.
Lincoln is on the penny and five dollar bill.

▶ 4. Read *A Picture Book of Abraham Lincoln* by David A. Adler.

▶ 5. Read *Martin Luther King, Jr.* by Margaret Boone-Jones. Also, read *What Is Martin Luther King, Jr. Day?* by Margot Parker.

Who Says "Caw, Caw"?

| claw | hawk | jaw | crawl | draw | lawn | yawn | fawn |

Write the spelling words that **end** with the **aw** sound.

_____   _____   _____

\- - - - - - - - - - - -   \- - - - - - - - - - - -   \- - - - - - - - - - - -

_____   _____   _____

Write the spelling words in the boxes below. Then, **write** them on the lines.

Learn at Home, Grade 1

Shopping With Cents

Add the cost of two things. **Write** the total in the box.

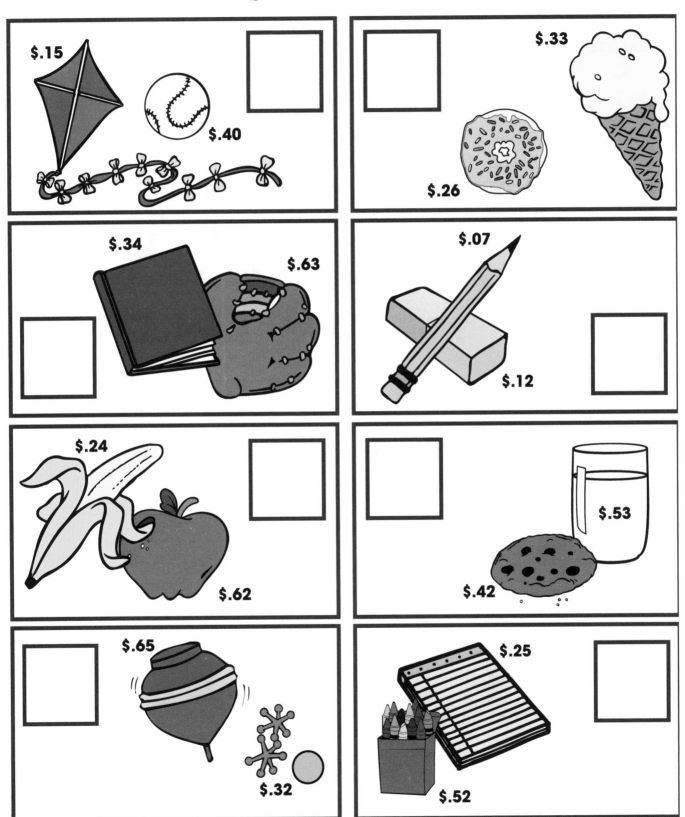

George Washington

1. **Connect** the dots, beginning with number 1.
2. **Color** the dollar bill.
3. On the lines below, **write**:

   George Washington was our first president.

cut

Learn at Home, Grade 1

Abraham Lincoln

1. **Write** the words from the box beside the correct pictures.
2. Then, **color** the pictures.

log cabin   top hat
White House   ax   book   beard

Abraham Lincoln as a boy

_____

_____

_____

Abraham Lincoln as President

349

Clara Barton

1. **Color** the medicine bottle brown.
2. **Draw** a bandage on the man's leg.
3. **Color** the cross on the wagon red.
4. **Color** Clara Barton's bag black.
5. Now, **color** the rest of the picture.

Learn at Home, Grade 1

Martin Luther King, Jr.

Color the picture of Martin Luther King, Jr.

MARCH ON WASHINGTON

Learn at Home, Grade 1

	Language Skills	Spelling	Reading
Monday	Help your child develop vocabulary through reading poetry and discussing the meaning of unfamiliar words.	**Y as a Vowel** Pretest your child on these spelling words: party cry candy dry bunny fly baby my Teach your child *y* as a vowel. Help your child to group the words according to the sound *y* makes.	Read *If You Give a Mouse a Cookie* by Laura Joffe Numeroff. Discuss the events in the story and examine the pictures carefully. On a long strip of paper, have your child draw the story events. Then, staple the ends of the paper together to make a circle. Tell your child that *If You Give a Mouse a Cookie* is a circle story because the events of the story could keep repeating.
Tuesday	Continue reading and discussing poetry with your child.	Have your child write the spelling words in sentences.	Point out to your child that the boy's single act of sharing started a whirlwind of activity. With your child, brainstorm variations on the story. Ideas include *If You Give a Cat a Dish of Milk, If You Give a Dog a Ham Sandwich* and *If You Give a Rabbit a Piece of Carrot Cake*. Have your child choose the title he/she likes best and write his/her own story following the pattern of *If You Give a Mouse a Cookie*.
Wednesday	Read and discuss poems written in different styles and from different eras.	Have your child say and spell each word aloud into a tape recorder. Then, let him/her play the recording back for practice. Have your child complete **Why Is Y a Vowel?** (p. 356).	Have your child write the name of the main character in *If You Give a Mouse a Cookie*. Under the character's name, have your child write the qualities of the character (*kind, reckless,* etc.). After each quality, have your child write an example that demonstrates that quality.
Thursday	Have your child write his/her own poem using the style of a poem he/she likes. Your child may keep the pattern but change the topic. Encourage your child to use the best words to "make pictures" with his/her words.	Use a sheet of grid paper to make a word search puzzle for your child. Let your child find his/her spelling words in the puzzle.	Teach your child about the use of commas. Call attention to the sentences that begin with *if* or *when,* pointing out to your child that the clause is always followed by a comma. Have your child create his/her own *If...* or *When...* sentences, based upon the story written on Tuesday.
Friday	Have your child read his/her poem to you. Then, help him/her edit the poem. Help your child publish his/her poem with illustrations.	Give your child the final spelling test.	**Poetry:** Read poems about mice. Discuss their meaning and rhyme with your child. Have your child memorize and recite the poems with expression.

Learn at Home, Grade 1

Math	Science	Social Studies
Shapes Have your child identify geometric shapes, listing as many descriptors as possible. **Example**: A triangle has three points, three sides and no rounded edges. Two triangles make a four-sided figure.	**Sound** Teach your child that sound is produced by vibrations. *See* Science, Week 33, numbers 1–4.	Read with your child about the first woman in space, Sally Ride. Discuss the history of space travel. Have your child complete **Sally Ride** (p. 358).
Let your child use a geoboard to make different geometric shapes and record them on dotted paper. *See* Math, Week 33, numbers 1 and 2. Ask your child: *How many different-sized triangles can you make on the geoboard?*	Have your child make a musical instrument with vibrating strings. Provide different sizes of boxes, rubber bands and tape. Let your child design an instrument that actually works and plays at least two different notes.	Discuss other famous Americans. Have your child choose one person to read about and talk to your child about what he/she learned. Have your child complete **The Person I Most Admire** (p. 359).
Have your child sort the shapes from **Attributed Shapes** (p. 357) in inventive ways, such as straight sides and no straight sides. Write each category your child names on an index card. Repeat until all possible ways to sort seem exhausted. Choose two of the index cards to label a Venn diagram and sort. Let your child discover what to do when a shape fits in both categories. *See* Math, Week 33, number 3. (no sides / large)	Teach your child to make a telephone out of two cups and a length of string. Discuss how sound travels along the string and quiet conversation is amplified. *See* Science, Week 33, number 5.	Discuss American holidays, including Memorial Day, Flag Day, Labor Day and Presidents' Day. Help your child research the history behind several of the holidays. Have your child complete **A Year Full of Special Days** (p. 360).
Gather objects and containers with the shape of a geometric solid. Identify spheres, cones, cubes, pyramids, cylinders and rectangular prisms for your child. Examine shapes with your child and locate geometric shapes such as circles, squares and triangles on the faces of the solids. Have your child draw ten objects in the room that contain a geometric shape.	Brainstorm with your child examples of pleasant and unpleasant sounds. Then, have your child pair the sounds and write sentences for a book about sounds. **Examples:** A train makes a loud whistling sound while a chick makes a soft peeping sound. An angry cat howls while a contented cat purrs. My brother yells at the ball game, but he speaks kindly at home.	With your child, read about the life and work of the current president of the United States. Then, have your child write a letter to the president, including the information learned.
Have your child cut out geometric shapes from construction paper. Have him/her use the shapes to create a design or picture and glue them onto drawing paper.	Continue the sound activity begun in yesterday's lesson.	Explain to your child that the president cannot read every letter he receives or solve every problem the country has. Therefore, senators are elected in each state to help him/her. Discuss with your child issues which are important to him/her (environmental issues, homelessness, etc.). Then, help your child write a letter to your senator asking for a change. Have your child complete **Make Your Vote Count!** (p. 361).

TEACHING SUGGESTIONS AND ACTIVITIES

Spelling (Y as a Vowel)

BACKGROUND

Your child already knows that *y* is a consonant. Explain to him/her that in some words *y* acts like a vowel. At the end of a two-syllable word, *y* sounds like a long *e* as in *happy*. When *y* is the only vowel and it is not followed by a consonant, *y* sounds like long *i* as in *my*.

Math (Shapes II)

BACKGROUND

Using the basic shapes (circle, triangle, square and rectangle), your child will explore problem solving and spatial relations.

▶ 1. Make a geoboard on a 10" square of plywood. Hammer 25 nails in five even rows and columns, leaving a 1" border around the edge of the wood. On the completed board, allow your child to experiment with rubber bands, making geometric shapes by stretching the rubber band around the nails. Next, show your child a drawing of a simple shape for him/her to recreate on the geoboard in various sizes.

▶ 2. Create a record sheet that looks like a geoboard. Using the geoboard and several colored bands, ask your child to make two identical rectangles using different-colored bands on the geoboard. Then, have your child draw the same rectangle on the dotted record sheet. Have your child make squares, triangles and other shapes. Challenge your child to make a square with 9 nails inside, 16 nails inside, etc. Then, have him/her make a record of each.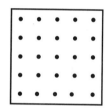

▶ 3. Have your child color and cut out the **Attribute Shapes** (p. 357). Then, have him/her use the blocks in some of the following activities to practice problem solving:

    a. Sort the blocks into categories of color, shape or size.

    b. List every attribute possible on individual index cards.

    Venn Diagram

    c. Put the attributes on a Venn diagram and sort the blocks. Some blocks may fit in both categories and, therefore, are placed in the intersection of the two circles.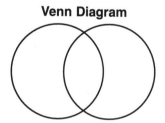

    d. Make a one-difference train. Choose any attribute block to begin the train. Follow it with a shape that is different in only one attribute.

    Example: A large red circle is one different from a large red square. The difference is in the shape—the size and color are the same. Continue placing blocks one different from the previous block.

    e. Make a two-difference train.

Learn at Home, Grade 1

Science (Sound)

BACKGROUND
Sound is part of the science of physics. Sound is produced by motion. When an object moves, the air surrounding the object vibrates and sets off sound waves that move through the ear and send messages to the brain. Sound can travel through many things. If we could see sound moving through the air, it would look like ripples in a pond moving away from a stone thrown into the water.

▶ 1. Have your child place a hand on his/her throat while speaking. Explain that what your child feels is his/her vocal chords vibrating. The vocal chords pass the vibrations to the air as waves of sound.

▶ 2. Show your child how sound waves travel. Fill a large metal bowl with water. Tap the side of the bowl with a metal spoon or knife. Point out the ripples that travel out from the center. Explain that they resemble sound waves.

▶ 3. Have your child feel vibrating objects that produce sound, such as a bicycle bell, stringed instrument, drum or metal stick striking a triangle.

▶ 4. Show that sound can also move through other things besides air. Put a ticking clock at one end of a table. Have your child put his/her ear to the table at the other end. The ticking will probably be louder because sound moves better through a solid than through air.

▶ 5. Give your child two plastic cups. Help him/her pierce a hole in each one with scissors. Have your child cut a piece of fishing line about 10' long. Instruct him/her to put one end of line through the hole of one cup from its bottom side and to tie the line to a paper clip inside the cup. Then, have your child do the same with the other end of the line to the other cup. The line must be pulled tightly between two people. One person speaks into a cup while the other person listens from the other cup.

Learn at Home, Grade 1

Why Is Y a Vowel?

Week 33

Write the spelling words in which the **y** sounds like a long **i**.

party cry dry candy bunny fly baby my

Write the words in which the **y** sounds like a long **e**.

Use the spelling words to complete each sentence below.

1. Michael had ice cream, cake and _____ at his _____.

2. I watched the birds _____ into the bird feeder.

3. The _____ ate the lettuce in _____ garden.

4. When the _____ is hungry, it may start to _____.

5. Jerry and Debbie helped me_____ the dishes.

CARROTS LETTUCE PEAS

Learn at Home, Grade 1

Attribute Shapes

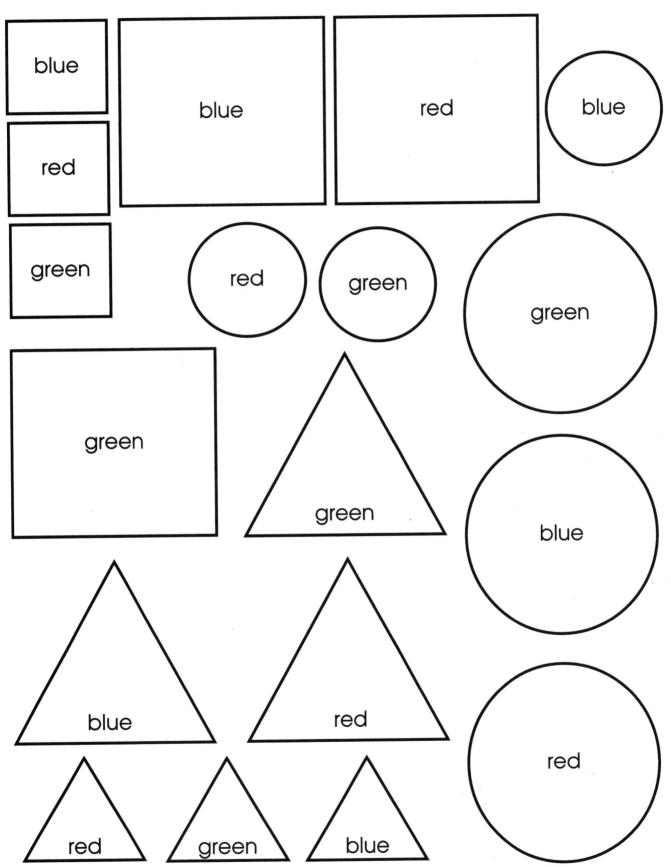

Sally Ride

Color the picture of Sally Ride.

Sally Ride

First Woman in Space - June 1983

358

The Person I Most Admire

1. **Think** about the person you most admire.
2. **Complete** the sentences below.
3. Then, **draw** a picture of yourself with that person.

The person I most admire is _____ .

I admire this person because_____

_____ .

A Year Full of Special Days

Color and **cut out** each holiday stamp below. **Glue** each one in the box that shows the month that holiday is celebrated. Then, **color** the stamps.

January	April	July	October
February	May	August	November
March	June	September	December

M.L.K., Jr.'s Birthday | Valentine's Day | St. Patrick's Day | Easter | Mother's Day

Father's Day | Independence Day | Halloween | Thanksgiving | Christmas and Hanukkah

Learn at Home, Grade 1

Make Your Vote Count!

Write a letter to your state senator about a problem our country has. Ask your senator to work to solve that problem. **Mail** the letter to: Senator _____ , U.S. Senate, Washington, D.C. 20510.

_____
(date)

_____
(address)

_____

Dear Senator_____

_____

_____

_____

_____

_____

_____

Sincerely,

_____

	Language Skills	**Spelling**	**Reading**

Monday	Have your child pick a topic about which he/she would like to write. Ask your child to think of words that tell about it. As your child says the words, have him/her write them on the chalkboard. Then, have your child use the words to write about the topic.	**Position Words**
		Pretest your child on these words:
		   right left
		   now next
		   after before
		   last first
		Teach your child the position words. *See* Spelling, Week 34, number 1.
			Library and Reference Skills
			Help your child select a nonfiction book. Review the parts of the book with your child: cover, title page, table of contents, body of text and index. Teach your child how he/she can find this book in the library. Read *Mama Do You Love Me?* by Barbara M. Joosse.

Tuesday	Have your child edit yesterday's sentences. Talk about changing sentence order to make a clearer story.	Have your child write the spelling words in sentences.	At the library, teach your child how to use the card catalog and computer system. *See* Reading, Week 34, numbers 1 and 2. While at the library, have your child look for books he/she would like to read. Have him/her write down these titles and keep this list for book ideas over the summer. Have your child find *Mama Do You Love Me?* in the card catalog at the library.
Wednesday	Have your child pick a new topic and brainstorm what you both know about the topic. Write key words on the chalkboard for your child. Then, encourage your child to refer to those words as he/she writes a story about the topic.	Have your child spell each word aloud while tapping keys on a piano or tapping two blocks together. Have your child complete **Correctly Positioned** (p. 366).	Ask your child where he/she could find the spelling of a word or find a word's meaning. Show your child a beginner's dictionary and teach him/her how to use it to locate words he/she wants to spell. Make a list of ten words for your child to find in a dictionary.
Thursday	Show a detailed picture from a book. Discuss what is happening in the picture. Have your child make up a story to go with the picture. Then, have him/her edit the story's punctuation and spelling. Have your child copy the story neatly and attach it to a photocopy of the picture.	Have your child draw a picture for each word showing an object in the position. Make sure your child incorporates the word in the drawing.	Have your child locate specific books on the library shelves and write down the title and author. *See* Reading, Week 34, number 3. Have your child complete **Library Scavenger Hunt** (p. 367).
Friday	Give your child time to finish the story begun during yesterday's lesson.	Give your child the final spelling test.	Read the book *Mama Do You Love Me?* together, with you taking the part of the mother and your child taking the part of the child. Have your child follow the pattern of Barbara Joosse's book to write his/her own version of *Mama Do You Love Me?*

Learn at Home, Grade 1

Math	Science	Social Studies
Problem Solving Draw a 2 x 2 grid. Ask your child to count how many squares there are. Encourage your child to look beyond the four obvious squares to see the large square that outlines the whole grid. Next, draw a larger grid (2 x 3) and have your child count again. Continue increasing the size of the grid and having your child record the total number of squares in each grid.	**Earth Science** Teach your child that beneath its top layer, the Earth is primarily made up of rock. Rocks can be as large as mountains or as small as grains of sand. Look at pictures of mountains and discuss the colors of the rocks on different mountains. Tell your child that some people like to climb mountains for sport. Some people also like to collect rocks for fun.	**Your City and State** Use local and city maps to help your child locate your home. *See* Social Studies, Week 34, number 1.
Have your child use manipulatives to solve this problem: *Build a staircase using six blocks. There should be three steps. How many blocks would be needed to build ten steps?* Have your child analyze the staircase step-by-step. Without building it, have your child tell you how many blocks are needed to build twelve steps.	Go for a walk at the beach or in the woods. Help your child collect a variety of rocks in a bag. Take the rocks home to study. *See* Science, Week 34, numbers 1 and 2.	Take several day trips to explore the region surrounding your home. Have your child record regional characteristics and points of interest in a journal.
Have your child draw a picture to solve this problem: *You are building a 4-sided bird house. An adult cuts a board into four even-sized pieces. How many cuts do you need to plan? How many cuts would be needed to make the sides for a 5-sided bird house? 6-sided? 10-sided? Using the pattern, can you predict how many cuts would be needed for a 100-sided bird house?*	Using a magnifying glass, observe the rocks collected yesterday. Have your child sort the rocks into groups. He/she may sort them by color, texture, size and any other way he/she finds them to be alike. Have your child label each group of rocks and make a list of words that describe the rocks.	Teach your child about your state's flag, bird, flower and motto. *See* Social Studies, Week 34, number 2. Have your child design a flag and motto for your city. Have him/her choose a city flower and bird. Discuss why they would be appropriate symbols for your city.
Have your child choose a strategy to solve this problem: *Your younger cousin was staying at your house. She missed her four cats and three birds and decided to draw shoes and hats for each pet. She asked for your help to figure out how many feet and heads there are altogether. Write an explanation of how you solved this problem.*	Teach your child that rocks change. Your child may have noticed that some rocks fall apart more easily than others. Explain that water and wind may change rocks. Discuss how rocks at the beach can be smoother from the effects of the wind and water. *See* Science, Week 34, numbers 3–5.	Explore the possible recreational activities available in your area. Have your child write about the interesting aspects of your area. *See* Social Studies, Week 34, numbers 3 and 4.
Pose this problem when the whole family is sitting at the table. Ask your child how many feet he/she thinks are under the table. Have your child tell how he/she solved the problem. Then, have him/her think of other ways to solve it. Then, have him/her determine how many feet there are after someone leaves or another person comes.	Explain to your child that people may change rocks, too. Show your child pictures of a brick layer, a miner, a sculptor and someone pouring cement. Discuss how rocks can be useful. *See* Science, Week 34, number 6.	Discuss with your child how people in your area work to make a living. Discuss the difference between urban and rural areas.

TEACHING SUGGESTIONS AND ACTIVITIES

Spelling (Position Words)

▶ 1. Put a variety of objects on the table. Give your child directions for moving or pointing to certain objects. **Examples:** *Move the pencil next to the marble* or *Point to the block to the left of the ring.* Then, give your child the same directions again, spelling the position word instead of saying it.

Reading (Library and Reference Skills)

▶ 1. **Field Trip:** Go to the local library with your child and teach your child how to use the card catalog. Explain to your child that the card catalog is arranged alphabetically. Each book in the library has three cards in the card catalog—one listed by its author, another listed by its title and a third listed by its subject. Help your child look for a book in the card catalog by title, subject and author. Point out to your child that the book's location (similar to an address) is located in the card's upper corner. Explain that nonfiction books are in numerical order according to subject, and fiction is ordered alphabetically by the author's last name. Ask a librarian to teach your child about the Dewey Decimal system of grouping nonfiction. Teach your child to use the library's computer search system as well.

▶ 2. Allow your child to get his/her own library card if he/she doesn't already have one.

▶ 3. Give your child enough information to find a specific book. (Information can be hints about the content of a familiar book.) When your child locates the book, have him/her write the author's name followed by the book's title. Remind your child to capitalize the first letter of the author's first and last names and every important word in the title.

Author
Wanda Gag

Title
Millions of Cats

_____   _____

_____   _____

Math (Problem Solving)

BACKGROUND
Problem solving is not limited to math. The strategies learned in mathematics will enrich all areas of problem solving. Problem-solving strategies include *guess and check, draw a picture, use a model* (manipulatives), *make a chart, look for patterns* and *act it out.* Teach your child a strategy by posing a problem and showing your child which strategy to use. Explain, however, that some problems are solved using two or three strategies.

Learn at Home, Grade 1

Science (Earth Science)

BACKGROUND

The Earth's surface is made up of rocks, minerals, soil and living things. In this unit, your child will explore and compare the components of the non-living surface of the Earth. He/she will gain an understanding of how rocks and soil are made and how they are useful.

▶ 1. If you have mountains in your area, go for a hike with your child on a mountain trail. Point out the rocks that make up the mountain and have your child compare them to the loose rocks. Collect a variety of rocks to take home and study. Visit other accessible habitats around your home to study the variety of rocks there.

▶ 2. Visit a rock shop with your child to see the variety of rocks and learn about different types of rock. Ask the store owner to teach your child about the hobby of rock collecting.

▶ 3. Provide your child with rock polishing materials obtained from a rock shop or provide your child with a piece of fine sandpaper to work on the surface of a rock. Explain to your child that he/she may change the surface of a rock by polishing it much like the wind and water polish the surface of rocks.

▶ 4. Explain to your child that as rocks are tumbled around by the water at a beach, they become smoother and rounder as well as smaller. Tell your child that the sand on the beach is made up of tiny rock particles.

▶ 5. Put several small jagged rocks in a plastic container with a lid. Add water and take turns shaking the container for several minutes. Have your child look at the water in the container. Ask your child why he/she thinks the water is cloudy. If the rock particles are not visible in the water, pour the water through cheesecloth and have your child observe the residue.

▶ 6. Tell your child that people make changes to the Earth at a very fast rate. Road builders use explosives to tear down a rock wall in no time. Explain that natural changes happen more slowly although occasionally a natural change will happen quickly as in the case of a volcano, earthquake or avalanche.

Social Studies (Your City and State)

BACKGROUND

Share with your child the qualities that attracted you to the area in which you live. Work together to research the immediate area as well as the state in which you live.

▶ 1. Gather maps of your city and state. Write to or visit the chamber of commerce of your city (town) to ask for information about the area. You will be able to obtain information about travel, festivals, entertainment, maps and much more.

▶ 2. Duplicate your state flag and help your child color it appropriately.

▶ 3. Have your child write to relatives who live far away and describe the attractive features of your area. Have your child invite them for a visit.

▶ 4. Have your child create a travel brochure for your city.

Correctly Positioned

after	last	right	before
first	left	now	next

Read the sentences. Use spelling words to complete the sentences.

1. Buck will read the _____ story.

2. We must go to the bus stop _____ .

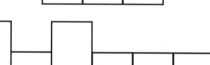

3. We must get some logs _____ we can build a fire.

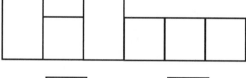

4. That is the _____ slice of pizza.

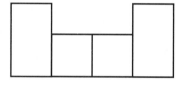

5. Plant the flowers to the _____ of the tree.

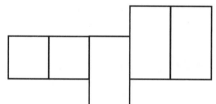

6. This was the _____ time she sang by herself.

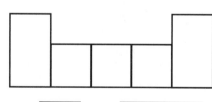

7. Go to the _____ , not the right.

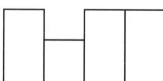

8. She will go to bed _____ she brushes her teeth.

Learn at Home, Grade 1

Library Scavenger Hunt

Go to the library. Find a book whose cover has one of the
pictures below on it. **Write** each book's name.

Find a book whose title has one of the words below in it. **Write**
each book's name.

1. the _____   3. a _____

2. in _____   4. of _____

Find a book whose author's last name starts with one of the
following letters. **Write** each book's name.

1. B _____   3. S _____

2. T _____   4. H _____

	Language Skills	**Spelling**	**Reading**
Monday	**Story Elements** Assess your child's writing for any skills that need to be reviewed this week.	Pretest your child on these spelling words: said　　　and was　　　have you　　　come are　　　will Read and spell each sight word together with your child.	With your child, brainstorm different kinds of books, such as riddles, sports, tall tales, fairy tales, picture books, cookbooks, how-to books, poetry and information books. Have your child think of the title he/she read this year and under which categories they fit. Encourage your child to select a book from a category he/she hasn't chosen from yet. Read *Swimmy* by Leo Lionni.
Tuesday	Fold a sheet of paper into thirds. After reading a story, have your child draw a picture of what happened at the beginning of the story in the first third of the paper. In the second third of the paper, have your child draw a picture of an event from the middle of the story. In the last section of the paper, have your child draw the story's conclusion. *See* Language Skills, Week 35, number 1.	Have your child write the spelling words in sentences.	**Field Trip:** Go to the library with your child. Show your child the locations of picture books, riddle books, books about animals, sports books, fairy tales, poetry books and cookbooks. *See* Reading, Week 35, number 1.
Wednesday	After reading a story, have your child identify its setting, problem and conclusion. Have him/her write each in a complete sentence. *See* Language Skills, Week 35, number 2. Have your child complete a **Story Map** (p. 372).	Have your child spell each word aloud while using sign language to form the letters. Have your child complete **It's in Sight** (p. 373).	Gather several books by authors whose last names begin with different letters. Have your child arrange the books in alphabetical order by the author's last name. Then, have your child write the titles and authors of the books in order.
Thursday	Have your child brainstorm ideas to complete the story map.	Give your child a large sheet of butcher paper or shelf paper. Have him/her create a graffiti mural by writing and painting the words with crayons, markers and paints.	Help your child find other books by Leo Lionni. Make a list of books by the author. Then, look through the books together to compare the artwork. Choose one to read.
Friday	Using ideas from the story map, have your child write a story.	Give your child the final spelling test.	**Field Trip:** Visit an aquarium. Look for the animals mentioned in *Swimmy*. Discuss the meaning of the word *survival*.

Learn at Home, Grade 1

Math	Science	Social Studies
Draw three horizontal lines on drawing paper. Have your child draw one vertical line intersecting the horizontal lines and count the number of boxes created. Record the number (0) at the top of the line. Tell your child to draw a second horizontal line and count the boxes (2). Ask: *How many vertical lines will make 16 boxes?*	Obtain a sample of rich garden soil if possible. While it is still fresh from the garden, allow your child to inspect the soil and describe the things that make up soil. Possible elements include rock particles (sand), dead plant parts, live plants, water, worms, insects, twigs and stones. *See* Science, Week 35, numbers 1 and 2.	**United States** Look at a map of the United States. Help your child identify your state and the surrounding states. *See* Social Studies, Week 35, numbers 1 and 2.
Pose this problem to your child: *The sum of three consecutive numbers is fifteen. What are the three numbers?* Have your child use manipulatives and the "guess and check" strategy. Then, ask: *The sum of four consecutive numbers is eighteen. What are the four numbers?*	Read with your child about the work of the earthworm. Help your child understand that the earthworm feeds on the plant matter in the soil and enriches the soil's nutrients with its castings. As the earthworm digs, it leaves holes in the soil which allows air and water to move easily. *See* Science, Week 35, number 3.	Discuss what makes the U.S. a good place to live. Have your child complete three sentences that begin *I am glad I live in the United States because....*
Hide the following coins from your child: one quarter, one dime and two nickels. Tell your child that you have four coins totaling 45¢. Challenge your child to figure out exactly what coins you are hiding. Encourage your child to use the "guess and check" strategy with coins as models. Pose additional coin problems with different combinations.	**Field trip:** Visit a farm. Have your child prepare questions ahead of time about the composition and care of soil. Ask the farmer to explain the characteristics of healthy soil and the benefits of crop rotation.	Ask your child why the United States of America is a good name for the country. What would it be like if the United States were not united? *See* Social Studies, Week 35, number 3.
Set out a box of Unifix cubes or pattern blocks to play a game of clues. Hide some blocks (fewer than ten) in a paper bag. Give your child one clue at a time about the bag's contents. Have your child use blocks as models to figure the number and color of blocks in the bag. **Example:** *I have two colors. I have an even number. I have three yellow. I have two more blue than yellow.* As a challenge, have your child write clues for the game above.	Have your child grow the same type of seed in two samples of soil. One soil should be dark and full of nutrients. The other soil should be light and sandy. Have your child keep track of the growth and compare the soils.	Help your child research some of the natural attractions of the United States, such as Yellowstone, the Rocky Mountains, the Appalachian Mountains, the Tetons and the Redwood Forests. Help your child plan an imaginary vacation to these places. Plan the route and itinerary of your trip. How you will travel, where you will go, what you will see, the order in which you will visit different places, etc.
Assign values to the letters of the alphabet. Keep the values below 5¢. **Example:** A=1¢, B=2¢, C=3¢, D=4¢, E=5¢, F=1¢, G=2¢, etc. Ask your child to find the value of his/her name and other familiar words. Challenge your child to find a word with the value of 15¢. Then, have your child write clues for a word of his/her choice. Have him/her give clues to its value, its beginning letter, and so on and give the clues to someone else to figure out the word.	Brainstorm with your child a list of things found on the farm. Have your child sort the list into living and non-living things. Have your child write a thank you letter to the farmer he/she visited on Wednesday.	Treat your child to an ice-cream cone. Tell your child that the ice-cream cone was introduced at the St. Louis Fair in 1904. Talk about other food products that originated in America. *See* Social Studies, Week 35, numbers 4–6.

TEACHING SUGGESTIONS AND ACTIVITIES

Language Skills (Story Elements)

▶ 1. Tell your child that every story has a beginning, a middle and an end. Ask your child to think about what happened in each part. Guide your child in his/her responses. In the beginning, the setting and problem are usually established. In the middle of a story, several events occur. At the end, a conclusion or solution is usually reached. Discuss the three parts in a familiar story, such as a fairy tale.

▶ 2. Use the Story Map on page 372. Read unfamiliar stories to your child and discuss them. Then, have your child identify the setting, problem, characters and solution.

Reading

▶ 1. Before you go to the library with your child, make a list of some books and library locations. Make an activity like a scavenger hunt. See the sample activities below:

Find A Light in the Attic in the poetry section. Write the full name of the author.
Find a book about your favorite sport. Write the name of the book.
In what section would you look if you wanted to make an apple pie?
Copy a riddle from a riddle book.

Science

▶ 1. Begin a compost pile in your yard. Put yard waste in a pile or large box. Add some worms found in the dirt. Keep the pile in a partially sunny location and water it if it gets dry. Have your child observe the pile throughout the season and watch the size of the pile decrease as the yard waste decomposes. If you stir the pile occasionally, the decomposition will not smell and it will work faster. Discuss the benefits of using a compost pile.

▶ 2. Have your child compare the composition of rich soil to that of poor soil. There should be less organic material in the poor soil and more non-living material.

▶ 3. Have your child observe the body and movements of a worm under a magnifying glass. Find a resource book in the library and identify the parts of the worm's body. Have your child describe in writing how the worm moves.

Social Studies (United States)

▶ 1. Collect pictures of symbols representing the U.S. (Declaration of Independence, the flag, the Constitution, the White House, the Capitol, the Seal and the Statue of Liberty). Read about the history of each symbol and how it came to be important to this country. Discuss the patriotism that unified the 50 states into one cohesive unit.

▶ 2. **Art:** On a sheet of 18" x 24" paper, have your child display the symbols of the U.S. Provide scissors, glue and colored paper for your child to copy the symbols that represent the U.S. and glue them on to the large paper. Write *Symbols of the U.S.* at the top of the paper with a black marker.

▶ 3. **Art:** Make a large collage banner of the U.S.A. On a sheet of shelf paper, glue large cut-out letters spelling *U.S.A.* Have your child look through magazines and brochures for pictures that are typical of America. Tell your child to cut them out and to glue them inside and around the block letters.

▶ 4. Following is a list of food products that were unknown in Europe before the discovery of the New World.

corn	turkey	peanuts	sweet potatoes
pumpkins	squash	string beans	lima beans

Have your child find a recipe using one of these products. Have your child gather the necessary ingredients and make it.

▶ 5. **Cooking:** Make peanut butter with your child. Put a few raw peanuts into a powerful blender. Turn on the blender until the peanuts are completely pureed. Add salt to taste. Spread the peanut butter on crackers and enjoy.

▶ 6. **Cooking:** If you want to cook an "All-American" meal, *The Frugal Gourmet Cooks American* by Jeff Smith has some excellent recipes, including the history of some of them.

371

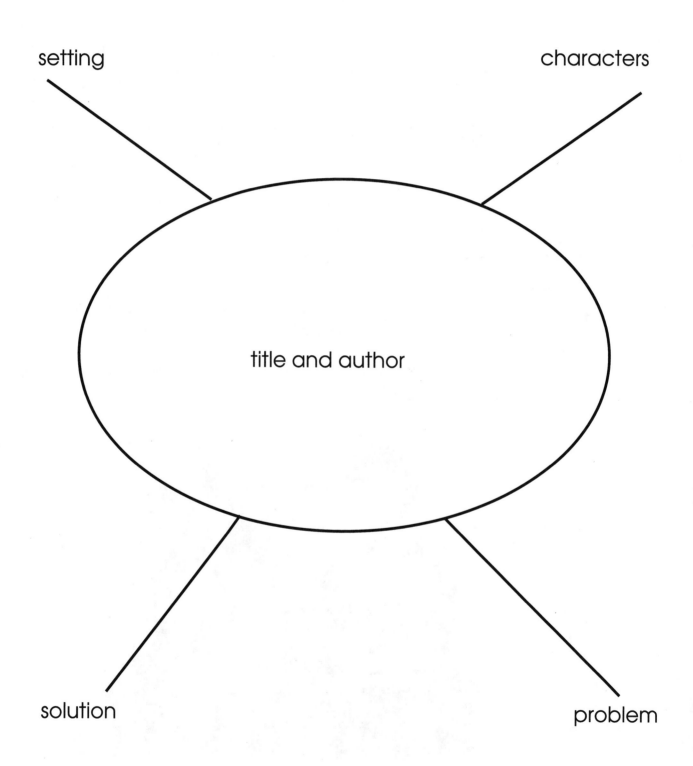

setting

characters

title and author

solution

problem

Learn at Home, Grade 1

It's in Sight

Write the spelling words in alphabetical order.

said	was	have	you
and	are	will	come

_____   _____   _____

- -

_____   _____   _____

_____   _____   _____

- -

_____   _____   _____

_____   _____

- -

_____   _____

Use the spelling words to complete the sentences.

1. Andy and Amy ___ ___ ___ ___ three kittens.

2. Jan and Donna ___ ___ ___ going to the horse show.

3. The girls ___ ___ ___ boys wanted to play the same game.

4. Sam ___ ___ ___ ___ that he can play the drums.

5. ___ ___ ___ ___ you be able to ___ ___ ___ ___ to my house?

6. Do ___ ___ ___ like to go camping in the forest?

7. The puppy ___ ___ ___ asleep in the basket.

Language Skills	Spelling	Reading

Monday

Review Week
Write sentences and/or stories for your child to put together and sequence. *See Language Skills, Week 36, number 1.*

Review Week
Review *r*-controlled vowels. Draw three columns on a sheet of paper. Draw a star at the top of the first column, a bird at the top of the second and an orange at the top of the third. Give your child past *r*-controlled spelling words. Have your child write the words in the columns with the same vowel sounds.

Review Week
Review homophones with your child. Read *There's a Nightmare in My Closet* by Mercer Mayer.
Have your child complete **Different Meanings** (p. 378).

Tuesday

Write a short story on the chalkboard. Leave out some periods and capital letters. Have your child read the story and use colored chalk to add capital letters and/or periods where they are needed. *See Language Skills, Week 36, number 2.*

Review long *u* and *oo*. Help your child make a crossword puzzle using words containing the *oo* sound as in *cool* and *oo* as in *look*.

Review prefixes with your child. Write five sentences, leaving out a word in each that begins with a prefix. Write two choices at the end of the sentence. Have your child copy the complete sentence, filling in the blank space with the correct word.
Example: The cat was _____ to climb down from the tree. (unable disable)
Read *The Little Engine That Could* by Watty Piper. *See Reading, Week 36, number 1.*

Wednesday

Read travel brochures with your child. Help your child make a list of adjectives found in the brochures. Then, he/she can write words that are synonyms together on the list. *See Language Skills, Week 36, number 3.*

Review the *aw* sound. Draw a crow on tagboard and cut it out. Give the pattern to your child to trace around on black paper twelve times. Have your child cut out the crows and use a yellow crayon to write words containing the *aw* sound on each one. Help your child put them together with a brass fastener to make a *CAW Book*.

Review drawing conclusions with your child. Read *Who Sank the Boat?* by Pamela Allen.
Have your child complete **What Will They Do?** (p. 380).

Thursday

With your child, brainstorm a list of summer words. Have your child sort the words into nouns, verbs and adjectives.

Review *y* as a vowel. Say several spelling words with *y* in them. Have your child tell if the *y* is a vowel or consonant. Give your child *y* spelling words and have him/her spell them orally.

Review syllables with your child. Read *The Doorbell Rang* by Pat Hutchins.
Have your child complete **Take One or Two** (p. 381). *See Reading, Week 36, number 2.*

Friday

Make a plan for summer activities with your child. Include time for reading, writing and playing. Help your child write goals and daily routines as guidelines.

Review the words from the past 8 weeks with your child. Write spelling words on small cards. Say a word and have your child find that word and spell it aloud. Test your child on the words he/she found the most difficult.

Have your child add the books he/she has read in the past 9 weeks to his/her "reading caterpillar." Read *Millions of Cats* by Wanda Gag.

Math	Science	Social Studies
Review Week Review column addition. Have your child gather signs of summer, such as seeds, leaves and twigs. Have him/her form three small groups of these objects, count each group and write the quantities in a column. Have your child add the numbers, then count the objects to confirm. Repeat with different sizes of groups. *See* Math, Week 36, number 1. Have your child complete **Tall Number Tales** (p. 382).	**Review Week** Review magnetism with your child. Provide magnets, iron filings and magnetic and non-magnetic materials and allow your child time to investigate the properties of magnets and to develop his/her own activities. Encourage your child to discuss his/her findings with you.	**Review Week** Review the names of some of the Native American tribes with your child. Make up a chant to help your child remember some of the names.
Review linear measurement with your child. Gather several twigs of various lengths. Have your child use a ruler, meter, yardstick or a non-standard unit to measure and compare the twig lengths. Then, have your child measure and compare the heights of plants outdoors. *See* Math, Week 36, numbers 2 and 3.	Help your child define *repel* and *attract* as they relate to the north and south poles of magnets. Have your child complete **Attraction and Repulsion** (p. 383).	**Field Trip:** Arrange to visit an antique shop that has several objects from long ago. Have your child guess what they were used for and discuss what has taken their place. If there is an old mill or blacksmith shop nearby, arrange for a visit there. Have your child record what he/she sees there. Then, have your child think of an object we use now and create something that might replace it.
Review volume with your child. Fill a wading pool (or tub) with water. Provide a variety of containers for your child to explore volume. Encourage your child to make comparisons. Have your child make equivalent measurements, counting how many cups fill a quart or pint. *See* Math, Week 36, number 4.	Review simple machines with your child. **Art:** Have your child make an "inclined plane" painting. Cut drawing paper to fit the bottom of a baking pan. Mix thin paints. Have your child spoon a small amount of one paint onto the paper. Drop a marble in the paint. Then, have your child pick up the pan and tilt it back and forth, letting the marble roll and create a design. When the paint dries, repeat with other colors.	Review famous Americans with your child. Visit a local museum and spend time in the history section. Ask your child to tell you what influence he/she sees of famous Americans.
Review fractions with your child. Use sidewalk chalk and a meter stick to draw geometric shapes. Draw lines dividing the shapes into equal parts and have your child shade in fractional parts such as one-fourth or two-thirds. *See* Math, Week 36, number 5.	Review sound with your child. Help your child make a musical instrument and have him/her play it along with a familiar song.	Help your child make a mural. Write *Proud To Be an American* at the top of a sheet of shelf paper. Discuss with your child why he/she is proud to be American and have him/her paint pictures to show this.
Review money with your child. Help your child set up a summer store and price a variety of objects. Your child may practice counting money, adding values or making change. Encourage your child to use the store all summer, adding new objects as needed. *See* Math, Week 36, numbers 6 and 7.	Review earth science with your child. Help your child discover that soil holds water. On a sunny day, place a glass jar upside down on the ground, leaving it there for a few hours. When you return, have your child draw a picture of the contents of the jar. *See* Science, Week 36, number 1.	Have your child finish work on his/her *Proud To Be an American* mural. Then, review your city and state with your child. Have your child plan a summer vacation in which he/she visits a location in your state.

TEACHING SUGGESTIONS AND ACTIVITIES

Language Skills

▶ 1. **Game/Center:** Compose four different short stories and write them on heavy paper using large letters. Cut apart each story so there is one sentence per piece. Mix the sentences from all four stories in a shoe box. Have your child read each sentence, sort the sentences into the four stories and put the sentences together in a sensible story order.

▶ 2. Paraphrase a familiar short story, such as *The Three Little Pigs,* on an activity sheet. Leave out some periods and capital letters. Have your child read the story independently and, using a colored pencil, write the capital letters and periods where they are needed. Repeat this activity often to improve your child's proofreading skills.

▶ 3. Have your child make travel posters for familiar places, such as your backyard or a local park. Encourage your child to use descriptive language.

Reading

▶ 1. After reading the story, discuss with your child the quality of determination and how the Little Engine used it. Then, have your child think of a time he/she did something that he/she didn't think he/she would be able to do. Use that idea to create an "I Think I Can" award.

▶ 2. When you have finished reading *The Doorbell Rang,* discuss how the feelings of the two main characters changed over the course of the story. Record your child's ideas on the chart on page 379 (shown at right). *The Doorbell Rang* is also a good book to use when talking about the importance of sharing.

character	event	feeling

Math

▶ 1. Dictate column-addition problems one at a time. Have your child set up each one as a vertical problem and then solve the problem.

▶ 2. **Assessment:** Give your child a ruler. Have your child define an inch by pointing out its start and finish. Ask your child for another name for 12 inches. Draw some lines no longer than 12". Have your child measure and label them. Ask your child to draw specific lines (4", 8", 1", etc.).

▶ 3. Allow your child to explore with the measuring tape. Ask your child when a measuring tape might work better than a ruler. Guide him/her to discover that it works well on rounded objects.

▶ 4. Put a cup, pint, quart, half gallon and gallon container on a table. Have your child find out which container is equal to 2 cups. Remove the cup container. Tell your child to find out how many cups each of the other containers hold (without using the cup measure).

▶ 5. Draw two of each: circle, square and triangle. Cut out one of each shape. Cut each matching shape into two, three or four equal parts. Instruct your child to mix up the pieces, then reassemble the parts on top of each whole shape. Have your child name the fractions.

▶ 6. Challenge your child to find different ways to make various amounts of money.

Learn at Home, Grade 1

▶ 7. Have your child solve the problems below:

   a. Mike has thirteen cents. His sister has forty-six cents. How much do they have together to spend on their mother's birthday card?

   b. Sarah gave the baker fifty-five cents for six cookies. He gave her one cent in change. How much did the cookies cost?

   c. One lollipop costs eight cents. A piece of gum costs three cents. Popcorn costs twenty cents a bag. Melanie had a quarter. What could she buy? Make a list of the possible combinations.

   d. Holly earned a dime each time she emptied the trash. Holly emptied the trash five times in one week. How much money did Holly earn?

   e. Billy bought a bag of peanuts for fifteen cents and a drink for sixty cents. How much money did Billy spend?

   f. Mother gave Jane a quarter and Father gave her two dimes and a quarter. How much money did Jane have to spend at the fair?

   g. Pencils cost fifteen cents each. Teddy bought two. How much did he spend in all? He gave the clerk two quarters. How much change did he get back?

Science

▶ 1. The jar should contain water droplets that evaporated from the soil and condensed in the jar. Repeat the experiment with the jar in several locations throughout your yard. Place a jar in different locations, such as on the grass, in the garden, over a spot recently watered and over a sandy spot.

Circle the word that matches the picture. Then, **write** the other word in the blank to complete the sentence.

This is a present _____ your birthday.
four   for

Jane lost a _____ of new shoes.
pair   pear

We _____ in the car for two hours.
road   rode

The boys will either swim _____ go to the ball game.
oar   or

Let's _____ at eight o'clock.
meet   meat

The scrape on his knee causes a lot of _____ .
pane   pain

Old Mother Hubbard's cupboard was _____ .
bear   bare

Learn at Home, Grade 1

Feeling	Event	Character

Learn at Home, Grade 1

What Will They Do?

Read each sentence and question. **Draw** an **X** in the box by the correct answer. **Draw** a picture to answer the question.

The boy is putting on his skates.
What will he do?

☐ He will go swimming.

☐ He will go skating.

The girl fills her glass with milk.
What will she do?

☐ She will drink the milk.

☐ She will drop the milk.

The lady wrote a letter to her friend.
What will she do?

☐ She will go out and play.

☐ She will mail the letter.

The kids gave Sally a birthday gift.
What will she do?

☐ She will open the gift.

☐ She will run away.

380

Learn at Home, Grade 1

Take One or Two

Look at the picture on each cookie and read the word on it. **Cut out** and **glue** each cookie on the correct jar to show how many syllables are in the word.

1 Syllable

2 Syllables

cut -

bathtub

soap

pencil

skate

duck

mop

paintbrush

mailbox

pickles
PICKLES

yarn

Tall Number Tales

Read each story. **Write** the numbers in the box. Then, add to solve the problem.

1. Marty had 3 marbles. Jake had 7 marbles. John had 4 marbles. How many marbles did the boys have all together?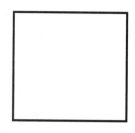

2. The soccer team won! Andrea made 2 goals. Michael made 3 goals. Sam made 3. How many goals did the soccer team make?

3. The first grade ran in three races. Team A scored 5 points. Team B scored 6 points. Team C scored 8 points. How many points did the first grade score?

4. We went to the farm. We saw 6 black pigs. We saw 4 black and white cows. We saw 6 brown hens. How many animals did we see at the farm?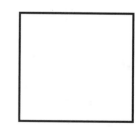

5. Mother picked flowers from the garden. She picked 7 pansies, 4 tulips, 4 irises and 3 daffodils. How many flowers did Mother pick?

382

Learn at Home, Grade 1

Attraction and Repulsion

Here are two bar magnets. Every magnet has a north pole and a south pole.

Attract - Repel

Hold the north pole of one magnet next to the south pole of the other magnet. What happened?

_____

_____

_____

Hold the north pole of one magnet next to the north pole of the other. What happened?

_____

_____

_____

Hold the south pole of one magnet next to the south pole of the other magnet. What happened?

_____

_____

_____

Unlike poles attract each other. Like poles repel each other.